PRESENTED TO:

Dave and Lisa

BY:

Marie Dukes

DATE:

2/24/19

OCCASION:

Friendship

ISBN 978-1-64349-649-8 (paperback)
ISBN 978-1-64349-651-1 (hardcover)
ISBN 978-1-64349-650-4 (digital)

Christian Faith Publishing, Inc.
832 Park Avenue
Meadville, PA 16335
www.christianfaithpublishing.com

Printed in the United States of America

from riches TO TRUE RICHES

Dear friends,
THAnk you so much for
your friendship & Support.
All my best
Marie Dukes 2/24/19

MARIE CATHRIE DUKES

DEDICATION

This book is dedicated to my exceptionally loving, caring and devoted husband, Charles, who is my rock and is always cheering me on. I love you very much, and I thank God for you. You are the wind beneath my wings, and your love shines through again and again. I admire your strength, your kind and gentle spirit. I thank you for helping me be who I am today. I want to spend the rest of my life loving you, and it pleases me greatly knowing that we will share the rest of our lives together.

To my beloved son, Ducarmel Didier Pierre (1967–2013), who loved me through the ups and downs of life. I will always love you and always cherish your loving memory in my heart. You were my first encourager when we found out that I had breast cancer. Your face was the first I saw when I awoke from surgery. You have always been my cheerleader when life got tough.

Ducarmel has given me three wonderful grandchildren. I dedicate *from riches TO TRUE RICHES* to Omar Leonardo Pierre (Mat), my first grandson. Mat, you are very smart and independent, you are talented and wise. I thank God for you, I am proud of you, I cherish all the wonderful moments we spent together, and I know that you will succeed in life, and I believe that you will accomplish everything that you set your mind to do. I love you and cherish you with every beat of my heart.

To Darien Drew Pierre, my second grandson, you are very smart. You are a genius, and like your father, you are soft, gentle, and tenderhearted. I thank and praise God for you. I admire your confidence in yourself, knowing just what your next step will be. I am so proud of you, keep up the great work you started. Every moment we spent together was precious to me. I love you and cherish you with every beat of my heart.

To Demari D'vyne Pierre, my only granddaughter, you are not only smart, you are also so beautiful. You are sweet, kind, open, and understanding. I admire your creativity and tenacity. When you start a project, you take all the time needed to complete it. You are very thorough. You have what it takes to make it in life; you have seeds of greatness in you. I praise God for blessing me with the gift of you.

I love you and I cherish you with every beat of my heart.

CONTENTS

FOREWORD

Everyone has heard of great heroes and heroines and others that have accomplished great feats, and some who have given us hope or courage. You are now going to embark on a true story that will do all that and more. Marie's story will capture your heart and stand your hair on end and give you goose bumps. Yes, even you tough guys will even shed a tear or two.

This lady comes out victorious in spite of all the obstacles hurled her way. Incredibly, it is her faith in God that sustains her, propels her, and jettisons her on to victory and success. She said what God says about her, her situations, and His power to overthrow anything. She quotes and applies scripture to the worse possible scenario and wins, and when she wins, she wins big. You might consider the possibilities after reading this spine-tingling, heartbreaking, victorious story.

I met Marie Cathrie Dukes in June of 1995. We both got hired at the same time at a transportation company. It was a difficult, challenging class we had to take. There were many hurdles to overcome or you could be terminated at the blink of an eye. You had to be very motivated to stay in the class. There were about fifty people per class, at the end maybe twenty-five of us made it. Rough and competitive. However, there was this kind of loud, petite, always well-groomed lady with great, long, and beautiful hair that I had come to dislike somewhat.

In our oral portion of the class, she *always* had the right answers and would yell them out, followed by a little laugh as the rest of us held up our hand with what was probably the wrong answer. She had this wonderful French accent that I love and wanted so desperately to hate but couldn't. There was no getting around it; she was really smart and had the memory bank of an elephant. (They have great memories, right?) Where I usually shined, I stood in her shadow. Yep, constant shade, all of us! Needless to say, she finished first in our class and later went on to be the best agent in the entire company with awards, trophies, and accolades.

Yes, the president of the company took her and her husband to lunch and dinner many times because she sold millions of dollars of product each year. Her picture was plastered all over the place and articles written about her accomplishments. You had to admire her, you had to respect her, plus she had this positively infectious personality. On her birthday in August, do you know she bought everybody in the class a gift for her birthday? Could I hate her anymore! She was perfect, flawless, and a bundle of energy.

Who would have guessed that little thing went through so much in her own country and in ours, and became a success story? Oh, did I mention she reminded me so much of my mother when I got to know her better? Guess what? My mom and Marie are best friends to this very day. Continue to read *From Riches to True Riches*, this book of triumph and faith.

Her sister in Christ,
Joanne Broussard

ACKNOWLEDGMENTS

As I think back to 1971, when I met Joan Franklin Henry, college professor, in comparison, I was a nobody. After hearing my story, she confidently told me, "You have to write a book, and maybe even more than one." I didn't believe that I could or that I would. But since then, people everywhere repeatedly told me the same thing. One coworker told me, "Marie, it would be selfish for you to keep this story to yourself, others would want to hear it." Many seeds have been planted. I feel blessed to have such people in my life who saw in me what I could not fathom. I appreciate each and every one of you whose inspiration, prayers, support and love blessed my heart and sustained me during the writing of *from riches TO TRUE RICHES*, you have made it a reality.

First, I want to thank my mother for raising me with spiritual values and always reminded me to have faith coupled with discipline.

Next, Joan, I thank you for being my first bestie in America and for believing in me. I want my friend back.

I am grateful for my family. You all contributed to my life story; every page of this book has you written all over it, you are a big part of who I am. I truly love all of you.

A special thank you to my twelve foster children who are and always will be in my heart. Your contribution is bigger than you can imagine. My love for you will live on forever.

Next, a myriad of surrogate daughters, my thanks go to all of you. We've comforted one another, we cried and laughed together, our bond of love continues to grow stronger every day.

I would also like to thank my pastors who have ministered to me, preached God's word, and corrected me when I was wrong. To my therapists who have helped in my recovery from depression, Marilyn Rainwater, I can't begin to express my gratitude. Even when you are very busy, you always stop what you're doing to give me a hug, inquire about my health, and answer any questions that I might have.

A big shout to you Lori Walcker. Throughout the process of writing this book, you were my techie whenever I couldn't find my way around my computer. You were my go to person; you never made me wait, you were always there. Also, thank you so much for all your help with repairing and putting the photos on flash-drive for my book. Superior job!

To Brenda Harris, my angel, my heart rejoices when I think of you. During my battle with cancer, when I was a stranger you welcomed me into your life. You comforted me with kindness and armed me with strength that helped me to fight. Thank you for your friendship when I needed it the most. I thank God for you.

Charlene, thank you for loving me and sharing your family with me, treating me like a sister, always caring about my health and offering comfort when I needed it most.

Special thanks to my niece Arvat McClaine, you are an inspiration. I admire your courage. Your strength was the encouragement that I needed to get me going. Thank you for your love and friendship.

I am immensely grateful to my niece Marie Immacula who was always there for Ducarmel, even when you were children. Your love for him was unconditional, you never stopped caring for him and being concerned about his well-being. You will always hold a special place in my heart.

Dot Logan, I can't find the right words to express my gratitude toward you. You and I became sisters in a very short time. You stayed by my side through my battle with cancer. You always know what to say or to sit by me quietly. I remember once, when I was at my worse and I refused to be comforted, my husband knew just who to call, and you came to console me. I thank you from the bottom of my heart.

To my grandchildren just for being you and the parents who were very generous with allowing the children to visit whenever I wanted. Do you realize how great that felt and how much I appreciate you? I love you.

To my two biggest cheerleaders, Mom Jeanne Kimble and my spiritual sister Joanne Broussard, you both knew, before me, that this book would be written, even if you had to drag it out of me. If you could, you would have written it for me, that's how much confidence you had about *from riches TO TRUE RICHES*. You have both helped, encouraged, and inspired me. Mom's own words and thoughts are all over this book. You've given me many valuable insights but allowed me to do it my own way. Without the two of you, there probably wouldn't be a book. I love and cherish you both.

To Minister Dwight Pledger, author, public speaker, coach, realtor, a man who wears many hats. Pastor Dwight is the founder of The Voice of Freedom. He ministers every Saturday morning at nine o'clock at KPRO1570 AM, inspirational radio located at 7551 Lincoln Avenue in Riverside, California. He is also my friend, coach, encourager, and my counselor. He has been telling me that I should write this book, and like I did with everyone else, I didn't listen. Once, he was giving the eulogy at a mutual friend's memorial service, and he said something that really got to me. He quoted Dr. Myles Munroe who said something about not taking your talents to the grave with you. After hearing his explanation about that statement, I decided to start writing the book. Without Pastor Dwight's coaching, it would have been impossible for me to continue my writing. He helped me through the whole process. I had residue of deeply rooted anger, abandonment issues that were in the way of completing the project, but through his counseling and coaching, I was able to get closure and make amends with the past. Thank you so much, my friend, I owe you a lot.

And lastly, to my husband, my soulmate whose love, prayers, and support are the things I needed most and was always available. I thank you from the bottom of my heart, and I love you.

CHAPTER 1

La Republique D'Haiti;
The chosen one and the left behind

Mapou Tree

For here we do not have an enduring city, but we
are looking for the city that is to come.

—Hebrews 13:14

My given name is Marie Caristille Thegenus. My birthplace is Mapou
Buisonniere, a commune of Leogane, fifteen long miles from Port-

Au-Prince, and I was born on August 7, 1947 at 5:00 o'clock in the morning, and I was delivered by a midwife.

In the Caribbean near Cuba, Jamaica, and the Dominican Republic lies the country named Haiti. There is a city, a coastal commune in Haiti, named Leogane. There are many communes in Leogane, one of which is Mapou Buissoniere, where I was born. This commune got its name because of the many gigantic "Mapou" trees in the area.

Most Haitians are Roman Catholic. There are some who worship as Pentecostal, Adventist, Baptist, and even Jehovah's Witness. Unfortunately, there are many who practiced voodoo as well. Some say in the millions! The foundations of voodoo are based in the tribal religions of West Africa, brought to Haiti by slaves in the seventeenth century. The people of Haiti perform strange rituals and dance wildly to a loud and incessant beat of drums. Potions are sold that truly promise love, money, and yes, even death! As if this were not enough, I have also heard of practices involving cannibalism, witchcraft, and devil worship. Thousands of Haitians continue until this day to live in spiritual darkness. I would later learn that people should stay clear of these demonic practices.

The beauty of Haiti was complemented by tall palm trees, tropical fruit trees like guava, corosol, (soursop), cachiman (custard apple) papaya, mango, mamey, quenepe just to name a few. It's much like the island pictures we see in the magazines. It is believed that cachiman is native to the West Indies. Among other things, they cultivated luscious vegetables such as corn, tomatoes, okra, peas, potatoes, eggplants, l'arbre à pain, green banana, plantain, manyoc, and many others, like pomme de terre, du riz, malanga. The sweet potatoes, are purple on the outside and white on the inside, they are so delicious, almost like eating sweet buttery bread. Imagine having all this right in your backyards, at your fingertips, to pluck and eat at any time you wish.

Haitians also raised chickens, turkeys, and other small farm animals in their yards. Many of the homes are close enough to the sea where they go fishing for different types of fish, shrimp, blue crab, and crawfish. Many Haitians make their living as fishermen. My father's house was located in front of a river; we call it a canal (a small river), and the entrance to the canal is near the front of the house. Neighbors came often to draw water for drinking, cooking, as well as washing clothes. Most homes do not have electricity or indoor plumbing. They use kerosene lamps and candles. They wash their clothes by hand and hang them on the clothes lines in their backyard.

The water for drinking is collected mostly at night or very early in the morning when there is no activity upstream. The current is usually calm and slow at that time. The water is cleaner, and there is less of a chance for germs and bacteria. It is then poured into jars of clay that helps to keep it cooler and more palatable. Owning a refrigerator in Haiti is a luxury that most of Haitians cannot afford. Each day, during the summer, blocks of ice are purchased and kept in a cooler. Ice picks are used to chip off the ice in order to make cool and refreshing drinks.

Besides keeping the water cool, the clay jars allow for impurities to settle at the bottom. With a ladle, you can draw water and put it in pitchers or glasses for drinking. Each time the jars needed to be refilled, the residue that is settled at the bottom is removed and the jar cleansed. There are times when the water from the canal is muddy (mostly after the rain), slices of cactus (nopales) are added to it. The nopales helps to separate the mud from the water. The mud goes down to the bottom, and the water is then clean and safe for drinking.

Throughout the day, there are a lot of activities up and down in the canal, where people are crossing to go to the other side, swimmers, and others doing their laundry. All these activities contributed to the water being unsafe for drinking. People cross the river with their clothes on, so they get soaked, and it's almost like taking a bath. There is a so-called bridge (We call it a pon.) that people use to cross over to the other side without getting wet, but the pon is not too safe. It is made up of a long tree trunk of either a coconut or a palm tree laid on top of each side of the river bank, one end at the entrance on each side. When crossing on the pon, it is advisable not to look to the right or to the left, but go as fast as you can and keep your eyes fixed on the other end of that tree trunk. If you do not, you risk losing your balance and fall in the water. The currents can be violent at times; they can drag you a long way before you can catch yourself or find a branch to hold on to. It happened to me, I couldn't swim, I thought I was going to die.

There were soap vines (feuille de savon) on the slopes below the riverbank, on both sides of the canal, floating in the water. If you were taking a bath in the canal and you had no soap or did not want to use soap, you could rub the leaves together, rub them on your skin, and they would lather enough suds to wash the body.

My father, Desirus Thegenus, was by trade a butcher and farmer. He was a simple, quiet man, hardworking, and somewhat stern in his appearance. He was not particularly handsome by some standards, but was thought to be extremely fortunate to have married the talented and beautiful Denise Tilmeuse Rocher. In a previous relationship, he had fathered ten children. All of them were adults before we were born and they had families of their own; therefore, my sister and I never became close with them. We did see them infrequently, but they never became a part of our life.

My mother Denise Rocher, in addition to being beautiful, was quite fashionable. She was admired by all. How many Haitian women owned a sewing machine and could design and make a beautiful garment just by studying a picture? In the rear of our house, she operated a small boutique, which was quite successful.

Between my father and mother, they bore six children, my brother, Joseph Chantone, my sister Marie Anne, me, Marie Caristille, and other three children who died before I had a chance to know them.

I was told that when I was four years old, that my mother and father were separated. Their separation also resulted in my sister Marie Anne and me being separated. My sister, Marie Anne, *"the chosen one"*, moved with my mother to the city, and I was left alone to live with my father in Mapou Buissoniere. How does one pick? How does a mother choose? What was the criteria? I am still puzzled!!! My big brother, Chantone was much older than my sister, Marie Anne, and me. He had already moved out, working and living on his own.

Until this day, I have no memory of the four years spent with my father. I have often wondered what those four years spent with my father were like. I would give anything to be able to remember that time spent with my father. Why can't I remember those years? It remains a mystery to me. Was it that I was so traumatized by the separation that I literally shut down and I am unable to recall that part of my life? Has the pain of losing my mother caused a block in my memory that remains until this very day? Could there have been something much deeper, more traumatic than or in addition to my mother leaving? I don't remember feeling loved, kissed, or cuddled as a child. Neither, when she left, or if she ever came back to check on me. I was the baby, for goodness' sake!

After my mother left, I am told that one of my cousins used to come over to my father's house to give me baths and comb my hair. The only thing I remember about that is that the person combing my hair was always very rough and it was a painful ordeal every time they combed my hair. I got the feeling that the person combing my hair did not do it out of love but out a sense of duty, and that makes me sad to think of it that way. I am sure that I was aware of the absence of my mother; the fact that she was no longer with me would have to have made me feel the loss.

At the age of eight, I was reunited with my mother and my sister. I was told then that I had a "new papa," and his name was Donte

Joseph. I had never attended school before. My mother had taken me to be enrolled at Sainte Rose De Lima, a convent, the most prestigious school in Leogane. I found myself face-to-face with the nuns. It was like waking up from a dream. They looked like angels. I was in awe of them and wanted to be an angel just like them. This was my first encounter with nuns. And that was my very first memory.

I was far behind in my grades. I did not even know my ABCs. I could not count. I am not sure if I was tested before being assigned to a class. The nuns insisted I stay after school every day for extra tutoring so that I could catch up with age appropriate classes. This was a private school, and there were no special education classes, so the cost for tutoring was in addition to the monthly tuition.

Papa paid for everything now, because my father did not pay child support (There are no child support laws in Haiti.), and papa had another family, this was entirely common in Haiti. This practice becomes more prevalent with the amount of wealth one possesses. From time to time, during the summer, my sister and I visited our father in the country for a short while.

I can also remember on one of our visits to our father during the summer, my cousin Leonie and I went fishing for shrimp in the canal. My sister didn't like to fish. Under the vines and weeds was where the fish and shrimps, blue crabs, and crawfish would hide. It was very easy to catch them; we just brought our baskets directly under the vines, shaking the vines and whatever was hiding in the vines would fall into the basket. When we lifted our baskets, they would be full of shrimp and other good stuff. We used to clean them, cook them with garlic and butter, and eat them. I like the shrimp better, and there is a season when the small fishes and shrimp were in abundance, and that's the best time to fish for them.

We fished in the small river (Petite Riviere). It gets its water from the overflow of the big river (Grande Riviere), which is about three miles away from my parents' old house. Once or twice during our summer visits, Leonie (who was older) took me along to La Grande Riviere to fish for shrimp. Our catch was at least three times as much as what we caught in La Petite Riviere. We had to walk about three miles each way, if not more, and all of this walking makes for strong little legs! There were times when our little journeys provided such meager rewards, that were it not for the fun and giggles we had, grown-ups would deem our forays to be of little value. In Haiti, children did not have playtime as we know it in other parts of the world. This time spent together with her really allowed us to bond. Because of the distance between Mapou, where she lived, and the city where I lived, we didn't see each other often.

We didn't see our big brother much either, he had gotten married and still lived in Mapou with his wife, Anita. I was ten years old when Chantone had his first child. It was such a memorable occasion for me when I was allowed to hold my first niece, Micheline. She was very small and beautiful. When I touched her tiny hands and kissed her face, she smiled at me and that stirred up so much joy inside of me. I loved her instantly.

We didn't get to bond with my brother's family because our visits to Mapou were far apart. Later when Micheline was all grown up, she and I developed a beautiful friendship that we both cherished. Micheline got married, and she was blessed with two beautiful children, Van Jr. and Tily. She was called to ministry and is now the pastor of a small church in Mapou, following in her mother's footsteps, who had founded and pastored that church for over fifty years. Praise be to God!

CHAPTER 2

My Life in Haiti;
Are we the products of our environment?

*It is the Lord who goes before you. He will be with you, He will
not leave you or forsake you. Do not fear or be dismayed.*
—Deuteronomy 31:8

Clearly, the time away from my mother caused some very deep psychological pain and has caused me to wonder if my mother ever really loved me. Why did she whip me so often? Oftentimes, she had me get on my knees so that my sister could whip me. Many times, my sister would resist at the risk of getting a whipping herself, but mother made her do it.

I remember always being sad and keeping my distance from others. Being constantly treated that way made me feel hurt and disappointed. The fact that I was a very sensitive child being treated like that made me feel that there was something wrong with me. The funny thing is that even though my mother treated me that way, I still loved her just the same. Was I not good enough? Maybe, that's why she had chosen my sister over me. There were times when I felt empty and numb. I tried to be good so she would love me and not leave me again. With my mother, good was never good enough, and no matter what I did I could never measure up.

How does a mother leave her baby behind? Did I cry myself to sleep? Did I find solace? And who comforted me? Why can't I remember, did something bad happen to me? I guess I will never find out, and maybe it's better that I don't remember.

As a child growing up, we went to church, we said our prayers in the morning and at night, we were taught to love God and have faith in him that was the extent of religion to us. Beside saying our prayers, I didn't know about having a relationship with God. We would pray for the things we needed. When something bad happened, or if we wanted something really bad, we were told to ask God for it, he will answer our prayers. I thought that was all there is to it. I felt disappointed when some of my prayers were not answered. When I asked God to have my mother stop whipping me and not make my sister whip me, instead of things getting better they seemed to get worse, because my mother went from just whipping to slapping me with her hand. I thought he was ignoring me and I had to endure that

25

kind of abuse for many years. I couldn't quite understand it, because as a child, I thought that God answered all prayers. Later, I learned that Christians do face trials'- James 1:2-3 "Consider it pure joy my brothers and sisters when you face trials of many kinds, because you know that the testing of your faith produces perseverance.

My father was considered to be one of the richest men in the area. He was well-known, but I did not know him very well, except for what I was told and very little that I observed during short visits. One of his enterprises was butchering animals and wholesale the meat to other businessmen, who in turn would retail it in their own supermarkets.

On occasions when I'd go visit my father, I remember seeing cows, pigs, and goats being slaughtered, but I didn't like watching it because it was too bloody. Seeing all that blood made me want to throw up. That was how my father made his living. Looking back, I remember feeling sorry for the poor animals that had to lose their lives.

My father was in a relationship with a woman named Virginia, but he never married her. My mother and father had never divorced. During one of our summer visits, I remember one of the few times speaking with my father one on one in which he shared the story about how he came to marry my mother. He had awoken from a dream where his deceased father, my grandfather, gave him twenty gourdes (Haitian currency equivalent to four US dollars).

Dreaming and speaking to the dead is one of the superstitious beliefs of Haiti. His father had told him to use the money to play at a cock fight. This was one of his pastimes when he wasn't working. He was assured that if he did play the money that Grandpa had given him (in the dream), he would win. He was to use his winnings to buy a ring and propose to a certain Denise Tilmeuse Rocher, my mother; and he won just as his father's dream revealed. He won big enough to purchase the ring; he proposed, and the rest is history.

Except for size and population, Haiti is no different than any other third world country. In those countries, the poor get poorer and the rich get richer. A country where men rule and women obey.

Men can have as many women as they can support; these are called kept women. The men have a family with these women, and many of them are put up in small houses in crummy neighborhoods, and some even live in upper class neighborhoods. While they live in rich neighborhoods in luxury with their legitimate families, their children (little princes and princesses) attend private schools, take pleasure in eating at expensive restaurants, shop at upscale stores, and wear top-of-the-line clothes. They delight in the better things that life has to offer, while many of the kept women's children are treated like paupers and second-class citizens.

Sadly, many of the homes look like shacks, put together with mud and straw and covered with palm leave; the floors are dirt, and some of them don't have any furniture. They sleep on the hard dirt floor on sheets or pieces of burlap and some used old clothes for a pillow. For many Americans, it is hard for you to think that children should sleep on the floor at night. Some adults have to sleep on the floor as well. It is a reality in Haiti. Having a solid roof over your head and a bed in every room for each person in your house is a luxury that most Haitians cannot afford. The most important thing for a lot of them is survival, not luxury. A bowl of rice that fills their belly is more important than going to sleep in a comfortable bed, with their stomach growling.

A house in an upper middle class consists of three rooms, maybe four, a living area and dining room combination, a master bedroom with a "paravan," which is a room divider that separates the room from the personal hygiene area. There is no commode, no sink or shower. Very few homes have indoor toilets with bidet, lavabo, and maybe a shower. Everyone in Haiti has a shower outside and an out-house in their backyard. The inside (toilet) personal hygiene with no plumbing consist of a lavabo, which is a two-tier cabinet. On the top first tier is where you put a cuvette, which is a face basin. There is also a pitcher full of water inside the basin, water to be used for washing the upper parts of the body and brushing the teeth. On the bottom tier you have a tall bucket of water to be used to wash the lower parts of the body. Under the bottom shelf, on the floor, there is room for a "vase" (not a flower vase), a bedpan that is used for urinating at night, since the facilities are outside. That area of the house is like your bathroom where you wash up and brush your teeth in the morning before you come out of your room. Because most houses don't have indoor plumbing, you take a bird bath every morning and shower later. Next is the children's room, a little larger, for most families, since all the children have to share it. Many of them have to share a bed as well.

My sister and I couldn't share a bed because I was a bedwetter. There were times my sister and I would fall asleep together in the same bed, she would wake me and my mother up screaming that the bed was wet. My punishment for that was a whipping and a bucket of cold water poured over my head, right in the middle of the yard for the neighbors to see, and all the children laughed at me. My mother did this to me every single morning, even on cooler days. No one was waiting to hand me a towel to dry myself off. I tried to stop wetting the bed, but I couldn't.

Mother would try anything and everything to make me stop, including making me sleep on the floor. I had to hang my sheets to dry and reuse them the next night. She said that I would stop wetting the bed when I get tired of the smell of urine. I felt embarrassed and ashamed, and the shame continued far beyond the bedwetting. I was made to feel unloved and worthless, that shame, those memories haunted me all the way to adulthood.

I was scared of Mother—one look from her will make anyone tremble and wet their pants. I was always expecting a whipping even when I hadn't done anything wrong. When she whipped me, I had to pretend it didn't hurt; because she said, crying meant that I thought that I was being wronged. When Mother sent me to get a switch and what I brought was too small, she whipped me harder and warns me that if I cry I would get another whipping.

The children's room did not have the Paravan, just beds. If you're lucky enough, your home will have another small room, like a big hallway, where the maid sleeps, if you have a maid. That small area is also used for storage. If you don't have the small room, she sleeps on the floor in the children's room. The vase (bed pan) that the children use for nighttime urination is stored under their bed. My bladder couldn't hold the urine long enough for me to make it to the bedpan.

You might have an indoor kitchen "la cuisine," but most people's kitchen is another small structure outside; for some people, it's like a hut. This is the kind of house the kept women with illegitimate children lived in. The men that kept these women and father their children do not live there. They come by whenever they want to. Mostly, I think, for quick sex and to give the women their financial allowances. Many women have to succumb to that kind of life in order to survive poverty; they don't have any other means of supporting themselves. There is no government welfare, no Section 8 to help them with rent payment, not even social security benefits. These women probably felt blessed to have been provided the opportunity to be kept by men in exchange for the use of their bodies.

The trophy wives know that their husbands are living a double life, but they are helpless. They have no recourse. There's nothing they can do. Women do not have rights in Haiti. They are treated just like another slave with a marriage license. They keep their mouths shut in fear of being beaten or left without any means of providing for themselves and their children. They don't want to rock the boat. Some live in mansions with butlers and servants, a nanny for their children. They belong to the elite class with all the privileges that came with it. Their job description is "look good for daddy." They must be ready to entertain and put on a happy face even after receiving a beating.

Spousal and child abuse is a trademark in Haiti. When the men face problems of any kind, they take it out on the women and children. Very few families are the exception, mostly the super rich are exempt; they must have other ways of dealing with their issues. The maids and butlers are treated like they're not human. They must refer to the master and mistress as *"monsieur et madame,"* the children as *"petit monsieur et mademoiselle."*

Some families are wealthy enough to have servants' quarters outside of the main house. The servants don't come inside the main house but to clean and serve meals. They also have other duties like washing clothes (by hand) and ironing; very few families have washers and dryers. The maids also iron men's underwear and bed sheets. Some maids do the grocery shopping and cook the meals, if the family does not have a cook.

There is a mandatory blackout every night in certain areas for approximately two to three hours. Those who do have electricity stay prepared. The maids make sure that the lamps are filled and they have enough candles handy, because the blackouts do not occur at the same time each night. Since most people don't have refrigerator, food shopping is done daily, especially for thing that are perishable. The food that is prepared must be eaten the same day or it will spoil.

There is a custom that was adopted, mostly among the upper middle class, where, if you cooked more than enough food for the day, the extra food is used to make a plate for the next-door neighbor on either side of your house whenever you could. My mother practiced this with a passion. Every time she was able, she prepared extra food on purpose so she could help others. This custom is a way of making sure that your neighbor doesn't go without while your supply of food is in abundance. Many people cannot afford to help. Most of the time, they are waiting and hoping that a neighbor would bring them a plate of food.

There were times when my mother would call in passersby to come in for a meal. She told us that we must share our overflow with those who are less fortunate. She said that when we help others in their times of need, it is like putting money in God's bank so we might make withdrawals later when we are in need. I think that is a great practice to adopt. As a child, it was very hard for me to comprehend that concept. It bothered me that we were giving away the little bit that we had, when our supply wasn't even enough to meet our own needs. It did not make sense. It has become clearer to me later, after I learned about God's mercies.

Mother had always said that if we give from our hearts that at some time in the future we would reap the benefits. That would certainly be the case when I think about that life and time that we experienced at papa's house.

CHAPTER 3

"New" Papa;
What makes for a real father!
You might have to look up!

*In my Father's house are many rooms; if it
were not so, I would have told you.*

—John 14:2

Donte Joseph, our new papa, was strikingly handsome, clean shaven. He was tall and slender, well educated, and he stood proud and confident. He was respected and well-known in the community. Papa was very courageous, sincere, and mature. He loved Mother, and he loved my sister and me very much. He was all the above things, but to me he was my dearly beloved "new papa."

He was the general manager at a distillery company. He was in charge of everything. Because of his status and position in the community, we were considered "rich." Our new papa provided a beautiful home and a safe environment for us to grow in. He didn't live with us all the time; it was primarily the three of us—Mother, my sister, Marie Anne, and me.

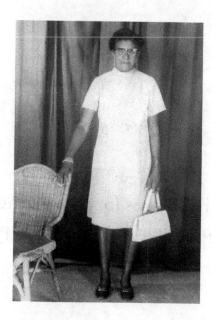

One of my earliest memories is my first experience with a death in the family. My maternal grandmother died at age 107. I remember her to be very beautiful. She was tall and slender, her skin was light, soft, and smooth. Her eyes were like amber; they were piercing and mesmerizing. My mother, a mirror image, perhaps a shade darker. Her passing occurred the same year Mother had moved me to the city to live with her and Marie Anne. I had only been enrolled a few months at the convent when we received word of her demise.

Mother helped us quickly pack our bags, and we waited anxiously for our taxi to arrive. The trip to Mapou Buissonniere is not very far, but a fifteen-mile trip over unpaved roads seems much farther. To avoid getting wet, we were careful to pick a sturdy bridge (*pon*) on which to cross the canal and walk one block east to grandmother's house.

When we arrived, my mother took us inside to Grandma's room to view the body and say good-bye to her. At that time, there were no morgues in Mapou. The body must be kept extremely clean. On the second day, it is covered with a large piece of plastic and iced frequently to keep it cool. The dead must be buried within a few days.

I remember being surprised at the sight of so many people gathering at Grandma's house. Some of them were inside, some slept on the floor, and others were in tents that were ready for the occasion. There were two big fire pits burning all night; the people talked, ate, and mourned. It was like clockwork. After the first group ceased crying, another group began, and they wept all night, each in turn. As an adult, I can see the drama of it all, but as children, our cousin victor, my sister, and other cousins were a little confused and frightened as well. We wondered if we were supposed to cry; we had never been to a wake before.

The funeral was held the next day. A long procession made their way to the mausoleum, which was located in the rear of Grandma's property. The inscription on her crypt read, "La Famille Rocher," and this elevated area featured a small cross and a sitting area with two rocking chairs. Smaller crypts were intended for other members of our family. I thought the really small ones were little houses. Later, of course, I found out otherwise. Tall leafy trees and beautiful flowers were almost everywhere, making it seem like a garden park. To me, it was a breathtakingly beautiful garden.

After the funeral, the people returned to the house for more food and fellowshipping. Grandmother, Francoise Rocher, was blessed with longevity. At age 107, she was still able to wash herself up and eat her meals without the aid of others. There was no wheelchair. Since there was no plumbing, she had to go outside to relieve herself, except for nighttime wherein she used a bedpan kept in the corner of the room. She was not sick; she died in her sleep of natural causes.

The next day, Mother packed our bags and we went back to the city, Leogane, and resumed our normal life. We had one servant and a *restavek* (a young servant that lives in but doesn't get paid). My sister and I were fortunate to have had expensive clothes to wear and to have gone to Sainte Rose de Lima, which was a private school in Leogane. Papa paid all our bills. He was always very nice to us and attentive to our needs, so we never want for anything. He provided a very happy and comfortable life for us; one would consider us privileged and blessed.

Mother always shared with others from the wealth of God's abundant gifts to us through our new papa. Papa came over to our house almost every day, whenever he came to spend time with us, he brought big bags loaded with food, candies, bonbons, and other gifts for us; he gave us dolls, barrettes for our hair, and different kind of toys. We didn't get an allowance, but from time to time, he gave us money too.

Whenever I found out that Papa was coming over, I immediately became excited and couldn't wait to see him. When Papa was around, I felt safe and protected because I knew when he came the whippings would stop. He always made sure that all our needs were provided for. Even though he had other children, he treated us like his own, his little princesses. I say that because we were privileged to have our hair washed and curled at the beauty parlor, just like grown-ups.

Oftentimes when Papa couldn't come home for lunch, Mother sent us to his job to take him his food; he always shared some of his food with us. Papa always made us feel very special and loved. At other times, he came home and we all ate lunch together; and after a very satisfying meal, he took a siesta, and many times, Mother joined him.

Papa seldom spent the night at our house. He was married and had another family who lived in another part of town. Papa was the only daddy we knew. I certainly believe that he loved us, and we loved him as well. The first eight years of my life were lost to me. The lost years were spent with my biological father and I don't know him at all; but I knew my Daddy, my "Papa", and I loved him very much.

As I looked back on it, the years spent with Papa were the best years of my life. I am grateful that he was part of my life. If I were asked to choose a father, he would be the one I would pick. I will never forget him.

I don't ever remember Papa being sick. I remember him as being a very healthy man. That was not the case with mother. She was always very sickly, and always in need of medical attention. Several medications were prescribed for her; we did not know what was wrong with her. Children were not privy to the things concerning adults. Whatever Mother was suffering from seemed incurable. I was afraid that she might die and leave me again.

I have learned that we must trust God in all things, He is our healer. Maybe Mother didn't trust enough because she spent a lot of money consulting with voodoo doctors instead of relying on God. They sold her different types of potions that were supposed to heal her and make her feel better, but none of them had proven to be effective. The voodoo doctors told her that she was being possessed by demons, and that a close family member had put a spell on her. They said that she was in danger in her own house, which made her afraid to be home alone; she had people keeping guard over her.

Mother believed the lies that the voodoo doctors told her. For a long time, she kept going to see them and never got better. I felt so sad watching her in bed suffering, and there were no outward signs of the sickness, except for her losing so much weight. She used to be a vibrant and active woman, always busy taking care of the important things, like her boutique, shopping for beautiful items to adorn her home. She looked sick, very pale, and anorexic; she wouldn't eat, and couldn't sleep.

Some thought that she was crazy. Her problem might have been mental or psychological, but in Haiti, mental health is not a priority. They rather think that people with psychological problems are possessed. They waste money in treatments that are not lasting. They allow voodoo doctors to perform spells and rituals. They read palms and tea leaves. It could be a matter of pride too. They don't want their loved ones to be labeled as mentally ill (*fou* or *folle*), so they don't seek help for mental health until it's too late then they end up putting them in a mental institution.

We were forbidden to go near mother's room. My sister was allowed once in a while to go in because they said she was older and she could handle it. Every time they allowed her to go in, I worried that she would be telling Mother things to make her mad at me. She often stirred up trouble for me, and I had gotten whippings for it.

During the time that mother was sick and couldn't get out of bed, my sister had the privilege of torturing me for bedwetting. I hid and stayed away from her. I cried out for help, but no one came to my aid. There were times when I got vengeful and beat her silly. She didn't have much power while mother was sick, because, after enduring so much pain at her hand, I became stronger.

When is enough, enough? It's one thing for my mother to beat me herself, but making my sister beat me was cruel, and even criminal. I developed a thick skin. I tried to cope with it for a long as I could, but when my mother was not looking, I fought back; and when I did, the cycle repeated itself. She would go and tell on me, she gets to beat on me again, and on and on.

The one good thing I had going for me was that I was smart. I got good grades, all As. They paved the way for me. They earned me favor with Mother every time. The only time my mother was nice to me or complimented me was on report card day, and I looked forward to those days. Our report card came once a month, and that's when I get a reprieve.

We went to church as a family, but we were not devout Christians. We were not born-again. Looking back now, I think her illness might have been caused by menopause. The signs were there: depression, anxiety attacks, fatigue, insomnia, moodiness, etc. I think I had heard it said that Haitian women didn't go through menopause until later than what we know it to be here in America. These women were still having children in their late forties and fifties. I don't believe that the physicians whom she consulted before the voodoo doctors ever gave her hormone replacement therapy treatment. She just had to suffer through it.

During the time of her illness, some of her Christian friends visited. They used to pray for her, laid hands on her. They kept vigil with her when she couldn't be alone. When they laid hands on her, they prayed out loud and sang praises to God for her recovery. Sometimes we were invited to go to their church. Mother was so weak she could hardly walk. Some of the male friends' brothers took her by the arms, one on each side of her, and helped her walk slowly. They carried her when necessary. After a while, she started taking some nourishment and was beginning to feel better. She was humming songs of praise, lifting her hands and raising her voice to the Lord.

One night the meeting was held at our house because mother had asked the elders if it could be done there. That night was when Mother got her breakthrough. She repented of her sins and invited the Lord into her heart, and my sister and I both dedicated our lives to the Lord as well. I was twelve, and my sister was fifteen years old.

When I dedicated my life to God as a young girl, I didn't have a full understanding of what salvation was really about. Looking back on it, I believe that I took that step because my mother did it and we had to follow. However, I felt good about that decision and the fact that I didn't have to worry about demon possession and going to hell was a big relief.

Even though God was in my life and I knew of him, I hadn't yet taken the time to know him in a personal way. It was very hard for me to completely understand it at the time, but I would later learn what it really meant to walk with God.

There was one thing that bothered me about my mother's decision to give her life to God. How could Mother, a Christian woman, live as a kept woman? It also caused me to wonder if her illness was in a way punishment for her sin. My young mind could not understand God's grace at that time. I guess she chose that life in order to provide for us, to allow us to attend school in the city, and to keep her in the lifestyle to which she was accustomed.

Papa was very good-looking. Mother was beautiful and sophisticated. Together they made a perfect pair. They probably met on one of her shopping sprees and decided that her life in the country was no longer satisfying and she wanted something better. We lived with Papa for what seemed to be a very long time, but it was only six years. I was a fast learner. I was able to catch up with my grades and was at the top in my class.

Mother's decision to move to the city was a good thing. It helped us to experience a better quality of life, and it provided us a great start for higher education. Fun and happy memories of my daddy "papa" will forever be in my heart.

When Mother got sicker, her relationship with Papa suffered a decline. Papa had spent a lot of money on real doctors and voodoo doctors. The bills might have been a little more than he was willing to handle. Another reason could be that mother had outlived her usefulness. Papa didn't come to see us as often as he used to. We didn't know why, but I am sure that he must have discussed it with Mother. Gradually, their relationship came to an end.

Mother later told us that Papa was not coming back to see us and that we were moving. He left us lots of presents, but he couldn't handle telling us the bad news himself. I was of course devastated. It was like the end of my world as I knew it. I felt like everything was taken away from me—my security, my safety, my joy, my comfort, my peace, and my happiness. This is yet another wound; the second time that I had been abandoned. I didn't know why. I wondered if I had done something wrong! I remember crying myself to sleep. The thought of not seeing Papa again made me feel like I couldn't go on living.

After the separation, we could no longer live in Papa's house, so we had to move. With no place to live and no money, my mother decided to send my sister and me to live with friends because that way we would be able to continue our schooling in the city. Mother decided that it was best for her to go back to her old house in the country where she could recuperate in solitude.

Going back to the country was a good move on her part. She joined a little church nearby, and she was able to get a lot of rest. Her Christian friends prayed and interceded on her behalf. Her health returned speedily, and after a few months, she fully recuperated from her illness and her broken heart. With the help of her new doctor and the support of family and friends, she was able to manage her health, and her walk with the Lord grew closer and stronger.

Mother sold some of the properties she owned in the country, including what she had inherited from my grandmother Marie Louise. She used the money to acquire an apartment in the big city, Port-Au-Prince, the capital of Haiti. Moving and starting over are never easy.

CHAPTER 4

Living in the Capital;
The suburban shift: A better environment
to raise the children

Go through, go through the gates; prepare the way for the people;
build up, the highway; clear it of stones, lift up a signal over the peoples.
                                                                    —Isaiah 62:10

Starting over in the capital city will not be easy, so Mother had to be frugal with the money because we had no other source of income except for the rental income she received from her remaining properties. When we had to vacate from our nice, beautiful, and comfortable home (Papa's house), our life was shattered. We became poor, living in a one-and-a-half-room rented apartment where all three of us—Mother, Marie Anne, and I—had to share one bed. Most of our furniture was left behind. We had to make do with much, much less. All our possessions had to fit in one room. It was a large room, but it looked very small in comparison to the house we just moved out of.

Mother was very good at decorating. She had a good eye for beauty. She took advantage of the occasion to display her skills. She arranged everything in such a way to make the room appear larger than it really was. Mother made one of the corners of the room to be our living room, our dining table in the opposite corner. She centered the bed against the other wall. The headboard was tall enough to allow for privacy when we had to change, since there was no closet. At the foot of the bed, she placed a big foot locker to be used for storing our good clothes. We wore uniforms every day. Our better clothes were for church. The half room was for everything else.

Our lives had been turned upside-down. This is the first time we didn't have a maid. It seems as if this would be the beginning of the end for our family. Only time would tell.

The landlord's son, "the prince," his name was Vital. His room was above our humble abode, for which we were thankful. Mother always told us to be grateful for what you have. From his balcony he could see all activity in our small porch-like area. I felt so embarrassed every time I saw him. When he was not looking at us, he was enjoying whatever view he had from his balcony. His parents, Mr. and Mrs. Cleophas Pierre, were Christians. They were hard working, Godly people, and they have helped us on many occasions. They've given us groceries when we had none. Often they would send their maid with plates of food for our dinner. In addition, they were very patient with us when the rent was late. The Pierres would always check on us when Mother had to be away to the countryside to bring back sustenance.

My new school was far, but I walked to and fro; 90 percent of children walked to school. Vital walked to school too. Every time I would see him on the way to school, he would gaze at me with his intense light brown eyes, and I went the other way. Then I realized, he was not in high school, he was in college. College de Saint Antoine was just a few blocks away.

We lived in this nice apartment for a short while, and we had to give it up for an even smaller one-room apartment because Mother couldn't afford the rent. The new apartment was in a neighborhood that wasn't as nice as the old one, and I had to walk farther to my new school, which was a public school. I adjusted well to public school, and I was ahead of everyone else. I was well respected by my teachers and my peers. I was very smart. I'm sure they could tell that I was poor, because sometimes I wore my private school uniforms with the logo on them as I did not have much else to wear. We didn't wear jeans and T-shirts.

Madame David, one of my teachers, befriended me. She was a widow with three daughters of her own. Gladys the oldest was around my age, Simone and Jasmine were younger. I was surprised and felt special when Mrs. David invited me to her house to spend time with her family. I knew Mother would object, so I told her it was for a school project and only a chosen few were invited. She ate it up like candy. She'd go for anything that would help to further my education. I always enjoyed spending time at their house. She would send me home with extra food, and she also gave me shoes and clothes from Gladys's closet. Gladys was a bit taller than me, but we wore the same size clothes and shoes.

We lived in the new place for a few months then we had to move again, and again. This is the straw that broke the camel's back. This place was like a shack. Again, we are reminded that we are blessed to have it. Don't get me wrong, I am not being ungrateful, just thinking of the good old days. Mother said that there were others that would love to have the crumbs that fell from our table. That was funny, what crumbs?

A lot of the times my mother went without and allowed us to eat whatever little bit that was available. I remember a time when we had nothing at all; it was after a devastating hurricane that had wiped out everything in our area, and our cupboard was empty. We had a good neighbor who wasn't doing all that well herself, but she thought of how bad life was going for us. She found some rice that was hidden way back in the cupboard, and it had started to spoil already. She didn't have anything else to offer us but the spoiled rice. She said that she remembered that my mother had helped her numerous times in the past. She felt uncomfortable that she didn't have much to offer, but that was all she had for her family and she wanted to share it with us.

Mother was grateful for God's provision. She washed the rice, but it had bugs in it. Rice bugs are the same color as the rice. They're not really bugs. They looked like tiny worms. The only reason you can see them is because they can float. That's all we had, so she cooked the rice, bugs and all. That was our supper. There was no meat. We gave thanks to God for it, and we just closed our eyes and ate it. My mother said, "Worms are full of protein." I laugh about that even now. How can I forget something like that! I have learned in everything, good or bad, to depend on the Lord.

Philippians 4:12 says, "I know what it is to be in need, and I know what it is to have plenty. I have learned the secret of being content in any and every situation, whether well fed or hungry, whether in plenty or in want." There were times when I cried myself to sleep because I was so hungry, but I still went to school and kept my good grades. That's all I had going for me. I wasn't about to mess it up. One way or another, God had always provided for us.

One day, I came home from school and Mother was fixing a scrumptious meal. It smelled so good, and I was so hungry I could eat a horse. Guess who was invited to dinner? Our old landlord's son, Vital. I was told that while I was at school, he came to our apartment. He brought bags of groceries, and gave mother money to keep us supplied for at least another month. Later, mother told us that he said that there was more to come, whenever we needed it. He had come to ask Mother's permission to date me. Of course, she agreed. He kissed me right then and there, and I spit and ran out of the room. That was the first time that I was kissed by a boy. As I was leaving, I heard my mother say to him, "She is shy. She'll get the hang of it." Mother could smell a meal ticket from a mile away. I think, that was her way of providing for us.

He was very handsome, quiet, and easygoing. He was humble and generous, but the magic was not there for me. Why didn't he pick my sister? They were around the same age, and she didn't have a boyfriend. Vital was a very nice and generous person. My thoughts toward him were not judgmental but prejudicial. I couldn't see myself dating him because he was a Jehovah's Witness when I was a Christian. The two shall not mix; we would be unevenly yoked, and the Bible warns us about that.

Mother said it was okay, so I guess we were dating, but I felt like I was cheating on God (2 Cor. 6:14). Our dating didn't last very long; we only kissed once, nothing else. Thank goodness, he didn't try to have sex with me. His religion forbids premarital sex; they even encouraged having a chaperone when people go out on dates. Mother would object to that as well, and that would definitely have been a deal breaker.

I graduated from high school when I was sixteen years old. It was common in Haiti for students to graduate at sixteen. If you are a slow learner, they would hold you back one, and even two years, if they have to.

I was very smart, with a high IQ. Given the fact that I started going to school later than the average children, the nuns still allowed me to move as fast as I could. It didn't take long for me to get on track and do well.

Things might be different now in Haiti, but fifty, sixty years ago when I was a child, almost 40 percent of the Haitian population was illiterate. They didn't have schools nearby, and even worse for the people who lived in the country.

I was born in the country, and my father was illiterate; he did not believe in formal education. He believed that if you have wealth, that's all the education you need. My mother, on the other hand, knew better. That's one of the reasons she moved to the city, where her children could get a good education. That's what she told us! My father's view on education was not the same as some of the other rich in Mapou. Many of them sent their children to school in the city.

Most parents cannot help their children with homework because they don't know how—it is like a different language to them. The native language is Creole, and that's what every Haitian speaks. French is learned when children go to school. Those who never attended school cannot speak French, nor do they understand it, so it's like a foreign language to them.

"Eyes in your books," Mother always said. I was very obedient when it came to school issues. I had never seen adults showing affection to one another. Boys did not interest me. I did not know how to give or accept affection. I thought that sex and kissing and physical attraction was something dirty. I had a one-track mind, and my books were my friends.

Many things have changed in Haiti since 1963, when I graduated valedictorian from high school. I did not deliver the closing statement at the graduation ceremony. Our graduation ceremonies, unlike other countries, are not grandiose. Graduates were not given a diploma at graduation. Here is the way they proceed: the finals are done at a neutral place, a government facility, where all students from the schools in the area gather in one big room. The student next to you is someone you've never met before, from a different school, whom you might never see again. Everyone is all dressed up, wearing their Sunday best.

This is the only time we are permitted to wear regular clothing. Most parents spent a lot of money to buy new clothes for this occasion (if they can afford it). Since my mother could not afford to buy me new clothes, Mrs. David bought me three brand-new dresses for the occasion. Having those dresses made me feel very happy and blessed.

Our finals lasted three full days, and after that, everyone nervously waits an entire month for the results. They announce the names of the successful candidates on the radio, in alphabetical order. On the day of the announcement, students gather together with friends and family, listening for their names to be called. This makes for some very happy and some not so happy students. Those who have succeeded are allowed to go on a picnic for graduates only. During the graduation ceremony, the valedictorian recites the memorized poem chosen for the occasion. In Haiti, students are thought to memorize all their lessons. Many students failed because they're unable to memorize their lessons; therefore, they failed their finals. Thanks be to God for having given me a very sharp memory.

Having graduated at age sixteen, I started college right away. Due to limited finances, I decided to become a teacher. With a two-year certificate, I could start teaching at a private school without credentials. That was my plan while I continued my college education. There are no grants or student loans, no jobs flipping burgers or washing dishes, so parents had to pay for the children's education. My mother was financially challenged at that time. Ever since her illness that almost took her life, our money situation had been meager, and even worse when I started college. We only had the bare necessities, borrowing from Peter to pay Paul. I went to my friend's house to study because I could not afford to buy my books.

God has always provided for us, and mother always had something up her sleeves. Without my noticing it, there was a new suitor coming around, and I was always the last to know. I didn't have a clue of who he was or what was going on. I thought maybe he was there for my sister, I was too busy to care. I was studying as hard as I could because I wanted to get my teaching certificate as quickly as possible.

Vital had invited me to go to kingdom hall with him as he always did in the past; the answer was always a big fat no. I always felt that going to a church that you think is bad for you would be like going against the grain, against God. This time was different. I wanted to know. I just wanted to see what that religion was all about. I wanted to see for myself, so I decided to go with him.

The welcome team was warm and courteous. He introduced me as his fiancée, but I did not consider myself as that. As far as I was concerned, we were just dating because mother said so. Their service was very different from ours; it didn't impress me at all. They called it a kingdom hall meeting. It was foreign to me. I would prefer to stick to what I know. I was vulnerable at that time. I was very weak when it came to walking with God, just beginning to walk by faith. I didn't want to be pushed into doing something that I don't know anything about.

Jehovah's Witnesses don't believe in being unequally yoked. After the meeting, all Vital wanted to talk about was for me to convert to Jehovah's Witness so we could get married. When I refused, we had a big fight and he left. I was too busy for that kind of commitment at that time, and furthermore, I was already married to my books.

I wasn't sure how mother was going take the news. I started to psychologically prepare myself for my punishment. When I told Mother that I broke up with Vital, she was disappointed that I didn't consult her first, but to my surprise, she wasn't upset. She told me not to worry, that she had a better plan for my life, and that a bigger door had been opened and she thought it was from God.

CHAPTER 5

Sleeping with the Enemy;
The worse nightmare.

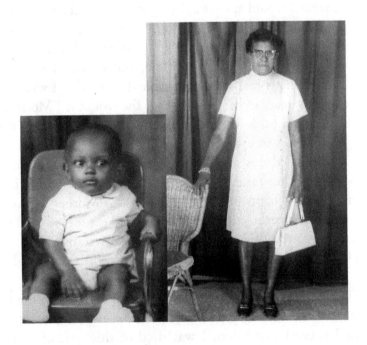

*He rescued me from my powerful enemy, from
my foes, who were too strong for me.*

—Psalm 18:17

Is it door number one or door number two? In the summer of 1965, in the hope of solving our financial dilemma, my mother forced me to marry Sully Pierre, a man I did not know, a man I did not love. There was no courtship period prior to the marriage. I was just told by my mother that I was going to marry Monsieur Sully Pierre, as if he were royalty. She said, "We had found favor with this rich man who wants to marry you. He said that you are beautiful, very attractive. Since you are a virgin and you are pure, he has chosen you to be his wife. All the preparations have been made for you and he to get married."

I was not allowed to respond. I was not asked if I wanted to get married. I couldn't agree or disagree. The decision was made for me. I felt cold, I had chills, I was frozen. I was so afraid that I couldn't speak because when I opened my mouth, nothing came out. To my mother, a refusal would appear as being disrespectful and ungrateful. I was very much afraid of my mother, so afraid that when I started my period, I could not bring myself to tell her that I had been bleeding. I was fifteen years old at that time, and I didn't know what it was. I thought that I had some incurable disease, that I was dying. I couldn't tell my sister either for fear that she would tell Mother.

I bled for almost a whole day, not knowing that it was a natural thing that happens in every young woman's life. That is so sad. We had never discussed this sort of things before. Could it be that since we depended on her for everything that she knew we would have to go to her when it happened? I had never seen Mother or my sister using any kind of protection or talk about that time of the month. That sounds very stupid but that's just the way things were. Adults only tell things on a need-to-know basis, when the time is right, not before.

The beatings had stopped then, but she would slap me in the face; that was her new way of disciplining me at that time when she thought I needed correction. I was tired of this type of treatment from her. The sad thing is that we never talked or bonded with each other—practically no emotions between us. We were almost like two strangers, two ships passing in the night. I kept my mouth shut for a moment, then she gave me that look, and I said, "*Oui, Maman*" (which means "Yes, Mother"). There was no way out for me, except to run away, but where would I go? Nowhere to run, nowhere to hide.

Things moved rather quickly. I was almost eighteen years old, married to a thirty-one years old man. A marriage of convenience to someone fourteen years older than me, and we had nothing in common. He was an atheist; he never went to church one day in his life. He was also involved in voodoo practices.

My mother told me that he has the means to take good care of me, all my needs will be met, and we would not be poor anymore.

Sully was a shrewd businessman who made his fortune in the transportation business. He was a man that had no regard for others, so he did whatever he wanted and whenever he wanted to do it. He did not care about other people's rights, or the law, because he had the government in his pocket. I found out later that he was so deeply involved into the voodoo practices that he had sold his firstborn to the devil.

Sully was smart and possessive, not a nice man, and always angry. He often took his anger out on me. He slapped me around. He raped me every night according to his many moods. I would be beaten whenever he felt I wasn't obeying his rules. This treatment made me feel alone, abandoned, and dead on the inside because I thought that God had forsaken me. I was miserable every day. I had no peace of mind. I never knew when something was going to happen. When I thought that the child abuse days were behind me, no more getting slapped, that, just maybe I could have a better life; I found out that I was coming out of the frying pan into the fire. Sully was much, much worse than Mother.

I felt like my mother had sold me to devil. She thought that because he had money, he would be a good provider. Maybe she wasn't aware of the kind of man he was. What Mother didn't know was that she sentenced me to a life of torture, torment, pain, and punishment. I was beginning to wonder where God was. Why had he forsaken me? I was forced to endure physical, psychological, and emotional anguish, always in fear for my well-being and, at times, even for my life.

Sully forbade me to have friends. I couldn't communicate with our neighbors. I was not allowed to attend church functions. I couldn't come out on our own front porch without him present. He did not even allow me to visit my mother. I was a prisoner in my own house.

I was a trophy wife. I was told how to act and when to act. He was the lion king, and I was his defenseless prey. We had servants to run the house, and I would be breaking the rules if I tried to run my own home. I would not dare to try to have a discussion with him. My so-called husband would slap me, kick me, and try to choke me if I did. I lived in constant fear. My whole body was covered with black-and-blue marks. If I cried when the pain was too hard to bear, he told me to shut up or worse would happen to me, to him that was a sign that I was being ungrateful.

My job was to always look my best for him, waiting for him with a smile on my face when he came home from work. When we socialized with his friends, whether we are at our home or away from home, I should not bring attention to myself. If I tried to mingle with others, he would say I am trying to embarrass him in front of his friends and that I should sit and be quiet, what I have to say is not important. There is always hell to pay afterwards. More beatings and expecting me to be ready for intercourse.

I think he was possessed by the devil. He always accused me of making him act that way. He said that he loved me so much and couldn't stand for other men to look at me with desiring eyes. He always made me promise to never leave him or look at another man besides him. My husband wanted me to always look perfect for him. He told me what to eat and when to eat, what to wear, when to sleep. (We took a siesta every day after lunch.) In Haiti, we refer to lunch as dinner and dinner as supper. Lunch was the heaviest meal of the day, and supper was always light. He would not let me eat late at night, that would be out of the question. He was always watching my figure, if I gained one pound that would be an unpardonable sin.

Sully would pick what I would wear to different functions. We socialized often because that helped boost his business. Part of his enterprise was to provide transportation for certain music groups to and from their gigs. He carried them to formal dances, different types of parties, but at other times it could be just to the groups rehearsal meetings. A lot of the times he sent his employees to do it, but at other times, he would take them himself.

We got free passes to different events. We would dress up, and of course he picked my outfits, complete with shoes and handbag. My clothes were tailor made for me. The seamstress came to our home to take my measurements and personally delivered what he ordered. My husband always chose what I wear for different occasions. He decides how I should wear my hair, up or down, the shoes style and height of the heels, he would tend to every detail, even the perfume he wants to smell on me. There were times when he would get me all dressed and changed his mind and we would end up staying home. He'd say, "You look too delicious, I don't want anyone to look at you tonight," and he would then attack me and rape me. I would not dare say no to him, couldn't even say I had a headache.

When we did go to these parties, there were times when he'd let me sit while he danced with other women. There were times when we danced the first dance together and he would ignore me the rest of the night, and I would go home upset. If I was extremely good, or if he planned to have his way with me later, he would save the last dance for me. Some of the times he would pick the last song, something to suit his mood, and he would say to me, "You know I picked this song because of you." I felt used. When I felt bold enough to talk back, I would tell him that I didn't believe him because what I know is that he is doing it for himself.

I was a naïve young girl, caught between an unstable husband and a mother who thought she was doing her best for her child or, just maybe for herself. There were times when I thought about that transaction, it made me feel more unloved and disgusted. My mother clearly loved my older sister more than me; I knew that she did it for herself. She was running out of money, out of options, and here is a golden opportunity to rid herself of her financial responsibilities. I can almost hear her think, "The girl is smart but naïve. She can't understand it now, but she'll thank me later." I never had the nerve to ask her if Sully gave her any money for selling me to him.

I did not get love from Mother, but her actions spoke louder than words. Her lack of love pushed me to acquire strength to do things for myself, take courage, and move on. I developed a sense of I can do anything if I put my mind to it and "give it an all you got" attitude and don't leave any job unfinished. Look back only long enough that you don't forget where you came from, but don't get stuck there.

Being unloved also thought me to remember how far the Lord has brought me from, to always look ahead and reach high. Always be your best and do your best. Don't be blinded by pride because even at your best there could be someone better than you, and at your worst there could be one lower than you. Don't step on him, use his situation as a lesson to encourage you to move up and make room for him too.

I really did not understand all that was going on. My life was in shambles, trapped with nowhere to go. I don't have any friends and was not allowed to visit my family. I was stuck in a mess that I did not create. I need to get smart and roll with the punches. I need to try to stop the beatings by being very obedient; it worked sometimes, but other times the demon in him had to come out. So I learned to pray in my mind and in my heart without making any noise. I found a place where I could go and be whenever I wanted to, in the arms of Jesus, where it felt safe. Whenever I go there, nothing else mattered. I endured my abuse and felt no pain. Being raped was expected, it did not faze me anymore. Instead of fighting it, I pretended it wasn't happening.

About sex? I was a virgin when we got married. No one had ever told me what to expect. We did not hear about it on the radio or see it on television programs. We didn't own a TV and I'd never seen any parents showing affection one to the other. As for me, it is as if sex did not exist. I thought kissing was unhealthy. Having someone else's spit in my mouth is just one way of exchanging germs. Dating was forbidden. A boy had tried to kiss me once, and from that first kiss I realized that I wasn't missing anything. The same goes for sex.

My first sexual experience was with my husband, and it was not a good experience. It did not seem like rape that first time. He sort of told me that it might hurt, that it would be uncomfortable at first but it would get better later and don't worry there would be some bleeding. I guess we can give him a little credit for that. But I wish he didn't, because right away, I got scared. *Pain* and *blood* are not my two favorite words. I panicked and I cringed. I could feel his weight on top of me. I held my breath, closed my eyes, and I felt ashamed. I thought of him more as an uncle. My first experience should have been with someone around my own age. Oh well! Who asked me to think?

This process went on and on for about one year and a half, and I never experienced the thrill, the ecstasy, or the fireworks that's supposed to happen between two people in the boudoir. Well, the worst happened: I was pregnant, but I didn't know it. He knew it. He gave me three little pills and a glass of water and he said, "Take this."

And I replied, "What are they for?"

And he said, "Take them now," in a loud voice, and made sure that I swallowed them. He warned me to never question him again, or there will be consequences to pay.

I found out much later what the pills were. They must have done their apparent miracle because the next day, after our usual siesta, I had menstrual cramping that lasted a long time. They were so severe that I did not get up for dinner. I stayed in bed until the following day, and my period came flowing down with a vengeance.

I guess this was a miscarriage or an abortion caused by the little pill. This happened almost every month. The little pills must have been the morning-after pill, and he was using it as birth control. I didn't know about that kind of things then; I am only book smart. My mind began to wander. I realized that my period always came after I took the little pills, so I decided not to take them, just to see what would happen. Even though he was standing right there and made me swallow the pills. This time I pretended to, but the pills didn't go down. We laid down as usual for siesta. When we woke up I was not cramping and my period did not come. He questioned me about not having taken the pills, but I lied.

"You were right there when I swallowed," I said. "Was it supposed to make my period come?" (I was laughing inside.) I didn't realize that my action was going to cause a lot more anguish for me. He slapped me.

"Are you making fun of me?"

I said, "No, I am sorry, just wanted to know."

I was pregnant again, but he wasn't so lucky this time, or should I say I wasn't so lucky. The morning-after pills did not work because I never took them. My curiosity caused all this.

I don't recall how much time had passed before he made his move. One evening, he took me to the doctor, who was one of his friends. He didn't tell me where we were going or why. When we got there, I was taken to a room in the back. I was told to undress and lay on the bed on my back. I was very scared. He and the doctor acted as if I wasn't even there. My feet were in the stir ups and told to bring my bottom way down to the edge of the bed and open my legs. Then I felt the pressure of the instrument going into me. I felt the pain with every stroke of the instrument scraping inside of me. I was crying unconsolably. I wished I had died. I guess that was an abortion and a D and C.

When he was done, we went home and I got in the bed. I was cramping a lot, so my husband gave me Tylenol. I bled for about two weeks. Refusing to eat, I'd gotten weak and depressed. I stayed in the bed almost paralyzed, could barely move. Sully must have talked to the doctor. One day he brought home a large bottle of some kind of elixir because he said I was anemic. He forced me to take it three times a day. When he went to work, the servants were to watch over me and make sure that I ate and take the magical elixir. One week or two later, I regained my appetite and began to feel better.

CHAPTER 6

A Son Is Born;
"The Gift of God!" Being a parent doesn't
come with a rule book

Let the little children come to me, and do not hinder them,
for the kingdom of God belongs to such as these.
—Mark 10:14

I am with child! I was thinking, for someone who is so smart, so shrewd, Sully was stupid. Why didn't he put me on birth control pill? Why didn't he use condom? I figured it out later: his deal with the devil was to sell his firstborn for worldly gain. Possibly, his contract precluded him from preventing conception! I am thinking he must have taken a chance with the abortions. Maybe that's the reason I almost bled to death. We will never really know for sure. Will we?

A few months after that deadly abortion, early in January 1967, my menstrual cycle didn't come. Sully gave me the three little pills. This time, I was more aware of what was going on. I wanted to maintain control over my body. Abortion is a sin against God and against my body, and I do not want another abortion. I hid the pills under my tongue, swallowed the water, and laid down for siesta. He did not take siesta this time; instead, he sat at the foot of the bed and watched me sleep. I was not cramping when I awoke; his wonder pills did not work, so he thought! He accused me again of not taking the pills.

I answered, "You're right. I didn't."

To my surprise, he did not slap me for talking back, but when we went to bed that night, he raped me one last time. He was very rough and forceful, so brutal that my vagina was raw and bruised. I was in such pain that I prayed that I would never again have sex for the rest of my life. I just wanted to die. I don't think he raped me for pleasure that time. Could it be that he was trying to cause me to abort the seed that was planted in my womb?

Since then, things were kind of quiet, maybe even nice. My husband started coming home late, and this went on night after night. Even though he came home late, I was still not permitted to go to bed without him. It was sort of a blessing that he came home late because I didn't have to see or talk to him. Maybe it was part of his plan. All I know is since the last brutal rape, we never had sex again.

Finally, one Tuesday morning, in March I recall, he woke me up very early and told me that his business required him to go out of town for a while and to send for my mother to come and stay with me. My mind was wondering why. He had never let me visit my family, nor could they visit me, the whole time we've been married. I figured it was part of the deal he made with my mother when she sold me to him. He gave me money and told me to go shopping for maternity clothes and flat shoes. He also told me not wear high heels while I was pregnant. When I heard that, I almost fainted. I say that because for so long he tried to prevent me from becoming pregnant, and now that I was he seemed to do all he could to make sure that I had the baby. I almost opened my big mouth to say something, but instead I remained silent.

What is going on? He has never allowed me to go anywhere without him, he has always picked the clothes that I wore. Is this a trick? Could this be a test to see how I would behave? So he left, while I was still in bed. I think this is the Lord's doing. He was protecting me from the power of evil. This man realized that he couldn't kill me, so he had to leave me.

When I got up later that morning, and after taking a shower, I went to the dining room for some nourishment. I noticed there was an envelope on the table with some writing on it. It says, "Read before you go shopping." So I opened it. The note said, "You are pregnant, take care of yourself. The house is sold. You can only stay another six weeks. Send for your mother to come stay with you for those six weeks and then go back home with her until I return. The maid has been paid for the next six weeks. Do not expect her to return after that time." No face-to-face goodbyes, no *au revoir*, no farewell, no "It was good raping you." And that would be the last time he communicated with me.

I started crying. I couldn't think. For a reason I can't explain, I was already missing him. My thoughts were racing. How am I going to function without him? It was as though I couldn't live with him but in that moment, I couldn't live without him. Just had a taste of freedom for two minutes. He has sent me shopping alone—I can pick whatever I want. What now? There had not been any physical, psychological, nor mental abuse for a while. What is going on? What is he up to? Is he leaving me? Is that why he wants my mother to come? Was he returning me for a full refund? I am almost sure he is leaving me. Is that good or bad? At this point, I am not sure.

I am sure my mother is going to be disappointed in me. It has only been one and a half year since we've been married. This seems like an eternity. My mother does not know what I have been going through, but I know she's going to think that I must have done something to make Sully angry. Can she try to be on my side for once? She has not laid eyes on me since the day I got married, not sure if she had inquired about my well-being. Why hasn't he brought me to visit her? Just maybe, this must have been part of their arrangement.

My mind was running away with me, I did not want to send for her, nor did I want to move back home with her. She'll make my life a different kind of hell. I often wondered if he was sending her money to help with her financial situation. Maybe the amount is bigger, or smaller, depending on how well I behaved. I never had the nerve to ask her. We will never know. Whether I want to or not, I need her to come so she can tell me what to do. I have never had to make any decision for myself all of my life. First my mother was the decision maker, then it was Sully. I am nineteen years of age, a grown married woman, but still a child, unable to move on. For the first time in my life I should feel free to live as I pleased, but I am still in bondage. God, please, help me! I felt betrayed and abandoned again!

I felt like the children of Israel. After Pharaoh allowed them to leave, when they were about to cross the Red Sea, they were too afraid to cross. I am frightened as well. I cried myself to sleep, and am not sure for how long. A knock at the door woke me up. I didn't want to answer the door because I was never allowed to before. I thought I was waking up from a dream, wishing that this day had never happened. I want this nightmare to be over. I decided to open the door, and realized it was not a dream, it was my mother. My worst nightmare.

I said, "It is so good to see you, Mama," standing there sobbing and with tears curling down my face. "How did you get here, Mother?"

She looked mad, and she had blood in her eyes. As if to accuse me of wrong doing, she said, "Why did you have to make Sully mad and mess things up"?

I replied, "What did he accuse me of, Mama?"

She hadn't seen me in almost two years. She didn't hug me or kiss me. All she cared about was accusing me of things she knew nothing about. She started telling all the lies that Sully had concocted against me. He said that I was disobedient, I refused to keep my mouth shut when he spoke to me, and he said the baby is not his (I would say not, it's God's baby.), etc.

She said, "Who do you think was paying for your college tuition and your books and the uniforms and food? I had been broke for a long time, and he has been a God sent to us." She finished by telling me that she didn't believe the part that the baby is not his. Furthermore, she said that I needed to get on my knees and beg him to take me back. And it would be a disgrace, an embarrassment to our family if I had to come back home to live with her.

58

She refused to let me explain to her what had been going on for the past year and a half. She preferred to believe what this liar had told her. Could it be that she didn't want to lose her meal ticket? I kept quiet and let her vent and playing the blame game. I later found out that he is the one who brought her over to our house. He did not have to leave town on business.

In an effort to calm her down, I admitted to her that I was wrong for disappointing her, that she knows what's best for me and I would be willing to follow whatever decision she made, to let her run the show.

Finally, after so many apologies for my behavior and so many tears, and admitting that mother is always right, she allowed me to speak. I told her all the nasty things I had to endure: the beatings, and how he kicked me in my stomach, the abortions, and all my pain and suffering.

She said, "Oh, he didn't tell me all that." I am not sure if she believed me or not. But at this stage of the game, I wanted to say to her, "Frankly my dear 'Mom,' I don't really give a damn." I realized that, as of that very moment, I was free, free at last, liberated, and even empowered.

Then I said to my mother "I don't want to be disrespectful, but I am not asking for permission. I don't want to be here one moment longer than I have too. I want to move back home as soon as possible."

What does moving back home mean for me at that time? More misery, a different kind of misery. My mother had no money; I did not have any money either. She is not in the best of health, and I am pregnant, which means more problems for the both of us.

I'm going to need prenatal care, money for hospital bills, and after the baby is born, baby food and everything else that goes with having a baby. Nothing is free in Haiti. We don't have a welfare system, no WIC, no credit cards, or help programs. The government does not make men pay child support. I don't have a job. What am I going to do? I didn't create this mess, Mother did it, let her "take one for the team"; not me.

We are back at my mother's house. I am three months pregnant. The big bad wolf is no longer in the picture, no more abuse, no more beating, no kicking, but we had no food. My beautiful home is gone, no servants, and I have no transportation. My mother only has a restavec (a live-in person, unpaid not a maid).

My situation reminded me of the children of Israel, who, when they came out of Egypt and came upon hard time and began to compare that with their life in Egypt (Numbers 11:5), they considered going back. So, for a moment, I thought to myself, should I try to return to "Egypt" or trust God for his provision? Egypt looked very good from where I stood. I didn't want to think about Egypt. If God allowed it, there must be a reason and that makes it okay. The Lord showed me that it was a good thing that Sully left me. I started going back to church and having fellowship with other Christians. Every time something bad happened in my life, I call on the Lord for strength, and feel a certain kind of peace that only God can give. I was learning to trust him more and more.

My mother found out later that the devil was behind all the previous events. They also had told her that Sully had sold his first-born to the devil. In my mind, I was thinking that Sully was trying to play games with the devil. Each time I became pregnant would be an opportunity for the devil to collect on the deal that Sully had made with him. And I was also thinking that his many attempts to cause me to abort was his way of delaying payment to the devil, and the reason he said that the baby was not his is because if he denies the child, the devil cannot touch what does not belong to him. Of course, there is no way I will ever know for sure what Sully's plan was, but at the time, this all made sense to me as I thought about my situation.

My mother made me fast and wear sackcloth once every week during the pregnancy. She was told that this should help to protect me and the baby from the enemy's attacks. That's what we were told, but what I believe is that my baby belongs to the Lord, and that's why the devil couldn't touch him. The Lord protected us because we were covered by the blood of Jesus.

I didn't get enough food to eat during the pregnancy. I was beginning to lose weight. I couldn't afford the prenatal vitamins, except for a few samples that the doctor gave me when I went for my visits. I was hungry all the time. My mother used to make soup with just water and a few vegetable leaves—that was our meal. There is a Haitian prayer/proverb combination that goes like this: "*Seigneur, donne du pain a ceux qui ont la faim, et donne la faim de toi, a ceux qui ont du pain.*" The English translations is "O, Lord, give bread to those who have hunger, and hunger of thee to those who have bread." I trusted Him, and He provided enough to sustain my physical need. Now, I hunger for Him.

My best friend at the time, Rita Cameau, came to visit me and noticed how bad things were for us. She gave us some money, and each time she came back, she brought whatever she could. She was like the ravens that God sent to feed Elijah (1 Kings 17:6).

I did not want my baby to be born in such deplorable conditions. Rita was godsend. She always had words of encouragement. She was much older than I and married with no children, so she sort of adopted me. When I was approaching my due date, Rita invited me to move with her and her husband in the city until after the birth of my child. Her financial situation wasn't all that great, but she was better off than we were. Many times while living with Rita, when there wasn't enough food for everyone to get a full plate, Rita sacrificed some of her share in order for me to get enough to eat. She also even helped to pay for some other bills I incurred.

At every stage of my life when I think I can't hang on any longer, almost at the point of giving up, God has always sent me a guardian angel just when I needed one most. Just when I thought I couldn't handle the pain one minute longer, he would take it away. I remember reading somewhere that if a pregnant woman fasted on a particular day of the week, that's the day the baby would be born. I decided to try it. I had chosen Tuesday—the same day I was already fasting and wearing sackcloth—that was also the day that Sully left us. I fasted not only because of what I'd read, but also because I would feel better if I fasted on purpose, rather than being hungry and not having any food to eat. I would soon find out that, what I'd read did come to pass. When I fasted, I concentrated on prayer and kept my mind focused on God, I wasn't hungry; God's word was my food.

On Tuesday morning, October 10, 1967, my beautiful baby boy was born. My labor started that Tuesday morning. The pain woke me up. I remember looking at the clock, and it was exactly twelve midnight. The contractions became stronger and more frequent as time went by.

Rita gave me some home remedy that was supposed to speed up the contractions. She made me walk up and down the stairs as many times as I could. It wasn't long before Rita and her husband were transporting me to the hospital. I was in labor for only five hours. My birth canal was too narrow, so they had to make an incision on the left side of my vagina to help bring the baby out. After a lot of screaming and pushing, my son was born. My son weighed seven pounds and a half, and he was named Ducarmel Didier Pierre. I felt an overwhelming sense of relief. After delivery, my son was placed in a small bassinette next to my bed, where I could see him. For fear that he would not be stolen or possibly switched, I kept my eyes on him constantly.

Two days later, I had to deal with another complication in that the doctor who delivered my baby forgot to stitch my incision, and the result was I contracted an infection that caused me a lot of pain. They stitched it the night before I was to be released. The next day, my son and I went back to Rita's house. The stitches came apart the next day. Because of the infection, the area was too tender and raw to hold the stitches, causing me to experience excruciating pain. I couldn't afford to go back to the hospital, so I bore the pain for a while. Eventually, with the help of home remedies, the area was healed, leaving a scar.

Before I was released from the hospital, they asked for the name of the baby's father, or the person responsible for paying the bill. Rita ask them to wait for a moment while she went to talk to a friend. Rita's friend was a hospital administrator, and he gave her a voucher for the total bill. My heart overflowed with gratitude for that act of kindness. That was definitely the mercies of God. I had never paid a bill before, my mother took care of everything and then, there was Sully. I didn't know what it would cost to be hospitalized for three days to deliver a baby, I am not even sure if I had given it any thought at all. But God took care of it.

I will never forget what the Lord has done for me. My debt has been paid in full, cancelled, just like that. It reminded me of the debt that Jesus paid when he died on the cross.

As we go through life's testing, we can rely on God for strength and perseverance. He is refining us through our toughest moments. Job 23:10 says, "When God has tested me, I will come forth as gold." We named my son Ducarmel Didier Pierre. I made Rita his Godmother, and we called him DD. He and I stayed with Rita for a few days then we moved back home with mother. I told her that it would only be for a short time until I find a job to support us. There is no AFDC nor WIC program in Haiti.

When I was attempting to breastfeed Ducarmel, the nurse discovered a cyst in my left breast. My doctor would not allow me to breastfeed. We had no money for baby formula. Mother could only afford one bottle of milk per day, so she watered it down to last the whole day. At night, she gave him weak tea, which had no nutritional value. We had no other recourse. The tea helped to appease him from crying all night, due to his hunger. As his mother, I felt so helpless, sad and depressed. I looked at the baby lying in the bed, looking so frail, with his diapers made of old sheets soaking wet because we couldn't change him often enough. His bottom was also red with a severe diaper rash. It was more than I could bare. I felt like I wanted to die. I prayed for the day to go by so I could sleep off my troubles, but when the night came, the depression and anxiety were like a sentinel hovering over me.

When I couldn't stand watching my baby suffer like that anymore, I decided that this couldn't be my baby. My baby would be well cared for in his own room, with his nanny at his beck and call, and I would be wearing silk pajamas and beautiful robes, sitting in a rocking chair singing him lullabies. This is not my life! This is not how I wanted to live.

Even though I was suffering on the inside, I came to the conclusion that it would be better for me to leave than to watch my baby suffer. I felt that my leaving would be better in that there would be more for them after I was gone. I decided that the time to leave was now, so I decided to let my mother know my plan. When I went to my mother's room, she was resting. I spoke in a controlled but firm voice because I did not want to be intimidated and lose courage.

I said, "Mother, you are responsible for the situation we are in right now. This baby is the result of your interfering in my life. This is your baby, not mine. You can do with him as you wish. I am leaving and never coming back."

I never bonded with the baby anyway. I didn't think he would miss me. The whole time during my pregnancy, I only felt hatred for Sully. Maybe I was hating the product of his loin. I know I kept a watchful eye on him in the hospital after he was born. I didn't want them to give me someone else's baby, but I'm not sure if I loved him or not, and in that I loved him as a child but not as a son. Without saying another word, I grab my bags and I left.

As I think back on the day I left my mother and son, I am sure my anger had a lot to do with my past relationship with Sully. From the time Sully left me until shortly after my son was born, if I was asked, in one word, to describe how I felt, the word would be *angry* in big bold print. In fact, angry would not have been enough because I was also mad, sad, disappointed, and resentful. So much so that if I had a gun I probably would have shot myself or someone else. I felt abandoned, forsaken, tormented, used, weak, and alone. I was sapped out of all strength, reduced to a shell of a woman and defenseless. My madness was such that I thought I was going to lose my mind.

I felt that someone had to pay for all the wrong that was done to me, including the time loss from birth to eight years old. I am not sure who to blame. It would be disrespectful if I blamed God or to be mad at God for allowing this atrocity. God knows best, and he is well aware of what I have gone through, and I must trust him and accept that in due time, all my troubles will cease.

I am ashamed to say that being pregnant with Sully's child felt like he was still in my life, like I was a surrogate waiting for the baby to be born so I can have my body back. When the opportunity came, I felt free. I was free to be myself for a change, with nothing holding me back and no one to dictate what I could or not do.

Even as I am sharing this part of my story, I am so ashamed of my action. I am so sorry that I behaved that way. My heart aches and bleeds because of what I have done. I am guilty and deserving death, but God gave me mercy. God allowed me another chance to be with my son later. I am so thankful for his forgiveness, and I praise him for delivering me from my shame and guilt.

CHAPTER 7

I Am a Kept Woman;
"Desperate times call for desperate measures."
No excuses

I know that nothing good lives in me, that is, in my sinful nature. For I have the desire to do what is good, but I cannot carry it out. For what I do is not the good I want to do; no, the evil I do not want to do—this I keep doing.
—Romans 7:18–19

Pretty woman! I moved back to Port-au-Prince, in the city, with my best friend, Rita. Life was much better now. At Rita's house, I was free to express myself. I was a little bit happy for the first time. When the time was right, I felt comfortable and started dating. It seemed as though I was mostly attracted to older men (like mother like daughter). I found myself falling for a married man, one of Rita's neighbors and her friend.

At Rita's recommendation, I was hired to teach kindergarten and first grade at a small private school about three blocks from where we lived. When I received my first paycheck, I sent most of the money to mother, for her and my son, and gave the rest to Rita. I didn't know anything about handling money, making a budget, or even balancing a checkbook; for that matter I never owned one. When I had money, I gave it to the adult in charge, mother or Rita.

My life was beginning to shape up. I had a job and some money, and I was beginning to think about going to get DD from Mother. My new boyfriend, Felder, was a married man with three children. He was a pharmacist, and he sold pharmaceutical products part time. Felder was a very handsome man, not too tall, and had a very friendly personality. He offered to get a house that would be my very own. I thought that was a very good idea because DD and I would have our own place and I could begin to be a mother to my son. I was so happy, smiling from ear to ear.

I am becoming a kept woman! As we were looking for my new place, I got news that Marie Anne's (my sister) husband, who had gone to the United States the year prior, had sent for her to come to New York. My mother and DD were moving back to Port-au-Prince to live in my sister's house so my mother could take care of my niece, Marie Immacula. I was invited to move in with them, and I accepted the invitation. After all, I would have the best of two worlds. I would be living under the same roof with my son and still live my own life, so I thought. The reality was I would be back under mother's roof, and she would be in control, again, so I had to watch out!

I feel myself beginning to change not for the better but for the worse. I was beginning to become more and more promiscuous. At one point, I found myself being in a relationship with two men at the same time, which is not my character. I had even gotten to the place where I didn't care about anything or anyone. I wanted to live my life my way, on my terms, with no regards to how anyone else felt. The change I was experiencing was gradual, but overtime I could see myself changing for the worse.

I am now dating two men, Felder and Gerard, and they are both married. Gerard was a multibusiness owner. He dealt with import and export. He owned shoe factories and stores. He had two sons in private university and a young daughter of twelve. I knew it was wrong, but I didn't seem to care how it was negatively affecting their families. They don't know about each other. They both give me money and allowing me to live the lifestyle that I'm accustomed to. Gerard was very rich, and he was also older than Felder. He allowed me to use his chauffeur for my outings. I think the chauffeur was his spy to keep tabs on me and my activities. I was becoming more promiscuous, almost like a call girl. Being a novice at this game, I need to learn fast how to play it.

Because I was living with my mother, Felder and I decided that a small apartment would be better than a house, since now we are only going to use it as our private hideaway, our rendezvous place and love nest. On one occasion, I spent the night with Felder (which was unplanned), something that I have never done before because I would have to explain to my mother what I was doing that was more important than being home with my family. The next morning, I had gotten up early so I could go home and change for work. As I was walking down our street, which leads to the main road to catch a taxi there, I saw a familiar vehicle. It was Gerard's car, and I noticed Gerard's chauffeur pointing to me, at that moment Gerard signaled for me to come closer.

"D'ou viens-tu si tot le matin, petite cherie?" he asked. (Where do you come from so early in the morning, little darling?)

I answered, "Je rendais visite a une amie, maintenant j'attend le taxi pour me ramener a la maison." (I was visiting a friend, and now I am waiting for a cab to take me home).

Then he said, "Edouard viendra te chercher quand l'ecole laisse sortir, au revoir." (Edouard will come to get you when school lets out, good-bye).

I said, "Tres bien, au revoir." (Very well, good-bye).

Right away, I knew that Gerard was upset with me. The moment he said that Edouard will be coming back, I sensed that I was in trouble. He couldn't let his emotions show because his children were also in the vehicle. When I got home, Mother was at the door waiting. Explaining my behavior to her was very hard, in that this was my first time and I hadn't come up with a good excuse yet. I was almost sure she knew, so I told her the truth and let the chips fall where they may. She gave me a dirty look and said, "Is that how you're going to live now?" Without giving her an answer, I rushed and got ready for work.

When I got off work, Edouard was waiting for me in front of the school. I got in the car and went to see Gerard. I had all day to come up with an explanation, but it was hard for me to lie, and the truth would not have been the smartest route to take if I wanted to keep the relationship. I made up a story about mother's sick friend. He had a doubtful look on his face, so I invited him to ask mother.

Mother sort of knew what I was up to. She liked Gerard, but I didn't think she would betray me. He often brought her presents, pastries, and fruit baskets, and other goodies. She called him a gentleman. Gerard and I spent the greater part of the afternoon together. We had a picnic by a brook, and afterward he took me shopping for delicate things for me to wear and him to enjoy.

There were times when he took the liberty of sending the chauffeur to get me without letting me know in advance. I did not like that at all because it made me feel like he owned me. Felder never treated me like a possession, so I felt like I could get closer to him; but Gerard seemed more like a sugar daddy, maybe that's just what he was.

I think I am taking my freedom a little too far. I am not proud of the happenings of my past, but the truth has to come out so that I could be free from the bondage of my past that is still hanging on and haunting me. By being naked with you, I feel shameful, but speaking the raw truth of what I've done is my way of showing how far has the Lord brought me from. At this point in my life, sin had a strong hold on me. I did not feel guilt, or remorse, for my behavior. Every time I went to the altar and asked God to forgive me, I go right back to sinning again. I kept going back into Satan's web of deceit. At times, I thought I would never be free from the clutches of the enemy.

My mother did not know for sure about my two affairs, only that I was dating the two gentlemen. I came and I went as I pleased, and Mother had stopped meddling in my life. I give her money, buy her nice gifts. We are becoming a team as far as her two grandchildren are concerned. They both called her mama, and I called her mama. It didn't matter because we both had their best interest at heart.

My new freedom seems to be getting me in a lot of trouble. I was becoming very nervous because my menstrual cycle was late, and my biggest fear was that I was pregnant again. It should not be a surprise that I was pregnant because I had been engaging in unprotected sex with two men.

Once it was confirmed that I was pregnant, I now was faced with the dilemma of determining who the father was. Since I was sleeping with two men, I decided to tell each one that the baby belongs to him. Neither of them wanted me to keep it, and they both gave me money for an abortion. They didn't even ask me how I felt. Their action made me feel cheap, soiled, and tossed aside, as if my feelings didn't matter at all. I have no one to blame for this sort of trouble but myself.

Gerard recommended a doctor and offered his chauffeur to take me there. I made the mistake of telling both of them when I was getting it done, and there is no way I was going to tell Mother because she would never approve of me having an abortion.

On the day I was having the abortion, I would not allow the chauffer to take me; instead, I took a taxi because I didn't want him to know my business, and he could be spying for his boss. Sadly, I only felt numb, almost dead inside, as the abortion procedure was taking place. I just wanted to get it done and move on. The evening after I had the abortion, both men showed up, at my house, at the same time. My secret was out—they know about each other now. I was embarrassed that I got caught. I was ashamed, and I didn't know how to handle the situation.

The richer one, Gerard, was so upset with me. I thought he was going to get violent, but he did not. I am sure both men cared for me, but I thought that Felder cared the more. Needless to say, my Mother found out as well. I was not sure how she was going to react. She surprised me when she said, "You know, little girl, God doesn't like ugly." I thought I had lost both of my men.

Felder came back the next day and told me how much he loved me. He told me if it was possible he would make me his second wife. He didn't want to lose me. We continued the affair for a short while. Things seemed to be different. I could not stop feeling the guilt and the shame. It was very hard for me to look at him with a straight face. I don't know why, but he still wanted me. Things between us were never the same after that, so I ended the relationship and we decided to stay friends. Since that night, I never saw Gerard again.

Feeling ashamed didn't stop the behavior. I was still going from one relationship to another. I had no remorse about what I had been doing. It was like a drug. I was like a hardened criminal, and the more I did it, the easier it got.

Shortly after the breakup with Felder, I realized that I was pregnant again. I thought best not to tell him. I would try to handle it all by myself. I confided in Frantz, a male friend whom my sister had introduced me to. Frantz told me about his best friend and coworker, Luckner. They work in the import and export business together. He said that Luckner, who was going to be a doctor, had some medical knowledge, and maybe he can help us.

Luckner knew of an injection that I could take if I am not too far along that would take care of the situation. Have you been counting? Is this what the third, fourth or the fifth abortion? I've lost count. I had become a baby killer and didn't realize it. I was told that if the abortion occurred before the end of the first trimester, it was just tissue, it's not a baby until after three months. I always tried to make sure that I did not commit murder, but not so. I now know that a fetus is a person at the moment of conception. I found that out later, and I know it now.

Frantz arranged for me to meet Luckner. The thought of him judging me made me nervous and embarrassed at the same time. What is he going to think of me? I almost backed out, but I felt that I needed to do this, and quickly.

Luckner was a nice and friendly gentleman, understanding and to the point. He asked many questions about my predicament. He seemed to care about the outcome of what we were about to do, and that he wanted me to be safe. We agreed on what, when, and where. He said time was of the essence, and he left. He did not ask for a fee or money to purchase the injection.

The next day, he returned. As planned, he gave me the injection, and he advised that we should know something within three days. And just as he said, three days later, I had the worst cramping ever. I felt nauseous and feverish. I didn't want Mother to know. I told her that I was sick, so I stayed in bed, hoping that she would not become suspicious. As I lay in the bed, I begin to feel the fetus beginning to abort, and I could literally feel it leaving my body. This went on for two days until the cramping subsided.

Luckner and Fanfan came to see about me every day. Such good friends at the time when I needed them. They were looking out for my best interest. I thank the Lord that even when I was breaking his laws, he still cared for me and protected me.

As you continue to read, you will discover certain areas in a few chapters where I was the most vulnerable, where I was very weak and carnal. Starting after I had lost my first true love, and later after the rape; the enemy didn't play fair. He was winning on every side. He dragged me through the mud. When I overcame one hurdle, and my faith got stronger and I was winning, then he came back stronger with new tactics to cause me to stumble. I had to overcome many

more hurdles, the enemy was winning again. I started to get desperate and discouraged; at times, I felt I was losing my faith I couldn't
get my strength back.

In some of the chapters my words are in a way "too explicit",
but only to express how deeply I was in sin, how voracious the enemy
of my soul. He knew he could not conquer so he hit harder. He won
a few battles, but not the war. God was fighting for me, His love for
me is greater than the enemy's hatred. At the end I was victorious.

CHAPTER 8

Romeo and Juliet;
Love unspeakable. "Purity of love"

Your lips drop sweetness as the honeycomb, my bride;
milk and honey are under your tongue. The fragrance
of your garments is like that of Lebanon.

—Song of Songs 4:11

Faith-testing times can be faith-strengthening times. Luckner! Oh! Oh! If I was asked to describe Luckner in one word, I would have to say "complete." Why? He was twenty-four years old, and he was indescribable. He is gentle, loving, kind, understanding. He is generous, smart, and he is gorgeous. He is the picture of perfection, and he truly loves me. We fell deeply in love. He was my first and only love.

The very first time we kissed is when I felt alive for the first time in my life. I was almost twenty-one years old, almost an adult. Twenty-one is the age of adulthood, in Haiti, the legal age of becoming an adult is not eighteen. You're still a child until you are twenty-one, and, you live under your parents' roof and obey their rules for as long as you live there. I had never kissed anyone so passionately before. He was so caring and gentle as if he knew that I was fragile and needed to be handled with patience and special care. He had awoken such passion in me that my lips quivered, and I trembled like a leaf. I felt the earth move underneath my feet. When I began to cry, he held me very tightly. He comforted me and made me feel safe. He did not try to take me to bed. I loved the way he kissed me, long and with such fervor. I felt intoxicated. It was very easy to respond to his firm but tender embrace. I could live a lifetime with just that, and still be satisfied.

We did not rush into anything, but later, when we finally made love together, it was magical, pure ecstasy. I felt like I was like a virgin, being touch for the very first time. I felt grateful. I finally felt loved. I felt our two bodies merge together like they were made for each other, like hand and glove. Afterwards, I felt spent, but needing to stay close to him, so close, that—I don't know how to explain this—it was like I wanted to crawl inside of him and abide there. We were so in love that we couldn't stand to be one minute apart from each other.

I never thought of looking at another man. I had finally found my home. To me, the whole world consisted of two people, just him and me. Luckner and I were together each and every day. Our days consisted of just going to work and being with each other every chance we got. I could tell that Mother was happy for me, and that I had finally found my true love. People called us Rodrigue et Chimene— that's the French version of Romeo and Juliet. In thinking back on my time with Luckner, it occurred to me that even though we never used protection, I never came up pregnant.

The magic continued, and on June 12, 1969, Luckner proposed to me, even though I was still legally married to sully. In Haiti, women do not file for divorce; it's left up to the men to put away their wives. I accepted his proposal, and he told me that he knew that I was still married and that we will handle that together later. We were so in love that we couldn't wait for the legal formalities to officially be over so that we could belong to each other in marriage. He suggested that we do a blood marriage, and of course, I agreed. I would have jumped over a bridge if he'd asked me to.

My fiancé picked the date, but he didn't tell me why until after the ceremony. My mother was away one evening. I think he probably arranged it with her so we could be alone to do this. On the dining room table, he had placed a diamond ring (I still have the ring as a remembrance of our love.), a piece of parchment, two small candles and a large one, a pair of white gloves in an opened red box, a new razor blade, matches, a saucer and a fountain pen, last but not least a Bible. We didn't wear tuxedo and wedding gown, but we both dressed to the decorum of the occasion. He took the lead all the way through.

First, he slid my hands onto the white gloves. We got on our knees and prayed. Then he lit one of the small candles and I the other. Together we lit the larger candle. We prayed again then we read a scripture passage; it was 2 chronicles 30, the entire chapter, all twenty-seven verses. I do not know why he picked that particular passage, but if it was good enough for him, it was good enough for me. After the scripture reading, with the blade we cut each other's ring finger and drew the blood and let it drip in the saucer and used it to write our vows on the parchment. We dipped our finger into the blood and smeared it as a fingerprint and signed it as our marriage certificate. This was the most romantic thing I had ever done. Luckner said that even though it was not legal, he thought that God would honor it. I did not believe as he believed, but I went along with it. I was not divorced from Sully yet.

We were married, in our hearts, in our thoughts, and in every way that counted except in the eyes of God and the law. At the end of the ceremony, Luckner said, "I have something to tell you."

I said, "Okay, mon amour, tell me."

He said, "All the papers have returned. My passport is in order with my visa, and the letter from the school. I need you to help me choose my travel date. I am going to send for you as soon as I can. In America, you can get a divorce, and we can live our lives together."

That's why he picked the Fourth of July for our wedding day— so we can celebrate our freedom and our wedding anniversary on the same day, Independence Day. I was happy and sad at the same time. This trip had been long awaited, and now the time is here.

I don't want him to leave me. I was beginning to have feelings of abandonment. My heart started pounding in my chest. I could hear every beat. I have just found true love and happiness, and I don't even know how long I am going to be without him.

This was a very sad moment for me, but in the long run, I know it's going to be good for us both. So we decided that Luckner would leave in the middle of September. We spent the rest of the night together. Before heading home, he said, "I have a present for you," and he gave me a package that contained a beautiful dress that was hand painted by him. He had also painted one for each of his two younger sisters, Monique and Jacqueline. He wanted us three sisters to dress alike when we accompanied him to the airport on his day of departure.

Luckner's siblings were comprised of two sisters and two brothers. He was the eldest of five children. His mom and dad accepted me as their own and showed their love and support. The whole family adored me. I always felt at home with them. I really felt so blessed for having them in my life.

On the day of Luckner's departure, September 13, 1969, his family and I accompanied him to the airport to say our good-byes. Everyone was sad, but I think I was sad the most. I couldn't keep my eyes dry. I remember watching Luckner as he headed toward the plane. I was wishing that I was boarding the plane with him. We continuously waved until he entered the airplane. I felt an overwhelming sense of emptiness because with him I always felt full and alive.

After the airplane left, we all went to Mom and Dad's house. They wanted me to spend the night, but I had preferred to be in my own bed. The sisters went home with me and consoled me, after which they went back to Mom's house. They would become part of my support team, as extended family. They did their best to keep me busy, while I waited to join my husband in America.

In the first letter that I received from Luckner, he said that he started writing it the moment he sat down on the plane. Believe it or not, until this day I still have some of the letters that I received from him. Here is one of his letters that I would like to share, it is written in French. It is a 5-page letter, although I am only translating parts of it.

New-York   ce   21 Octobre 1969

Mon idôle,

S'il existe quelque chose
d'inoubliable, quelque chose d'insondable, quel
que chose d'incomparable, c'est notre amour.
Franchement, chérie, tu es
animée du même désir que moi. À chaque fois
que je reviens du travail, j'ai une folle envie de
t'écrire. Si je ne t'écris pas chaque semaine,
c'est pour ne pas t'exiger trop de réponses.
Caty chérie, point n'est besoin
de te demander de tes nouvelles ni de te faire a-
voir les miennes. Tu connais les miennes ainsi
que moi et peut-être mieux que moi. Car nous sa-
vons tous deux que seule la rencontre de nos yeux,

79

peut nous rendre bien portant. Mais chérie, sois sûre que ce jour n'est pas loin, ce jour où je te prendrai dans mes bras, comme il m'est de coutume. Caty, mon amour, sois sans inquiétude car, tu sais les vœux que nous avons faits et lors même qu'ils n'auraient pas existés, sois sûre que toutes les minutes qui me sont libres sont consacrées à toi. A te dire franchement, chérie, jamais il ne me sera possible de te trahir, une minute de ma vie, ne fut ce qu'en pensée. Toute ma pensée s'envole vers toi Caty pour aller en toi admirer la douceur et la grâce.

Caty ma mie, secret !!! J'ai payé les 100 $ d'écolage. On m'a donné 3 mois pour apprendre l'anglais avant de commencer à fréquenter l'école. Eh bien, chérie, sois sûre que je suis à toi durant ces trois mois. Je vais faire de mon

mieux pour te faire rentrer avant la fin de ces
3 mois. Ne le dis même pas à Mémé. Je vais m'é-
craser, chérie, sois en sûre car, ceux en qui j'espérais
m'ont abandonné. Seul Pablo m'a promis son aide.
Cependant, j'espère y parvenir quand même, puisqu'en
à Dieu a guidé, guide et guidera toujours nos pas.

Caty chérie, que de fois ai-je rêvé
te voir près de moi. Que de fois ai-je revé te prendre
dans un doux enlacement et te dire Tu Es à Moi
Douce Mignonne. Enfin Caty, jour et nuit n'ont
fait que projeter ton image devant moi et lors, je ne
puis vivre.

Tu me dis, chérie, te dire ce
que tu dois dire à mes sœurs au sujet de Dide. Tu
dois tu les dire sinon la simple vérité car tu sais
très bien que je hais le mensonge et qu'un jour ou
l'autre je leur dirai tout.

Caty chérie, n'aie pas honte. Il suffit que je t'aime comme tu es, ma mignonne, tout le reste n'est que folie. Choisis le chemin de la vérité, dis leur ce qui est véridique et rassure-toi que rien ne pourra éteindre le feu de notre amour, de notre éternelle union. Si Dieu avait béni notre union, c'est dire que rien au monde ne pourra nous désunir.

Caty, ma douce adorée, crois en mon amour et oublie tout ! Tout et Tout !!!

Ma chérie, c'est à regret que je dépose ma plume aujourd'hui. J'aurais voulu y rester encore mais hélas, tu n'auras pas des yeux pour les lire.

Bye. Bye amour.

Tout en espérant te lire sous peu, je joins à ma lettre mille baisers parfumés que

mon cœur consent à te donner malgré la distance qui nous sépare et nous retient

    Bye . Bye Cœur

    Ton adoré :

  Loulou

    Embrasse Mémé de ma part
et mes salutations à tous les enfants.

    Excuse - moi j'allais oublier
de saluer Mémé tant ma pensée est occupée
par ta seule et unique personne.

    Bye.

Translation

New York This October 21, 1969

My idol,

If there is something unforgettable, some-thing unfathomable, something incomparable, it is our love.

We both know, darling, that you and I have the same desires; always, when I come home from work, my only desire is to write to you. It is of no use asking you how you are and telling you how I am. We both know that our feelings are mutual, we both know that the only thing that can make us feel better is being together, face to face. But be assured that it is not going to be very long before you will be in my arms again.

Caty, my love, don't worry, you know the vows that we made to each other, even if we didn't, be certain that every minute of my day is consecrated to you. You're always on my mind, you're all I can think of.

My darling, I dream of you often, I dream of taking you in a sweet embrace and telling you that you are mine. Also, Caty, day and night, when I see your beautiful face, I die; I can't live without you.

Bye. Bye. love

In the hope to hear from you very soon, I am sending you thousands of kisses that my heart allows me, though we are a long distance apart.

Bye. Bye. My heart

Your idol,
Loulou

When he wrote to us, he always made sure that we read our mail together. He sent the mail to one place so we can visit and bond more while we commiserated together.

He wrote me a letter every day during the first month. With one of his letter, he sent me one crisp dollar bill with a card that said,

> I love you and miss you so much that I only lasted one week in school. I have decided not to continue going to school and have found a job. This is your share of my first paycheck. Signed, your husband who loves you more than life itself. PS, I will get paid every week and I will send you some of the money.

Luckner's letters had stopped coming as frequently as before; instead of daily, he started to write to me every week, and we set a date and a specific time to talk to each other on the phone for one hour. On the first day of the month, with much anticipation and excitement, I would go to Western Union at six o'clock in the evening. I made sure to never be late and waited for my name to be called. When it was my turn, the operator would tell me which booth to go to, where I would wait for the telephone to ring.

When I picked up the receiver, Luckner would be at the other end, anticipating to hear my voice. I could almost feel his presence. We had that special connection, as we shared how we felt at the time. Our two bodies were intertwined together, in our mind of course, and we were one again in a place of our own. By the time we came back to reality, the hour was well spent. Most of the times the operator would give us a five minutes warning that our hour was almost over, but there were times when they would just cut our conversation off at the end of the hour, and all I would hear was the sound of air.

Saying good-bye after our phone calls was harder than I thought it would be. I always had trouble leaving the place. I needed extra time to compose myself. It was pure torture—I could not handle it. After three months of this torture, I suggested to Luckner that we should stop the phone calls and just write letters. Even though he wanted to continue our monthly phone rendezvous, he respected my wishes.

Luckner and I continued our long-distance romance by letter while waiting for me to get to New York. Suddenly, his letters came only once a month, and I am alright with that because I know he was busy working, but I am still disturbingly sad, trying very hard to cope with the situation.

My job at the private school is very much enjoyable. The time I spent with the children helped me to stop wallowing in my sorrows and shift my concentration to prayer. I had learned to create new projects and new games in order to keep my first-grade students occupied. I always felt happier when I was around them. The children's laughter fuels my spirit and fills the void in my heart.

The money that Luckner usually send for me stopped coming for two months. That was alright because I did not need it to live on. I had my own money, and my sister was sending us a check every month to help take care of the children's needs. We had more than enough to keep us supplied.

One day, to my surprise, I received a registered letter from Luckner. I tore it open. He had sent me enough money for my trip to America with instructions about whom to go to for arranging passage for me to travel to America. I followed his instructions to a tee.

Oh, happy days are here again. And now, praise God I can breathe again. My heart ached for him. I got on my knees and thanked God for his goodness and his favor toward me. I couldn't sleep at night. Being with him was the only thing I could think of. I wanted so much to experience what happily ever after really meant, what being with the only person that you love and want to live for feels like. I couldn't wait to feel his arms around me again, to hear him calling me (his) again. He used to call me "Ma Caty." I keep telling myself "to hang on, be patient, just a couple of months longer, real soon we'll be together and we will never be separated again until death us part."

CHAPTER 9

Now Faith;
The true sign of faith is taking the first step without knowing where the journey will end

*Consider it pure joy, my brothers, whenever you
face trials of many kinds, because you know that the
testing of your faith develops perseverance.*

—James 1:2–3

Mustard seed faith. The unexpected happened, my world has turned upside down, and it was being shaken to the very core. To me, this is worse than death itself.

This story, my story, is going to help you see now, in spite of your own "earthquake moments," your hurricanes, and your tornados, you can still find stability in God, grow stronger in your faith, and continue to serve the Lord with all your heart and soul. Sometimes, trials can be God's mercies in disguise. This could be his way of trying to draw us closer to himself. Stop resisting. When the storm is over, you will discover that only in his arms can you find rest and enough strength to carry you through.

Luckner sent me to see his uncle Jacques, who was a government employee. He would help me to obtain the necessary paperwork I needed to travel to America. Just before the paperwork was nearly completed, Uncle Jacques, for lack of a better word, *pissed* off the big boss. That is unacceptable! You can't have that in Haiti. One hundred percent loyalty or death. Sometimes, death comes even if you had done nothing wrong

One night, while Uncle Jacques was in bed, four government officials came to his house, dragged him out from his mansion, and hauled him away to prison. He was accused of treason, which was all a fabricated lie. I thought I would never see him again. Uncle Jacques had all my money, all of the necessary paperwork for my travel to America. He was the only person we knew that could move so quickly for us. We were only waiting for one final letter from immigration, and we would have been able to buy my ticket and make flight reservations for destination America. Now that he is in prison, I concluded that all was lost. We didn't have any more money, and no recourse.

The government contacts Uncle Jacques was using were his own. We would have to start all over again, having to hire a new travel officer, a stranger, someone we had never worked with before that would make matters worse for us. Also we feared that they could take all our money and disappear. That sort of thing happens all the time in Haiti. If by chance you should meet them again, they would threaten to report you to the government for something you did not do, and the government would believe them instead of you. Furthermore, we didn't have any more money.

I got desperate, I thought, "This is a God-size problem, one that only he can handle. He can do the impossible." Therefore, I got on my knees and prayed so hard until I fell asleep. The next day, the Holy Spirit directed me to go to the mountain on a three-day fast. My mom, my Christian friends, and neighbors were praying and fasting with me. I had decided that I would fast and pray until something happened. I had memorized Psalms 23, 91, 123, 136, 139, and recited them every time I fasted and every day since, even now. I was hoping for an instant miracle (like he sometimes does), but God did not answer, so I decided to be patient and wait.

The last straw that broke the camel's back came about when I received a letter from Paul, Luckner's oldest and best friend. The letter reads as such:

Dear Caty,

Luckner has been trying to reach you. Did you send him the red box with the white gloves yet? Please expedite, signed, Paul.

His letter did not make any sense. I had received Loulou's letter (I used to call him Loulou.), asking me to send the box with the gloves, and he also asked that I read our marriage scriptures every night because he had encountered some difficulties. At our wedding we vowed to never part from these two items, they are like the glue holding our hearts together. He seemed a little distant around that time. I wasn't sure what was on his mind, and I didn't bother to ask him. I knew he must have been busy. We had not spoken to each other for two months. It started shortly before I got the news about Uncle Jacques.

I found out later that because Loulou went to work instead of going to school and not honoring the conditions of his student visa, papers were being filed to get him deported. To save himself from having to come back to Haiti, he had to marry an American citizen. It was only a marriage of convenience, in order to stay in America. Most people would have done the same, including me. I wish he would have told me. Even though I would have been devastated, I would have understood.

I had a huge setback and did not want to live anymore. I begin to have anxiety attacks and fell into a deep depression. I cried all day and all night. I didn't want to eat. I felt cornered, like a caged animal. I began to waver in my faith, and everything seemed dark and hopeless. Satan had me in a state of despair, and I couldn't find the light. I couldn't distinguish night from day. I had been suffering from depression since the first time I was pregnant. When Sully had the doctor to yank the baby out of me.

I had been taking Valium and phenobarbital every day until I met Luckner. He was my first love, the only man that I felt safe with, and I have lost him. I might as well be dead. When I went to my job and resigned, they thought it had to do with my travel plans. In a way it did, but not in the way they thought. What I was about to do was selfish. I had become very selfish in my ways. Everything had to be about me, my pain, my feelings, but that's where I was at that point. I didn't think about my son, my mother, or anyone else. I am done with this side of heaven. I wanted to go home.

That night, I did not eat my supper, I asked Claudine, our maid, to bring a glass of hot milk to my room; and I told her, "You made it just the way I like." The milk is boiled with cinnamon bark and lemongrass, and it smelled and tasted delicious. I thanked her. When I was alone, I took an entire bottle of Valium. I went to my mom's room and told her that I was going to sleep-in the next day because I had a bad headache. She said okay, and this was my way of saying good-bye to her.

I believed that these suicidal tendencies are caused partly because Mother's interference in my life. Every time the pain gets unbearable, I wanted to die. I had never learned how to cope with difficult situations that I cannot resolve on my own. Satan tempted me. He wanted me to die. He kept telling me that I was worth nothing, my life was not important, no one cared if I lived or died. When all else fails, kill yourself, that was my only resolve. If I died, I wouldn't have to endure anymore pain.

The next day, I woke up in the hospital. They couldn't wake me up. They had to pump my stomach. I think my mother said twice. I don't know how much damage I had done, and they don't tell you much at the hospital, "You should feel lucky that you're alive."

My mother changed quite a bit. In the cab, on the way home from the hospital after my release, she spoke only four words: "Where is your faith?

"She said nothing for the next few days. She only came to the room to make sure that I was still alive. Then I got up one morning. I was in a fog for hours. I walked like a zombie and was feeling very confused.

Mother filled the tub with warm water and poured in some herbs that are supposed to help in these situations. After making me get in the tub, Mother bathe, dried me off, and put me back in the bed. Once in bed, the maid brought me a bowl of soup. Mother peeked in later. She said, "Get your strength for tomorrow we are going to the mountain."

There is a certain place where we go to fast and pray. It's not very far from our house. It's a little hill with a cross on it. We sat on the ground under a big tree that shades us from the sun. We feel safe and protected there, and we sense God's presence. We call it the mountain. We usually go early in the morning, stay there until noon, with no food, no drink. We pray, we sang, and we read God's word out loud. We agonized before the Lord, and brought our petitions to him, for he alone hears us. We always ended with a song of praise and thanked him in advance for what he has done and is yet to do.

As we prayed, we believed that the prison door would be open for Uncle Jacques, his shackles would be dropped from his feet, and they would find him innocent of any wrong doing. We went to the mountain for three straight days. I was dehydrated from lack of water, and because I was already weak from the overdose, I barely made it to the top of the hill on the third day. I fainted for a minute, and my mother got me up and I made it through to noon. I was determined to finish the three days. I thank you God for the strength to finish well. God does answer prayers, and miracles do happen! That is my true belief. He gives grace for every season in our lives and strength for every battle.

The morning after the three-day fast, I had been so tired that I slept through the night. I usually get up to use the potty, but that night, I didn't. A knock at the door woke me up. It was summertime, and the atmosphere was warm. I always liked the feel of soft sheets against my skin, and I pulled the sheet over my head, trying to block the noise. Then there was another knock, and I heard a voice outside, saying: "It is I, Uncle Jacques. Can you please open the door?"

I thought I was dreaming. My mother ran to the door and opened it. When he came in, he said, "I don't have much time to explain. I haven't made it home yet because something was pressing so heavy on my heart that I must come here first! I don't know what it was about, but I'm here. I had a dream last night that I was in shackles. Someone came into the dungeon where I was, and they removed my shackles and told me to rush here to you."

Then Uncle Jacques said, "That was a weird dream. I was not in a dungeon, and I wasn't in shackles. The boss, of all people, woke me up. He told me that I was free to go, so I ran out of there. I thought I was still dreaming until I got here. I only made one stop on the way. I went to my business mailbox where I had kept your travel papers. Here is the money and your papers. I wrote down instructions for you to follow. I love you and bon voyage."

Uncle Jacques being in my house with my travel papers was evidence of God's miracle and a clear answer to the prayers we prayed on the mountain. (You must understand that, when you go to prison in Haiti, that is the end of you. You don't come out.)

Do you believe in miracles? I do, and so should you. When I thought that all was lost and all hope was gone, God performed a miracle for me. He gave me a personal miracle. My faith had sustained me. Faith is the substance of things hoped for, and the evidence of things not seen (Hebrews 11:1).

CHAPTER 10

Coming to America;
"My dream is of a place and a time where America will once be seen as the last best hope on earth."
{Abraham Lincoln}

I took you from the ends of the earth, from its farthest corners
I called you. You are my servant, I have chosen
you and have not rejected you.

—Isaiah 41:9

America the beautiful! Land of the free and home of the brave.
My knowledge of America was limited, except for what I'd read in
history books. One thing was etched in my mind: the Americans are
free, privileged in every way, and able to do just about anything they
wanted to do. With regard to education and business opportunities,
all doors were opened to everyone who dared to take a chance and
walk in. *I dared!* To me, America was the land of milk and honey.
Everyone from everywhere wants to go to America. Hollywood,
the movie stars, the Grand Canyon, everything that I heard about
America impressed me. I didn't know how, but I knew that someday,
some way, I would go to America. The opportunity of a lifetime is
upon me. I'm finally going to get my chance, and now is the time

A lot of preparations were made for this day. Mother thought
that it was unladylike for women to wear pants, especially her own
daughter. For the first time I'm going to wear pants against her objec-
tions. My seamstress made this beautiful, very attractive green-white-
and-black pinstriped suit just for this special occasion. I only planned
to wear the pants and vest since it was a hot day. Mother had gotten
up very early and was gone before I woke up that morning. No one
knew where she went. I had a restless night, and the previous night
wasn't much better. I guess I was a bit anxious about what living in
America was going to be like. In addition, I was concerned about my
safety on the airplane. The truth is I had never been on an airplane
before.

Later that day, Mother returned, and in her hands she had one
hundred and fifty dollars. She said, "You are a lucky girl, and here is
some pocket money. I played *borlette* (the lotto), and I won all this
money for you, except $50.00 that I am keeping for myself." I smiled
at her and said thank you. We hugged, and tears came down both my
and her beautiful cheeks. I didn't cry as much as she did. I didn't have
to worry about ruining my makeup, because we were both blessed
with natural beauty, so we did not wear makeup.

My friends Monique and Juliana were waiting in the car to
drive me to the airport. I was worried that my mother wouldn't make
it back on time to say good-bye, but, well she managed to return

just in time. When I hugged my son DD, I felt very sad that I was leaving and wouldn't see him for quite a while. I also gave my niece, Immacula, a big hug just before getting in the car. I was beside myself with joy and excitement.

The drive to the airport was very slow because there are traffic jams as usual, everywhere in Haiti. Besides that, we were driving on dirt roads. It was a very uncomfortable ride, but that didn't matter, because I was on my way to America. The three of us cried happy tears. We hugged and kissed. We promised to stay in touch. Then I boarded the airplane, and Monique and Julianna went back home. I thanked God for making my dream come true and asked him to please guide the pilot and keep us safe during the flight. It was a short prayer that I whispered under my breath.

It was a very hot day. The skies were blue, and everything was beautiful all around me. I felt blessed, so grateful for the opportunity to travel and to be able to turn my life around, in hopes of being the woman and daughter God created me to be.

This was my first time on an airplane, and I wasn't sure what to expect. I only had one suitcase that my mother packed for me the day before. She made sure that I had everything I needed. In place of a carry-on, she used one of her old purses; it was kind of bulky, and in it she included my passport, legal papers, birth certificate, and other items.

Thank God! The plane, which was a 747, was ready for takeoff. I was getting very nervous about the plane departing on time. The captain welcomed everyone on board. He told us about the dos and don'ts, the approximate flight time. The flight attendants did their share of talking, and we took off. It was a little scary at first, but it didn't take too long for me to get the hang of it. We left around five o'clock in the afternoon, with a layover and plane change in Miami. I didn't know what that meant until we arrived in Miami.

To occupy my time during the flight, I reached into the big purse that my mother had packed. I had placed it under the seat in front of me. I pulled out my Bible. Mother had included it among my needed things. Luckner had given that Bible to me as one of my birthday presents (La Sainte Bible: Holy Bible); it had been a companion to me. I still have it until this very day. It is written in French, and I don't use it much anymore, but I will cherish it for the rest of my life. The dedication read, "A Caty dated August 7, 1969." That was the best present that anyone could have given me. I praise God for him and pray that he is well.

We had our usual snacks and drinks as we safely flew over the oceans. There were some small turbulences here and there, the regular fasten your seat belt signs announcements. As we approach the state of Florida, the flight attendants came to our seats with forms, those forms that everyone must fill out when crossing the border. I thank God that we landed safely in Miami, and our flight arrived on time. When all the formalities were done with, we were able to disembark the plane. I was surprised it was night. I thought that Haiti and Florida were on different time zone.

While in the waiting room, I was curious to find out about the flight to New York. I went to the reservation desk and inquired of the attendant on duty. There was a language barrier because I didn't speak English and she didn't speak French. They did find someone to translate for us, and I was told that our plane to New York was not leaving until the next morning. I was very disappointed when I found out that we had to spend the night at the airport. We had no place to sleep and had to keep an eye on our suitcases. It was quite an experience, but I made it through the morning. They announced over the intercom when our flight was about to board. Everyone rushed to get in line. I had already been issued my boarding pass, so I got in line behind the other passengers.

Apparently, most of them had flown before, so they knew what to do; I, on the other hand, had to ask a lot of unnecessary questions. I'd taken English in high school for two years. I thought I knew it somewhat. I tried it at the airport, but it was so different. I could not understand anything people were saying, so I just listened very carefully.

Breakfast was served on the flight to New York. The food didn't taste good at all, but I ate it because I was very hungry, and I knew this too shall pass. I was very tired. I slept through most of the flight. I got out of my seat a couple of times to use the bathroom. When I looked in the mirror, I saw that my eyes were all red from lack of sleep. We had snacks before arriving in New York, and I went back to sleep. The captain's voice woke me as we were making our descent into LaGuardia airport, and they welcomed everybody to New York. It was a smooth descent. Everyone was happy. I think I was the happiest. I made it! I had finally made it to New York, New York, the big apple. I said, "Thank you God!"

After departing the plane, the first question I had was, where do I go? I've never been to an airport as a passenger before. Where is my suitcase? I am sure they told us where to go, but did I hear or understood what they said? Of course not. While walking toward the baggage carousel, one lady from the plane asked me, "Are you new here? Are you alone"?

I said, "*Oui*," (yes) because I understood her French accent.

She said in French, "Did you just come from Haiti?"

I said, "*Oui*."

She said again in French, "Do you have family to pick you up?"

Before I could answer, I heard my sister and her husband talking. She said, "*C'est elle, c'est* Carie." (That's her, that is Carie.) My family used to call me Carie. My brother in-law, Menes; my sister, Marie Anne; her three-month old baby girl, Martine; and my brother, Chantone, came to pick me up. We had a happy group hug. They got my suitcase and took me to their home.

It was a beautiful, hot, and muggy day in New York city. We had a nice taxi ride as we reconnected with one another. It had been about three years since my brother-in-law came to New York, in 1967, the year my son was born. My sister followed her husband the year after, and my brother the year after that, and now me.

Luckner went to New York the same year as my brother. When he got there, he stayed in contact with my family for a while. My sister complimented me for my choice of such a perfect gentleman. He was much help to her during her pregnancy. She said she couldn't ask for a better brother. Luckner worked at night. During the day and weekend, he spent all his time at her house. He said my family was his family until we could be together. He kept her company throughout her pregnancy, took her shopping, picked up her medication when necessary. Shortly after the birth of the baby, about the same time he stopped writing to me, he didn't visit with her anymore. He stopped calling, and she didn't know why, until I came to New York and told her what had happened.

Life in New York was so nice. My sister introduced me to her friends. We shopped together. We took care of my little niece together; she was three-month old, and she had chubby rosy cheeks. She was always hungry. I loved feeding her. She was a good baby and a great eater. We went to the social security administration building so I could apply for a social security number.

The next week, we went out job hunting. There were plenty of job openings, but I was turned down everywhere we went. The problem was I couldn't speak English. After days of searching, a door was opened at a coat hanger factory. They decided to give me a chance. The hangers were very beautiful. There were red, blue, and white satin and silk hangers. We had to stretch the fabric on top of them, fold and tuck the fabric in and stitch it in such a way that the seam didn't show. This was my first job at a factory, and I was expected to move as fast as the older employees. I learned to do the work and I was good at it, but the boss said that I was not fast enough. They laid me off on the last day of the month.

By now, I've learned how to ride the subway to and from home and never got lost. I went out again searching for a new job. In less than a week, I was hired at a Paper Mate pen factory. A line of employees, including me, stood in front of a machine that moved from one end of a very long counter-like steel table, where a door would open in front of each employee. The pens were in view. They were very hot, and each employee must empty the machine quickly and close the door. If one person moved too slow, that would stop the flow of production. The machine would then start making a loud noise to warn that there was a weak link—and the weak link was me.

It was as if the Lord wanted me to be at this job a while longer. They started me working the night shift, which was a twelve-hour shift, from seven o'clock in the evening to seven o'clock in the morning, I could barely keep my eyes open, but I am moving a bit faster. After one full month, I still was not fast enough. This job was so hard, but I was very happy to be able to work and provide money to help support my mother and the children.

At the end of my shift one Saturday morning, I went to the time clock to punch out, but my time card was not there; that usually means either you are being let go or the boss wants to talk to you. In my case, I thought the former, even though my performance had been improving. I went to the office to see the boss, and he said, "Maria (I hate being called Maria, but that's okay as long as I'm not being fired.), you are improving somewhat but you are still too slow. I'm going to give you another chance. You are being moved to the day shift, and if you can't cut it there, I will have to let you go."

I am so glad that I had made a friend, who was also from Haiti. Her name was Louise. She has been working there much longer than I and spoke very good English. Having Louise nearby, at times when it was difficult to understand what the supervisor was saying, to translate was a blessing from God.

On Monday morning, I reported to work at seven o'clock. Same place, same station, different time. I thought I'd lost my night-time friend, but there was another English-speaking Haitian woman working during the day shift who volunteered to help me. Isn't God good? When a door is closed, he opens a window. In my case, it's the other way around; when a window is closed, he knocks down the door. I love God!

I feel that the Lord has been directing my steps along the way in order to bring me to where I am right now. I know he is not done with me yet, but I am beginning to see his footprints in the sand. My job at Paper Mate is harder than my first job at the coat hanger factory. I feel less efficient here than there. Why did the boss invite me to work the day shift? "I praise you, Father, Lord of heaven and earth, because you have hidden these things from the wise and learned and revealed them to the children" (Matthew 11:25).

You might remember the three dresses that Luckner hand painted for his two sisters and me. I was wearing that same dress on the day I was fired, and it made such a big splash. Right now, you may not believe what I'm about to share, but my new Haitian friend Zita had a dress just like mine. You'll never guess who painted it. Even as I am sharing this story, my emotions are welling up in me and I feel like I wanted to cry. The reason is Zita shared with me that Luckner is her first cousin, and he made an exact replica of my dress for Zita. To think I had worried myself sick wondering where Luckner was, and now standing next to me someone who can let Luckner know that I am in America. We immediately exchange contact information.

I thought I had lost him forever and had given up the hope of ever seeing him again, and now my hope has been restored. I could hardly wait to see my husband. When it was time for us to clock out, I noticed my time card was missing. I knew at that moment I had been fired, but that was alright with me because I felt that meeting Zita was the reason that God had given me this job.

I had asked Zita to give my phone number to Luckner, and she did. I was embarrassed to go home and tell my family that I was fired. I was wondering if I should give them the good news or the bad news first. The truth is my family adored my Loulou, so of course they'd want the good news first.

My sister was the only one in the house, so I went to her and said, "I have found my Loulou! Yeah!

My sister smiled and said, Yeah? Where? Is he here?"

"No," I replied. At that very moment, the phone rang. My sister answered it. She told me it was Luckner!

I was so nervous that I couldn't control myself, and I was extremely happy, just knowing that he still cared. Even though I wanted my man back, I had mixed emotions. After all, he was married, and legally belonged to another woman. What would I say to him? I felt like I was in a trance. Then my sister yelled at me, "Pick up the phone. C'est Luckner, il veut te parler." (It's Luckner, he wants to talk to you).

I picked up the phone and I melted like butter. I didn't accuse or ask any questions. With my voice very low, I said, "Je veut te voir, Loulou. Veut tu me voir aussi?" (I want to see you. Do you want to see me too?)

He said, "Demain matin, je vient te chercher." (I'm coming for you tomorrow morning).

And I replied, "A demain." (Until tomorrow.)

Then I gave to phone to my sister. I felt so weak for him that I couldn't speak another word, and I went to my room. If that was not a miracle, I don't know what is. I had believed that he was lost to me forever.

Again, I am asking you, do you believe in miracles? I do. God did it for me. He can do it for you too. Needless to say, this calls for a long night of prayer, soul searching, unnerving, gut-wrenching night of prayer. The next day, my long-awaited lover, my Loulou came for me. Neither one of us said one word. I don't know how he felt, but I didn't feel the way I thought I would.

Without saying a word, we got into a train, and I am not sure where it was headed. We rode in silence until the train stopped for passengers to disembark. Because the train was going too fast, I heard the brakes squeak and we bumped into—no—we collided into each other and both of us started laughing uncontrollably. In one moment, our eyes met, and we couldn't help ourselves; we hugged each other so tight as if we would never let go. We still didn't speak a word. We continued to hug, and we kissed. Then one of us broke the silence, not sure which one.

We got off the train and walked to the nearest park. We stayed awhile, and we left and got back on the train and rode awhile longer. Finally, we decided it was time to go for lunch. We shared our first meal together, and from there we walked to my sister's house. He visited with my sister for a short while and he went home.

This was on Saturday, and we met again the next day. This time, we both talked. I asked many questions, and he was truthful with his answers. I learned that his wife's name was Mazi and that he only married her to get his green card, and I understood but I wished he had shared that with me sooner. We could have handled it together. He also told me that he had to stay in this marriage for two years before he can obtain his green card. Once he gets it, he and Mazi will get a divorce, and he and I can finally be together again. That was good news, but there was also bad news. My husband would have to live together with another woman for two long years before we could be together again. That did not make me happy at all. I was not comfortable seeing him and being #2 in his life while he was married to another woman. But God is in charge, he knows what he is doing, and he is sovereign in all things.

CHAPTER 11

Vital to the Rescue, Again;
Frightening experience to live in the U.S.
as an "Illegal Alien"

When you pass through the waters, I will be with you;
and when you pass through the rivers,
they will not sweep over you.

—Isaiah 43:2

God is up to something! It's late October, even possibly early November 1970, and I had received a letter from the immigration authorities, informing me that my three-month visitor's visa is about to expire, and they wanted to know what my plans were regarding my return to Haiti. What they didn't know was that I had never planned on returning to Haiti. My plans are that I have no plans. I am here to stay; I don't want to go back to Haiti any time soon. The fact is I want to be an American, just like them.

My sister, her husband, my brother, and myself are all here illegally. We were all considered illegal aliens.

That fact causes us a tremendous amount of anxiety and fear. So, my brother in-law, who had a bad temper, started drinking and cursing at me. He said that I have been nothing but trouble ever since

I came here, and if they come looking for me, they'll know that he and his family were here illegally as well. The bottom line is we could all end up being deported. He told me to find myself somewhere else to live so we can send the letter back and say return to sender, no one by that name lives here. He grabbed another beer, drank it, and he left the house.

Two weeks prior to receiving the letter from immigration, my sister and I visited a family that we all knew as the Pierre family. The very nice people who used to be our landlord when I was in high school. In fact, they are the parents of Vital. Vital, the same guy who kissed me when I was in high school, he now lives with his parents in Brooklyn. He was engaged to a young woman named Cecilia, who was still living in Haiti. He was about to make travel arrangements for her trip to America. Once in America, they plan to get married.

When Vital saw me, he assumed that we could pick up where we left off, because the last time we were together, he wanted to marry me. Just that quick, he changed his mind about sending for Cecilia. The fact remained that I was in need of a sponsor in order to stay in America, so this made for very good possibility. Vital started coming to see me on a regular basis. Our courtship didn't last very long because my need to get married was immediate. He and my brother in law worked at the same textile plant in Brooklyn. He talked to my brother in-law about me all the time. Simply put, he was obsessed with me.

"He is mad about you," my brother in-law said. He also encouraged me to marry Vital, because if I didn't he might report me to the immigration department. Menes didn't want immigration to come after him and his family. Before I knew it, plans were being made for us to get married so I could get my green card and remain in America.

Look at God! He always had a ram in the bush. He has never failed me yet. God's provision has always been there waiting for me when I needed it. Vital and I were married by the justice of the peace in New York City on January 15, 1971. We rented an apartment in the same complex where my sister and her family lived. I am now twenty-three years old. This is my second marriage, besides the blood marriage with Luckner, and this also had been pre-arranged. There was no love connection between the two of us, at least for me. My new husband had to go back to work after the ceremony. I don't know why he didn't take the whole day off. I was feeling very depressed and abandoned after my husband left. The depression had already begun when I realized that this was déjà vu, another loveless marriage.

Feeling cornered with no one to turn to, nowhere to run, I felt trapped. It wasn't Vital's fault. He couldn't help himself—he was in love—and at the same time, he was trying to help me. Vital had to return to work. After he left me at the subway station to catch the train home, I felt so lonely. I did not plan this, but I didn't want to go home alone, so I called Luckner. I needed someone to talk to, to commiserate with. He and I are now in the same predicament.

We decided to meet. He rode the train for about fifteen to twenty minutes. We went to a hotel and talked for a very long time. All of a sudden, and without warning, our conversation shifted into our love and passion for each other beginning to stir. We both began to justify why it could be proper for us to become intimate, and in effect consummate our marriage. Frankly, it was way overdue because I had been in New York for almost five months and we had only kissed but not have intercourse. We knew that we had sinned against God and against our prospective mates. Luckner and I promised ourselves that we would not do it again until we were both free.

After a while, we both went to our prospective home. I was home in plenty of time to make dinner for my new husband. I am ashamed to say it, but I did not feel guilty for having slept with Loulou, my first and only love, my real husband.

I have repented for my sin. I know the Lord has forgiven me, but it pains me to offend my Lord. This marriage to Vital could not stand because it was based on lies. Vital and I argued and fought almost from the very beginning of our marriage. I often wondered if my marriage to Vital would have stood a chance if Luckner and I had never reconnected!

Vital seemed very happy to have me as his wife. Being with me was a dream come true for him. I didn't have much to offer him. I was grateful to him, but I did not love him. I didn't know how to be a wife. Even though I had been married before, I had never learned. Everything was done for me or to me in my prior marriage. Vital, I guess, expected me to be the perfect housewife like his mother (who could win housewife of the year award). I would be willing to learn, but we lived in the Bronx, and his parents lived in Brooklyn. We didn't visit them too often. His dad was disappointed in him because he was a drop-out from medical school and now works at a factory. His mom was upset that he didn't wait for Cecilia to get here instead he married a divorcee, me.

My mother was not a good role model in the marriage department. I had no one to look up to. There were no how-to books in Haiti. I am not excusing myself for what happened. I did the best that I could with the hand that I was dealt. I am doing my best to be transparent by sharing things that, as I look back on them, they still conjure up feelings of sorrow and regret. Luckner and I had kept our promise to never be together again, and until this very day we never saw each other again.

My marriage to Vital ended when one night he came home upset about losing his job, and he never told me why he lost it even though I asked him to tell me. I had dinner ready, but he didn't like what I had prepared. He threw his plate in the trash and was yelling at me, and I started having flashback of my life with Sully. He accused me of not paying attention to his needs. I went to my room and left him in the dining room. He then followed me and accused me of ignoring him while he was talking to me, that I was disrespectful.

Evidently, I must have said something wrong because he slapped me, and I fell to the floor. He kicked me and hit me repeatedly. I cried, and before I was aware of how long the argument and the beating had lasted, there was a knock at the door. Someone must have called the police. He took a long time to go to the door. The knocking got louder, and the voice said, "This is the police, open the door." He opened it, and the police man inquired about what was going on.

He talked to the policeman, but I didn't say one word. The policeman approached me. He didn't know that I couldn't speak English, and he said, "Is there anything you'd like me to do?" The next thing out of my mouth—I remember as clear as day—was, "I want to go back to my sister's house."

He asked, "Where?" I pointed to my sister's apartment, which was down the stairs from ours, and he went with me to her house and she communicated with him for me.

After talking to my sister, the policeman understood what was going on. We decided that I was going to go spend the night at my father-in-law and mother-in-law's house, to give us both time to cool off. When I arrived, they were both surprised to see all the bruises on my face. They tried to console me. They made me hold a bag of frozen peas against the bruises. They gave me hot milk with honey and sent me to my husband's old room.

That happened Friday evening, and on Saturday morning, my husband came to visit his parents. I'm not sure if they called to tell him that I was there. He pretended not to know, and he saw my coat on the back of a chair and asked, "Is my wife here? She had the police at our place last night, and she left without telling me where she was going."

Mom said, "No, she's not here."

He replied, "Isn't this her coat? I recognize it."

So I had to come out of hiding. He apologized and promised never to hit me again. He even reminded me that before we got married I had told him that if he ever laid hands on me I would leave him. He begged me not to leave him, but what he failed to understand was that he only had one chance with me and he blew it.

He said, "I am going to leave. You can stay here as long as you want. I just wanted to make sure you were okay."

His dad walked him out, and they talked outside for a long while. When he came back inside, he and mom gave me some valuable counsel about living happily ever after. Mom let me borrow an outfit of hers, and we talked a while longer. I asked them to let me stay until Monday. The rest of the weekend with them was very pleasant, and on Monday morning, after having a hearty breakfast together, Dad took me back to our apartment. He didn't stay long because he had to get back on the train to go to his job. After Dad left, Vital was not home, not sure where he was, I went straight to my sister's house. I couldn't wait to talk to her.

I spent the day with her and my little niece, Martine. I told her that I didn't want to be married to Vital anymore. She had to help me leave. She talked to her girlfriend Sonia who was willing to let me room with her for a while until we come up with a better plan. The next week we went to visit Sonia just so that I would know where to go, because when I do leave, my sister won't be going with me, and she didn't want me to get lost. She was afraid of Vital. She didn't want the neighbors to tell him they saw us leave together. While we are making plans for my moving, I realized that my period was very late. I went for a checkup, and it was confirmed that I was pregnant. The move had to be postponed.

When it rains, it pours. As if I don't already have enough on my plate! What am I going to do? Children are blessings from the Lord. I have been blessed with a fertile womb. The Lord allowed me to conceive, but time and time again, I disappoint him by having these abortions. This marriage is not working, and I have no way of supporting myself and a baby.

My troubles with immigration are on hold for the moment. Vital had filed papers for me to be able to stay in the United States, and within two years I would get my green card. However, I must stay with him in order for that to happen. What is more important? My well-being or the green card? I had decided not to live with a man who beats me and that it would not be in my best interest to have the baby. I refused to allow a repeat performance of what Sully had done to me. So I cried out to the Lord: "I need you Lord. I need a way out."

Our God is an awesome God, and he is a way maker. He creates a new way where there seems to be no way. He gives grace for every season in our lives and provides strength for every battle. My sister and I went out shopping for groceries. In the middle of the afternoon, and as we were waiting in line to pay for our food, we saw someone who looked familiar. When we got closer, we knew it was my best friend from Haiti, Rita. We had lost touch with each other. She came over to my sister's house. We caught up with the ins and outs of each other's life, and again she was in the position to help me with my situation. She offered for me to move in with her and her sister Micheline. They were both now divorced and living alone in Jamaica, Queens. My troubles are almost over.

My sister and I decided that it would not be fair to trouble them with the responsibility of taking care of me, plus with a baby on the way; it would be too much of a burden. She remembered an old remedy that would solve the baby problem. What you do is to put seven types of beer together in one pot, boil them down to equal a half of a cup, and drink it while it's still warm. So we went to the store, got the beers, and boiled them down. This concoction smelled very strong and tasted awful. I forced it down and almost threw it up. Then I had to lay flat on my back and wait for the results. I waited three days, and nothing happened. It was too late. This remedy works well only if you just missed your period, I am told. Plan B was to have an abortion.

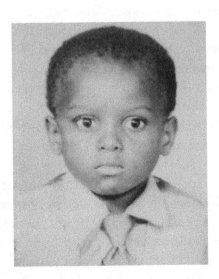

My one bag was packed, and on the dining room table, I placed my wedding ring and all the other jewelry that my husband had given me. I also wrote a good-bye note that read, "I am sorry. This is not the life I want to live. Good-bye."

My appointment for the abortion was that morning, and I was told that I would be able to leave right after. When I left the clinic, my next stop was to Rita and Micheline's house. I'd placed the house keys next to the note. I left the jewelry because they were very expensive. He had charged them on a credit card; perhaps he could return them and get the charges off of his card. He did not need to be in debt on my account.

All hope of obtaining my green card was gone. Vital can make one phone call to immigration and report me and they would be looking for me. The abortion was done, and I took a taxi to Rita's house in Queens. She, Micheline, and I had a nice dinner that evening, and we reminisced before going to bed. In the middle of the night, I felt chills, hot and cold, very uncomfortable. I called for Rita, who came into the room where I slept.

She touched my forehead and screamed, "My Lord, you are burning up!"

I told her about the abortion, and right away she knew that it was an infection. We don't have any money for a hospital visit. She said, "I'll take care of you my long, lost friend and daughter."

She put me in a tub of cold water to bring the fever down. (Rita used to be a nurse in Haiti.) She gave me two penicillin tablets, and she said, "I always keep a bottle of penicillin for a rainy day, and this is a rainy day." We went back to bed, and by morning the fever had broken. She gave me another dose of penicillin, and said, "Thank God, the worst is over."

That day, we received a phone call from my sister to tell me that she received a telegram; it read, "Son sick in hospital. Send money." My son, DD, was in the hospital. He was jaundiced again. Most of the times when you receive a telegram from Haiti, it causes fear because rarely it is good news. It's usually about an urgent matter, like someone has died or is very sick. I panicked and began to have feeling of guilt because of the abortion. I thought, "Why didn't God kill me instead of my son?" I thought this meant that God was trying to get my attention. I begin praying for the Lord to intervene on my son's behalf, that God would not allow any evil to prevail against my son.

My sister went to the bank for me that same day and sent the money for hospital bills. She also sent some extra money to help provide for both of our children. Marie Anne called back later to let me know that my husband was looking for me. He told her that he would rather die than to live without me, and that he is not going to die alone. He would first find me, kill me, and kill himself with the same knife. He even showed her the knife, and he repeated the same thing to my brother in-law, Menes.

She said, "We all thought he was crazy."

She also mentioned that she didn't think he was working anymore. He left early in the morning and came home very late at night and plays the music very loud until the morning hours. She also added that he might have been drinking. She suggested to me that if I wanted to come over, that I should do it after he leaves to go look for work and that I should let her know when so she can call to tell me when he's gone. I had left a few things at her house and wanted to get them back. We decided on a day for me to go over to her place. It's going to be hard visiting with her from that time on because an encounter with Vital could be deadly. I was also afraid of being reported to the immigration department.

CHAPTER 12

A Brown Winter Coat, Black Boots, and One Hundred Dollars; "Flight for your life." Out of the frying pan into the fire

*And the God of all grace, who called you to his eternal glory
in Christ, after you have suffered a little while, will himself
restore you and make you strong, firm and steadfast.*

—1 Peter 5:10

I know that I have faith and I trust God. He has shown himself mighty in my life. As I walk down the crooked, rocky and broken road of life, as I climb my faith mountain, things sometimes get really tough. I think I'm practically there, I can almost see the top; then I get tired. There is no sign of a resting place nearby, and I forget that the Lord is my resting place. I try to climb higher. Then I lose my footing and fall into the deepest pit. It feels like I'm being swallowed up alive. I have to look up, constantly remind myself that the "Lord", He alone is my anchor. He alone can redirect my steps and allow me to start again.

Los Angeles, California, 1971! My sister and I started our visit with food, and our favorite drink at the time, malta. We discussed my son, DDs, illness, and how he had gotten better, after having been released from the hospital. He had a relapse a few days later, and the doctor said there was very little hope for him. God has spared his life, and now he was doing much better.

We were chatting while I sorted through my things, and inside that big purse that Mother gave me as carry-on, I found a torn business card that was taped together. I looked at it funny as if I recognized it, and, of course, I did. That card belonged to Joseph, the man who came from California to visit his family that lived next door to my mother in Haiti. My sister didn't know about him. She was already in New York when he came to Port-au-Prince. So I explained to her what took place when his cousin brought him over to our house to introduce him to us, and right away she said, "Our problem is solved. You are going to California. Immigration won't know to look for you there. Call him." We called him that very moment.

When he answered, I introduced myself and reminded him of who I was. I explain my situation to him and reminded him of the card he had left and his offer to help me if I ever needed anything. Well, I said, "I need to run away from home."

He said, "I'll send you a ticket."

I replied, "That won't be necessary, I have some savings. I have enough to purchase my own ticket, but thank you anyway."

"Let me know when you are coming so I can pick you up at the airport." He finished with, "Here is my address. Send me your picture so I will recognize you at the airport."

I did not have any pictures at that time. Marie Anne and I went to a photo booth. We took a few pictures together and separate. So I sent one picture to Mr. Joseph B. and told him my intended departure date, which was April 3, 1971.

I had gained weight since I came to the United States. These pounds added up really fast, some 60 pounds in about eight months. I weighed 115 pounds when I left Haiti, and at that time I was at 175 pounds. I never thought that I was fat; no one told me that I was. My sister was even bigger than me. She hadn't lost all of the baby fat after giving birth to Martine. She weighed 200 pounds. I didn't think that was fat. I just got lost going from the land of not enough to the land of plenty. Caught up in the luxury of having so much, and so many choices.

In the good times in Haiti, we only ate three meals a day. Now besides the three meals, we have two to three snacks (and we were supersizing before McDonald knew the word). I'd forgotten about self-control. The more, the merrier. If it tastes good, have seconds. When we got too big for our clothes, we donated them to the Goodwill and bought bigger sizes. I remember that when I came to New York, I was wearing dresses size 3, and when I left New York for California, I could barely fit into a size 18. I was very hippy, so my pant size was even larger. My bra size was a 32A and grew to a whopping 38D.

When I lived with my sister and her family, most of the times we would eat breakfast twice. We got up around four o'clock at dawn. We fed the baby, prepare sack lunches for her husband and our brother to take to work, and ate breakfast before we returned to bed. When we got back up around eight or so, we ate another breakfast. Later, we would have our morning snack, then lunch, then our afternoon snack. We ate dinner when the men came home. Sometimes, we would have a final midnight snack before going to bed.

Who's looking? We didn't have a scale in the house, and for that matter we didn't care. We ate like porky the pig! We did not know to care. After being deprived for so long, unconsciously, we probably thought that it was about time that we got our fair share of food. We deserved to be fed right and to eat well. Unknowingly, we were hurting our bodies, and we will pay the consequences for our greed later.

The truth is we were both dealing with some strong underlining anxieties and issues, and were using food to medicate. We were not in control of many things in our lives, but the one thing we had control of were the choices about what we could eat. We didn't see the picture because we were in the frame, but looking back on it, that was part of what was driving our lack of control around food.

When I went back to Rita's house, I explained to her what had transpired. She didn't want to see me go, but she was happy for me. We promised each other that we would stay in contact with each other. Three or four years later, I went to Miami, Florida to visit Rita where she had moved to so she could be closer to Haiti in order that she could go home to be with her elderly mother. The friendship between Rita and me is very rare; it is genuine and solid, never ending.

April 3, 1971, if my memory serves me, was shortly after that massive Los Angeles earthquake, which was a colossal disaster that destroyed many homes and ruined many lives. When I found out about the earthquake, I wondered if God was warning me not to go to California. I was running out of the frying pan into the fire. Looking back, I was literally going from one disaster into another, one was physical and the other psychological, and they were both bad. Could it have been just my imagination runnin' away with me? I was an adult runaway.

I left LaGuardia Airport on April 3, 1971, in pursuit of a new life, one better than the one I had, so I thought. My flight arrived on time in Los Angeles International Airport. I was very happy to find someone waiting for me when I got off the plane. Some people waited by the baggage claim area, but Joseph came all the way to where everyone was coming out of the plane. He was holding a sign with my name on it: "Marie Pierre."

Let me clarify something. My last name did not change when I got married the second time as both my first and second husband had the same last name. It was common in Haiti.

I went to where Joseph was standing, and we shook hands and walked toward baggage claims area. We talked about the flight while waiting for my suitcase. We waited a long time because it was a full flight. I'm sure the other passengers carried a lot more baggage. I didn't have much in my suitcase, when I left Vital and my old life. For some reason, I was feeling nervous and almost claustrophobic, I couldn't wait to leave the airport.

I only brought what I needed: it was a brown winter coat, a pair of boots, and one hundred dollars, the money that my mother had given me when I travelled from Haiti. We went straight to the baggage claims, picked up my luggage, and headed to the car. As we left the airport, Joseph looked over to me, and he said, "You seem nervous. Are you alright?"

I replied, "I am okay. I am just missing my family and doing my best to adjust to this new environment."

He kept trying to make conversation, and I didn't want to be rude. So I started talking about how much prettier California seemed to be compare to New York. It was a beautiful spring afternoon. Many flowers were in bloom, and they brought new life, beauty, and love. I love flowers. Gardening is my favorite pastime, and some even say that I have a green thumb. I was daydreaming a bit about a rose garden, when Joseph announced that we had arrived.

My heart started to beat very fast. I was curious and nervous at the same time. He had told me that we were going to his brother's house. I didn't feel comfortable with that because I would be around people that I didn't know. I wondered what he had told them about me. He knocked on the door, and a nice lady opened it and said, "Entrez, Joseph. C'est la fille de qui vous nous aviez parlez?" (Come in, Joseph. Is this the girl you had told us about?"

He said, "Oui, elle s'appelle Marie. Marie, c'est ma belle souer Flo." (Yes, her name is Marie. Marie, this is my sister in-law Flo).

I said, "Bonsoir, madame. Je suis enchantee de faire votre conaissance." (Good evening, madame. It is a pleasure to meet you.)

She invited us to sit. We sat on the sofa in the living room for more than five minutes, and no one spoke a word. I was beginning to wonder if people in California didn't talk, but before my imagination could run too far, the woman said, "*Excusez moi.*" (Excuse me.) She got up and left the room. When she came back, her husband was with her.

He said to Joseph in English, "Sorry, brother, we can't help you. She can't stay here."

I understood the words, but I did not really know what he meant.

Then Joseph said in creole, "*An allez*, Marie", (let's go, Marie) as he was walking toward the door, and I followed him to the car. He drove silently for about one mile, then he broke the silence as if disappointed and said, "I tried to get them to let you live there until you get a job and get on your feet. The wife thinks you are too beautiful. She wouldn't trust her husband with you."

Instead of being flattered, I was insulted. Tears ran down my cheeks, and I didn't say a word; in fact, I was quiet during the drive to the house.

Welcome to California, mademoiselle! A chubby woman was waiting for us when we arrived at Joseph's house. Her name was Mildred, and she was also Haitian. Mildred had a live-in job.

She went to her employer's house on Sunday nights and retuned on Friday night or sometimes Saturday morning. She spends the weekends at Joseph's house. Joseph was a Christian. He was somewhat of a Good Samaritan, who tried in his own way to help people who were in need. I guess I was one of the needy people too. At what cost? I only needed God. He alone knows my troubles, and he alone can deliver me from them.

Mildred had prepared dinner that night. The three of us ate as we watched TV. I offered to do dishes, but Mildred wouldn't have it. This was a small one-bedroom with one bath house. There was a living room, a small kitchen with barely enough room to put a small dinette. I would say a single person's pad. There were twin beds in the bedroom and a sofa bed in the living room. That night, Saturday, April 3, 1971, my first night in California, Mildred and I shared the bedroom. Each of us slept on one of the twin beds, and Joseph slept on the sofa bed. Sunday morning, we got up, ate breakfast, and we went to church. The three of us spent a quiet day together. They were getting to know me and I them. I didn't ask too many questions, and I did not know what to ask.

The evening came. Mildred had to go to work, Joseph always picked her up and took her back to her job. So, on the April 4, 1971, I went with them to drop Mildred off. It was probably around seven or eight o'clock at night. When we got back to the house, it was almost bedtime. I went to the bathroom to get ready for bed. When I came out to the living room, Joseph had already turn down the couch. I thought it was for me, but he told me that "the lady" should stay in the bedroom. I didn't argue with that. I said my prayers and I thanked God that I had a place to stay. I wished Joseph good night and went to the bedroom. I didn't feel scared, not thinking of any monsters hiding under the bed or inside the closet. There were no red flags warning me to sleep with one eye open. I guess I was still that naive little girl, trusting and believing that all people are good and decent.

In the middle of the night, while sleeping I heard someone groaning and making funny kind of noises. I thought I was having a dream, but I wasn't. Then I realized there was something heavy lying on top of me. I tried to move and couldn't. I woke up fighting and screaming, and scratching. That pile of blubber was Joseph on top of me. His penis was inside of my vagina—he was literally raping me.

I said stop, but he kept moving faster and breathing hard. I said, "Please don't do this to me, get off me. Did you invite me to live here so you can have your way with me?"

He said, "I wanted to make love to you. I wasn't raping you. I loved you ever since the first time I laid eyes on you."

I kept screaming and tried to push him away from me. He was too strong, and I was unable to fight him off. Finally, in a loud and sturdy voice, I said, "I get it. This is what you want in exchange for your helping me? You don't make love to someone without their permission. This is called rape. If this is what you want, go on take it. I have survived worse than this."

He was already done by this time. He was lying on his back. He was either feeling remorse or proud of himself. Either way, I was violated. I was raped, shamed, degraded on April 4, 1971, the day after I arrived in Los Angeles, California. What a way to start a new life.

I had no family, no friends, and no place to go. My only possession was a brown winter coat, a pair of black boots, and one hundred dollars. I could not speak English. I didn't want to let him get away with what he did to me, but I was at a loss as to what I could do about it. I got out of the bed and went to the living room. He stayed where he was.

I was up the rest of the night, contemplating what to do next. Should I call the police? What is their number? I did not know then that 911 was a universal number. If I called, what would I say? Would they believe me? Would he lie to make me look foolish? Would they believe him or me? I did not want to take a chance. Where is the nearest hotel? I only purchased a one-way ticket to Los Angeles. I could not go back to New York even if I wanted to. I didn't have any money, and even worse, I was scared that Vital would find me and kill me or have me deported.

So I prayed. "Lord, show me what your plan is in this. I don't understand why I am here. Give me your peace to help me continue this journey I am on."

I had fallen asleep on the sofa. Then I heard him moving around in the other room. It's Monday morning, and he had to get ready for work. When he was leaving, he came to where I was and said, "I am going to work. I will be back around five o'clock." I ignored him and he left.

When I was sure that he was gone, I picked up the phone and called my sister. She was happy to hear from me and that I made it safe in Los Angeles. We chatted, and she said, "What is wrong? I hear a sadness in your voice."

I did not tell her that I had been raped, just that I was homesick. "I wish that I could go back to New York."

She said, "We both know that you can't." She told me that Vital had moved out of the apartment and went back to live with his parents. I didn't feel like talking anymore, so I told her that we would talk another time.

All is not lost. I had some really good news. After talking to my sister, I called Mr. Kaplan, the attorney that was handling the papers for my green card, to let him know that I left my husband and I will no longer need his services. He told me unless my husband came to him personally to withdraw his sponsorship, he was still on the job. And, so far, Vital had not been to see him or called.

He said, "In fact, while Vital was signing the petition, he had included the final papers as well. Vital didn't know it, but whether you stayed with him or not, you can still get your green card. I will keep you posted on the progress. Call me if there are any other changes."

I called my friend Rita to tell her about the rape. She was devastated. She would have liked me to return to New York. We decided that I should take a few days to decide what would be better at this time. I was mindful to keep my talking to a minimum because these were long-distance calls.

Time had gone by so slowly. My head was hurting really bad, probably from lack of sleep, and I had not eaten anything all day. I lay down on the couch for a nap and did not wake up until Joseph came back from work. He was loaded up like Santa Claus on Christmas

Eve. He brought flowers, bags of groceries, and a gift-wrapped box. He put down the groceries and handed me the flowers and the box.

"This is for you," he said, "and I promise I will make it up to you. I know it's soon, but I want to marry you."

I said, "I am married already, and if you were the only man left on the planet, I would not marry you. Take your flowers, your gift, and give them to someone who cares. I just want to find a job. I will stay here, but the moment I can get on my feet, I will leave. I promise you that, and the sooner the better."

I continued to live in this compromising situation for one and a half long years. Joseph continued to take advantage of the fact that I had no place to go by forcing me to have sex even though he knew that I detested him for what he was doing to me. Having said that, in my eyes I still considered what he was doing as pure rape plain and simple.

When I did get a job, I worked the night shift, so I would not be home when Joseph was there. When I could feel myself falling into depression, I would always find some kind of project to shift my mind away from my problems. I decided to plant a garden. So I found a place in the backyard to plant a beautiful garden. This type of work has always made me feel better and even brought me peace. It is a form of therapy and bring about a spirit of calm.

The soil was rich. My tomato plants were thriving. I also planted squash, two types of squash (the yellow crooked neck and Italian squash). It was a generous harvest. I gave most of it away to the neighbors. There was a small area of dirt near the front door. I thought would look pretty with some colors. I planted two rose bushes, a yellow, my favorite color and a pink, and I added some colorful annuals and some bulbs.

Even though the gardening helped some, the truth is my depression did not leave completely; in fact, it came back, and I was having multiple anxiety attacks. I thought that my life was being wasted, and I didn't want to live anymore. I was even contemplating suicide.

Suicide is a sin, I told myself. I tried to talk myself out of it. Then I realized that my period was late, so I went to the drug store and bought a pregnancy test. Yes, you guessed it, I was pregnant, again. What now? I don't have any money, except for the hundred dollars that my mother had given me. One hundred dollars, I repeat it's one hundred dollars! That is not enough to start a new life. I don't know where a hospital is, and if they accept illegal aliens without money. I don't want to tell Joseph that I was pregnant because he would probably make me keep it and even try to convince me that I should marry him and live a miserable life for the sake of the baby.

There are times, when, looking back, I wondered how my life would turn out if I had chosen a different route. We will never know, will we? Was I too selfish, stubborn, fearful because my life was being controlled and dictated by other people. I just wanted a normal life for a change. Is that too much for me to ask? I was hoping that going to California would give me a fresh start in life, but up to now, it seems as though I'm just repeating the pattern my life has taken for as long as I can remember. Surely things will get better, but only time will tell.

CHAPTER 13

Getting Free from My Rapist;
"Wolf in sheep's clothing"

It is for freedom that Christ has set you free. Stand firm, then, and do not let yourselves be burdened again by a yoke of slavery.
                                        —Galatians 5:1

Decisions! Decisions! Decisions! One morning, after a long sleepless night, some old remedy that I had heard of came to mind. They said that quinine pills would cause miscarriage, but I didn't remember how many pills would be effective. So I went to the drugstore and purchase a bottle of quinine. When I got home, I took five pills (that's half of the bottle) with a glass of warm milk (They always say that warm milk helps to expedite things.), and I lay down and waited. They said that it would take from two to three days, depending on the number of pills taken.

In two days, nothing happened. I cramped a little but nothing else. I took the rest of the pills, and on the third day, more steady cramping all day long and nothing else. The next day, I went back to the store and got another bottle, but this time I took the entire bottle. I lay down on the couch, and I did not eat, did not even water my garden. I just vegetated and was feeling very depressed. If my memory serves me correctly, I got up once to use the bathroom, and that's the last thing I remember, until I woke up in the emergency room at Los Angeles General Hospital.

The doctor said that I could have died but thank God I didn't. He also wanted to know what had happened, so I gave him all the details. I explained to him that I had taken quinine on two separate occasions in the last five days. The doctor said that it was the pills working, but I was so weak, that's why I passed out. He also told me that it was dangerous, and he instructed me to never do that again. He then showed me the tiny fetus; it was in a jar containing some kind of fluid.

Joseph looked at me and said, "You killed my baby." Quite frankly, I don't even remember how I responded to his statement, but I do remember thanking God for once again sparing my life. Thinking about Joseph, he appeared harmless, he wasn't violent; just another ordinary face. That's only the outside, who can know the thoughts of a man? The rape wasn't reported. He is free. But, am I?

When I went home the next day, I began taking inventory of my life and realized that having abortions had become a big part of my life. It was like a recurring nightmare, something out of my control; almost as if I were addicted to having abortions. I knew that it was wrong and that I was jeopardizing my health, but I couldn't seem to break the cycle.

When I look back on how it all got started, there is a part of me that wants to blame Sully for not only the first abortions but for every subsequent abortion. The truth is that I cannot continue to play that blaming game anymore. Sully is no longer in my life, and I cannot continue holding him responsible for my ongoing choices. I am now in control, and I own the fact that I am as big a killer as Sully was. I am responsible for the part I played in these abortions. Having said that, I know that in my heart of hearts my desire is to once and for all stop taking the life of unborn children.

I am becoming a kept woman again. I say that because my actions will reflect some of the things kept women do. The first thing I did was I had a long overdue conversation with Joseph. First thing is I let him know that I was tired of being forced to have sex, and from now on he would have to make a request and I would have the final say on when we would have sex. The next thing I said to him is, "The only reason that I am living here is because I have no place else to go." Also, he would have to agree, that our lives would be independent of each other's. I was going to find a job, work as hard as I could, and move as soon as it is humanly possible.

He said, "Wouldn't you rather go back to school and get your degree? As smart as you are, you can take accelerated course and be done in no time. I would pay for it.

Yes, I was smart, but I allowed pride to get in the way. I said, "No, thank you." Looking back, I should have accepted. Then he said, "The offer stays open, but I will take whatever you offer as long as you don't leave me. Here is a credit card to use however you want, and you don't have to spend any of your own money. I will even send the monthly allowance to your mom for you." I didn't really want his guilt money, but it was an agreeable deal.

I found employment almost immediately. It was not what I really wanted but anything will do. My first job was at a convalescent hospital, as a dish washer. Minimum wage at that time was $1.25 per hour, more than I've ever earned before. I opened a bank account with my first paycheck.

Every month, I sent most of my money to my sister, first to pay her for anything that I might have owed her and the rest for her to save. I wanted to make sure Joseph couldn't touch my money because at that time I didn't think I could trust him, but I later found out that when it comes to money Joseph was more trustworthy than my sister. She and her husband used all my money, and it took a long time for me to get any of it back. She blamed it on her husband, and I believed her.

The arrangement with Joseph is working out fine. I feel like a prostitute, but at least I get to choose when my body could be used. I made another request of him, which was that I wanted to learn how to drive and buy my own car, and of course he granted my request.

After I learning to drive, I immediately obtain my driver license. He had an old Ford in the garage. He got it fixed and gave it to me, just to use when I leave, the car had to stay with him. Of course, I had no problem with the conditions he laid out. He took me shopping all the time and bought anything I desired—clothes, shoes, purses, and everything to match. If I knew then what I know now, I could have gotten rich off of him, but the truth is at that time I was very naive and didn't think it was right to take advantage of people. I also know now, as a Christian, not only that we shouldn't take advantage but we should let the Lord fight our battles. The way I have chosen is much better, because I can say that God was my strength. God was my source, and I made it because God was always on my side.

I was very good at my job. I had integrity and speed, and I was obedient to those that were over me. I was soon promoted to setting tables and helping with the serving of food to the guests and patients in the dining room.

I had two bosses, Mr. Prince and Mr. Roth. They were brothers-in-law. They both admired me for my strength and courage. They knew a few things about what was going on in my life. They were both old enough to be my father. I told them about my living conditions, and the arrangement that I had made with Joseph. I've even told them about been forced to have sex against my will, and how we were living on a verbal arrangement. I also asked them to please give me as much overtime as they could because I would rather be at work than to be at home and available to Joseph. There were times when I worked two, three shifts back to back. I was almost never too tired to work the extra shifts.

While working these many hours I hardly ever ate; as a result, I lost a lot of weight. I also noticed that I was looking much better with less weight on my body. The weight loss also caused me to be more conscious about my eating habit. I love that. Because it's just like when we choose to follow God and live for him, it has to be on purpose. You can check yourself to see your progress, if you are flaking off or working hard at it.

I am an "all or nothing" kind of person, even a little extreme in some areas of my life. When I am serious about something, I give it my all, sometimes I go overboard. My losing weight is a good example, because once I started dieting, I rapidly lost ninety-eight pounds. Losing that much weight even became a problem because overtime, I became borderline anorexic. The truth was I was suffering from a serious eating disorder, and I was clueless that I was causing harm to not only my body and also to my mental and emotional well-being.

One year had passed since I came to California, I remember it so clearly as if it were yesterday. It was around income Tax Day, April 1972, and I thought I had saved up enough money to allow me to get my own place. When I told Joseph of my intention to move, he begged me to stay.

He said, "Have I not been good to you? What would it take for you to stay, even for a few months longer?"

I said, "Nothing." Then I thought about it for a moment and said, "I wanted a brand-new vehicle, an Electra 225." They were very popular that year.

He said, "You got it."

Shortly thereafter, he took me shopping for it. I test drove a white Electrac 225, my favorite car and color at that time. I let Joseph know that was the car I wanted. He went inside with the salesman to write it up, while I stayed in the lot admiring the car.

Suddenly, I ran inside just as he was about to sign on the dotted line, and I said, "Stop! Thank you. You have passed the test. Under different circumstances, I would stay for nothing, but I must move. I thank you for all that you have done."

I started looking around for a place closer to my job, since I was going to be without transportation. One day I noticed an advertisement in the newspaper for a one-bedroom apartment in Brentwood. It would be a long walk to my job. When I went to inquire about it, the lady who came to the door told me that they didn't rent to blacks and slammed the door in my face. I was not offended. I did not even know that I could be. I wasn't aware of discrimination laws. Law or no law, people should be able to choose who they want to rent their properties to. She was rude that's all I held no grudge against her. I understand now why people get upset when they have been discriminated against. We didn't have to deal with discrimination in Haiti, it was more about whether you were rich or poor.

Two months had gone by, and I couldn't move. It was very hard to find a suitable apartment within my price range, let alone in the ritzy area like Brentwood. I put a note on the bulletin board at work, "Marie Pierre is looking for small inexpensive apartment or room for rent." About one month later, one of my bosses asked me in to the office for a chat. I was not sure why but hoping it was about a raise.

He said, "What's that I hear about you looking for a room to rent? Why don't you stay here in one of the vacant rooms until you find an apartment? I was going to offer you Myrtle's job anyway. She is leaving next month and can train you prior to her departure. You're a fast learner, you'll do well."

"Myrtle's job!" I exclaim "That's perfect, thank you for trusting me."

He added, "You'll get a ten-cents raise but your duties will change. You'll have to pass out meds to the older patients. Some of them are on insulin. Would you be afraid to administer insulin?" I let him know that I was willing to learn. He said, "I know." How exciting! I will be earning $1.35 per hour. I was pleased. As usual, I did well at this job.

After that meeting, I couldn't help but give God praise for his many blessings in my life. Now I have a new and better position, a raise and a free room.

Not only were Mr. Prince and Mr. Roth were brothers-in-law, but they were also co-owners of two businesses. And now that I live in one of the facilities and the other one is not very far, they allowed me to work at both places. They sent me to where I was needed the most, sometimes one of them dropped me off and the other picked me up.

I also had a side job with one of the residents, whose name is Bernard. Bernard was blind. His daughter paid me to take him to his doctor's appointments, Braille classes, and at times I take him to the park, overall just being a companion to him. There were times when we got back late for my shift because we had to take the bus. I started looking for a jalopy. My boss offered to pay for the car and deduct the money from my paycheck. I couldn't ask for a better boss.

Our real boss is God, and he is the one who chooses the earthly authorities over us. That's why we owe respect and obedience to them—we work for them as unto the Lord. I thank God for being my keeper and my provider.

Now I have a new job with people who love me, my own car, a place to stay, and I can also eat at work for free. In addition to that good news, a certified letter came for me from Mr. Kaplan, my New York attorney. Immigration made an appointment for me to appear before them on October 2, 1972, in Port-au-Prince, Haiti for the issuance of my green card. I must go to New York to his office to sign final papers to take with me to Haiti.

I moved out of Joseph's house and I thanked him. I told him that I was going to live at my job and that I was still looking for an apartment. He said he would keep an eye open in case he sees a For Rent sign. I said, "Thank you."

By the way, he said, "You can use the credit card to purchase some furniture and pay me later."

I had to find an apartment for my son and I to live in. I cannot bring him to live at Brentwood Manor, a retirement home for the elderly. I had to find something before I left for Haiti, and time was running out.

I have worked very hard all my life. Beginning at Brentwood Manor, and later at Golden Manor. In addition to working at both manors, I took on private duties, working as a nanny for a very rich psychiatrist in Hollywood. Once or twice each month, I spent the weekend with his only daughter, whose name is Melody. Melody's quarters consisted of a bedroom suite, a playroom, private bathroom, and of course my room and bath. We only came out for meals. She always referred to me as her older sister. When Melody wasn't staying with her father, she was with her mother, who had legal custody of her.

Her father was a very nice person to work for, and never once did he make me feel less; in fact, we ate dinner at the same table. He was happy to have found someone that his daughter liked. I was told that they had interviewed many others before me. I loved being there. After working so hard, I welcomed a weekend of fun and games with my little sister, Melody.

CHAPTER 14

Mother and Son Finally Reunited;
The greatest gift ever is the love and the bond between a mother and her son.
Something no one can take away

Make every effort to keep the unity of the spirit through the bond of peace. There is one body and one spirit—just as you were called to one hope when you were called.
— Ephesians 4:3–4

Voyage back to Haiti! I will surely have to let go of some of my jobs when my son comes to live with me. I probably should say that I will need to shift some of my jobs to accommodate for the care of my son. I finally found a nice one-bedroom apartment off Pico Boulevard and La Cienega, not far from Marvin Avenue Elementary School, where DD would be able to attend kindergarten. I felt elated about being able to move into my new apartment.

Shortly thereafter, I traveled back to New York to meet with my attorney and obtain my immigration papers for myself and my son, Ducarmel Didier Pierre. I didn't realize how much I loved him until now. Knowing that we were going to be reunited sort of revived me.

My love for him and being with him is all that I could think about at the moment. I was away from him for much too long and trying to prepare a place for us was constantly on my mind. It was finally going to happen.

I was picked up by an old friend of my sister, named Leon, whom I met while living with my sister in New York. After picking me up from the airport, he invited me to stay at his house in Nyack during my visit in New York. When we met one and a half year ago, there were sparks between us. I had found him very attractive, and the feelings were mutual, but that's all it was nothing else. When Leon found out that I had left New York and moved to California, he got my phone number from my sister and called me. We kept in touch with each other. He and I started a long-distance romance. I often wondered, can a relationship that started long distance grow and flourish without real in person time together?

I was so desperate for companionship, for a soft touch, and for some strong but gentle arms around me. Every time Leon kissed me, I melted like butter in the sun. This happened in the fall, but it sure felt like summer. He wined and dined me, as well as taking me to the theater, and for long walks in the park. We liked many of the same things, the same songs, and many of the same foods. We both thought we were falling in love. I also wondered if it was even possible to fall in love so quickly? The time spent in Nyack, New York with Leon somewhat answered both of those questions. As to if long-distance relationships can flourish, I believe they can. Both parties must work very hard at it and be strongly committed. As for falling in love quickly, it is possible, but I am not sure.

Everything between Leon and I felt so real, as if we've known each other for an eternity. Our time together went by very fast, and we savored every moment. He was my chauffeur to and from visits to my legal appointments. He was also the one who drove me to the airport when I left for Port-au-Prince. Before leaving, we promised each other that we would continue our relationship until we decide how we would make it permanent.

Leaving New York was not easy, I was missing him before he even left the airport. I was happy to be going to Port-au-Prince, but anxious about the reunion between my mother and me. The trip back to Haiti went very well. The taxi took me to my mother's house, and since she knew I was coming, had the maid to make my room ready. I had not seen my son and family for over two years.

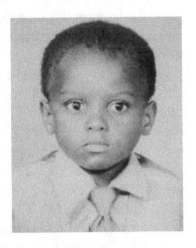

When DD came to greet me, I hugged him very tight and cried. He said, "Bonjour, ma tante." (Good morning, Auntie.") He called me auntie and refer to my mother as mama; he thought that I was his auntie. I also gave him and my niece the gifts that I had brought for them from America. I hugged Mother and gave her gifts and money. There was a lot to do before I reported to the immigration authorities on Monday. Many family members came to visit and were expecting gifts or money as well. I gave mother money to distribute among them because she knew better how to make sure each person got what they needed.

My son and I got in the taxi and went to the immigration office. I was sort of scared and didn't know what to expect. Things are very different in foreign countries. Every government employee wanted, and in fact expected you to grease their palm, for doing a job that they have already been paid to do. I felt obligated to give them the amount of money they requested because I wanted to make sure that they didn't put my papers in the bottom at the pile, never to be found. I didn't mind paying it, but I still think that was robbery, plain and simple.

The meeting was very brief because all the proper papers were in perfect order. They probe into your background, your finances, how you live, every aspect of your life. Then after, reviewing our paperwork we were given final approval. Once again, God took care of everything. I had waited a long time to see my son and be with him, and now that we're back together again, I was very happy and not only me but DD was happy as well. Once in the cab on the way back to my mother's house, I told Ducarmel that I came to get him and take him to America with me.

I looked at him and said, "Is that okay?"

He responded with a happy voice. "I am going to America!"

I said, "Yes, you are." That made him very happy.

My son and I came to Los Angeles, California, on October 12, 1972, two days after his fifth birthday. We went to our new apartment and started our new life together. It was not as easy as I thought it would be, and truth be told, I was very afraid. It was very hard for me. I now had to be responsible for the well-being of another person, a small person that I really did not know very well. I would have to learn his likes and dislikes, his favorite toys, foods, and any other aspect of his life. This is not like playing games with a little rich girl in Hollywood. I am going to be raising this child all alone and would be responsible to teach him right and wrong.

The thought dawned on me that, like mother like daughter. I had left my son behind for over two years. I had never thought about it like that before. Just as I had been left behind at age four, so was DD even though my situation was somewhat different. The bottom line is my son had to be without his mother at a time when he needed me most. I had gone to America to make a better life for us. Mother might have thought that way as well when she left me behind. My heart was beating so fast, and everything started to come back. All at once, I began to panic and get anxious. My imagination was running away with me once again. Different thoughts were flooding my mind with doubts and uncertainty. I am not cut out for motherhood. Am I going to be like my mother? What does it take to be a good mother? Are there any set rules to follow?

Then I thought, what about money? He is too young to stay home alone when I go to work. I'm going to need a babysitter. Maybe I need to cut back on my hours, but if I do, I won't have enough money to afford the apartment and the lifestyle I want for us. We lived in a very nice neighborhood, and the rent was high. I didn't think of all that when I moved there.

What about school? He doesn't speak English. What if the other children make fun of him? He didn't say much, so I didn't know what was going on. Maybe he is lonely, missing his mama. My little boy didn't seem happy anymore. He didn't like the food. He was missing his mama. I wanted to be a good mother, but I didn't know how. What should I do? Somebody, help me please!

One day, he came home from school crying. I asked him what was wrong. In reply, he asked me why I kept speaking like I do, why I don't speak like the people at school. I spoke to him in French, our language, he couldn't speak English yet. For that matter, my English wasn't all that great either. That was his first time going to school. He was in kindergarten. I didn't know if they had English as a second language for his age. I had to attend night school when I first came to California to learn English as a second language. I went to his school and spoke to his teacher about the matter. I was assured that they would handle the situation.

Somebody help me! I need a little help here. I quit my job because I had found something better. I wanted to go back to school. Someone told me about a government program that had something to do with on the job training (OJT), which was available to low-income applicants only. I applied and was accepted into the program. It was at the Watts Skills Center, which was located in a very bad part of town. I didn't know anything about good or bad neighborhoods. I thought that's just the way they were.

On my first day of school, I found out that not only did I have to qualify financially, but that I also had to take a placement test. I don't know how that's going to be possible; I could barely speak and understand English. If there is a will, there is a way. I wanted to be a clerk stenographer, which was one of the more difficult tests. They test your knowledge of English, math, grammar, typing, and filing. Except for math, I was deficient in all of them. I also had to do an essay. I had only been in the US for three years, give me a break! My English was not proficient enough for the class of choice. They called me into the office for a meeting to discuss my scores, which except for math, were all somewhat marginal. The professors of my other classes didn't see a big problem. It was Mrs. Anette Thomas, the stenography professor, who was going to make or break the deal, it entailed shorthand and advanced English.

I had only taken English as a second language at night school for a short time, not even a full semester. You can't understand shorthand without already knowing long hand. They wanted me to choose a different course, like file clerk or just be a typist, something easier. But I refused. I told them being a clerk stenographer involves typing and filing as well, so why can't I do it all and qualify as a secretary? I was a fast learner and asked if they could give me a chance at it for a couple of months, after which I could be reevaluated.

Mrs. Thomas, the stenography professor, was at the meeting also. She said, "This is going to be like suicide. It's going to take a lot of hard work. If she is willing I am going to take a chance on her," and so she did. I thank God for her.

I studied hard. She stayed after class almost every day to give me some extra help. She gave me and the committee a progress report weekly. I made it through and passed the two-month trial period, and eventually graduated. I was in the top 5 percentile of my class; out of forty students I ranked second. As a reward for my great achievement, I was chosen to spend a day at Mayor Bradley's office, observing and helping the secretary as she performed her duties. The job placement office called me in and sent me on my first interview at a firm in Culver City. I was hired on the spot as a clerk stenographer.

I forgot to tell you, in case you didn't guess already, the on-the-job training program pays as you learn.

My car got broken into while parked right in front of the school. The thief took everything he could, including the tires. At that time, it was the worst thing that could have happen to me because I depended on my car to get back and forth to work and school. That same day, I began to search for another car. My search took me to a Pontiac dealer on Crenshaw Boulevard, where an elderly sales person took a liking to me and gave me a great deal on a used car. Life is good! Things were working out better at school for DD and me, but he was still missing his mama.

My phone love affair with Leon is still on. My sister and her husband bought a triplex on Seventh Avenue, a duplex in the front and a two-bedroom in the rear that she and her family would live in. One of the units was already rented, and they wanted me to move into the other one. Moving in there was a good thing, in that it helped my sister and DD and me as well, an added bonus would be that the children would have an opportunity to play together.

My job at the firm did not offer many benefits, so I found another that did. I worked now for Los Angeles Unified School District at Virgil Junior High School, where I would be working as a clerk stenographer. Again, things were going well, so I thought. my frequent bout with depression had subsided for a while, but I could feel myself beginning to fall back into that depressive state. I did my best to keep it under control because I didn't want to jeopardize my employment or my ability to care for DD.

I needed and purchased a new vehicle, which was a Pontiac Firebird, a car that I really enjoyed owning. I felt that I deserved a new car since I worked hard and could afford it. I always felt guilty and needed to justify spending money on myself. I'd always pinch my pennies, shopped at secondhand stores, mend what was broken and find a way to make it new again. Never turned away a hand-me-down whether it is clothing or furniture. I'd never planned to be rich, just wanted to be a good steward of the treasures that the Lord had entrusted to me. I always thought that the funds could have been put to better use. You could say that I had poverty mentality. Maybe so, maybe not. I needed to trust God more. He had always provided abundantly for me, and he is not about to stop.

Even though things are going okay, I'm still depressed and struggling as far as being a mother to my son. Why can't I have a complete family? I felt something was missing in my life. I felt lonely, empty, and incomplete, and I just needed some companionship to be added to my life. I was beginning to have anxiety attacks, and the depression had gotten so bad that one of my friends suggested that I should see a psychiatrist.

I went to see Dr. Pender, who really didn't do anything for me but take my money. Mental health was not included in my benefit package at that time. When I sat on his couch, I didn't know where to start, what to say to Dr. Pender. I wasted forty-five dollars every time I went and had gotten nowhere. I managed to tell him about my son, our background, and about how he was born. I also mentioned the rapes and abortions. He concluded that I needed to be on medication and that my ability to function would be greatly affected, so much so that someone else would have to take care of DD.

Why didn't I think of it before? Was he thinking that I was a danger to my son? He made me put my son in temporary and voluntary foster care. I felt really bad having to place my son in foster care, that's like abandonment. He's only been with me two years and now I'm giving him up to live with a perfect stranger. My hope was that his foster mama would love and take good care of him.

The good news is Mrs. Ida Mae Lamette was a very good foster mother to DD, and she was an older woman I even called her mama, because in some way she filled a void and DDs need for a mother figure and a grandmother figure as well. She had been providing foster care for a long time. She had no children of her own. She and her husband filled the void in their life by raising other people's children. I think she had adopted one of her foster children.

With voluntary placements, I had to pay the county for his care. I felt good about providing financially for my child. I was allowed to visit whenever I wanted, and I did frequently. DD was seven years old at the time, and he adjusted very quickly. There was another boy living there as well, giving him a chance to have a brother, an older brother who was two years his senior. DD adored Mrs. Lamette and enjoyed having a big brother. Mrs. Lamette probably reminded him of my mother. I was glad for that, but I think he liked being with her more than with me.

I attended church services with them, Sunday dinners, and other activities. I was part of the family. I think this was the best for my son since I couldn't be the mother he needed. For many years, and even until this day, I look back on my relationship with DD, and it makes me sad because I so wanted to be a better mother. Why I wasn't is still a mystery. All I know is that I love my son, and nothing can ever change that.

CHAPTER 15

Home Again;
There is no other place like "Cali"!

By wisdom a house is built, and by understanding it is established;
and by knowledge the rooms are filled with
all precious and pleasant riches.

—Proverbs 24:3–4

Love or lust. Leon was moving from Nyack, New York to Dorchester, Massachusetts. He thought that it would be nice for us to go there together. I thought, "Great idea, just what I needed, a change of pace." In hindsight, I have concluded that to get back together was a very bad decision. I didn't put the welfare of my child first. I thought, since he was so happy and Mrs. Lamette was taking good care of him, he would be alright. I didn't take into consideration the fact that I would be over three thousand miles away.

I told my son about the trip, and he was okay with it. What was I thinking, he was just a child, how could I expect him to understand that kind of stuff? This is again abandonment. I returned my new car to the dealer and it was costly to return it or I would have ruined my credit. I sold what I could of my furniture and gave away the rest. My bank account was emptied out except for one hundred dollars to keep the account open, and that's exactly the amount of money I came to California with almost four years prior. I asked for a leave of absence from my job. Thank God that I was thinking ahead, because that would prove to be a very good move on my part. I didn't know it, but with the school district, my job was on hold for me for thirty-six months without losing seniority, what a deal!

Just a few days before Christmas of 1974, I travelled to Massachusetts, trying to find true love. Leon performed magic in the bedroom, but love, on either side, I'm not so sure. When he touched me, our bodies merged together like hand and glove; it almost felt like I was back in the arms of my first and only love, Luckner, my Loulou. He made me scream and begged for more just like Loulou. I think Luckner was the yardstick that I used to measure other men with. Later on, I'd became more promiscuous, in that I was comparing current sexual experiences with the experience I initially had with Luckner. My relationship with Leon did not last very long. Probably because it wasn't based on true love—the real glue that keeps hearts beating together.

While in Massachusetts, I worked at Youville hospital in Boston as a nurse's aide. I had prior experience in giving bed baths, emptying bedpans, checking vital signs, tube feeding etc. The money I brought from California was gone in no time, and my paychecks were spent to help with the household expenditures.

I was not aware that we were going to share a house with his brother and his wife. They had recently been married and his wife, Marlene, was now with child. They couldn't afford this big house alone; instead of getting a one-bedroom apartment, which was more like what their salary would support, they went beyond their reach and big brother had to come to the rescue and I was right in the middle of it.

I was not happy from the very beginning, and within three months, the honeymoon was almost over. We were fighting about every little thing. We never got to go out alone. We always had an audience, no privacy even when we argued. Once, we went to a birthday party at his brother's friend's house. We were all dancing, and before the song was over, he wanted to leave. When I asked why, he said, "You are embarrassing me." He didn't like the way I was dancing.

He didn't talk to me all the way home. He followed me to our room, where we argued violently, and he hit me in the face, and that brought back the memories of my life with Sully. I had promised myself longtime ago that never again would I allow any man to physically abuse me. I tried to slap him back, but he grabbed my hand and hit me again.

He said, "I am sorry. Now see what you made me do?"

I got my purse, took his car keys, and left. I went to my friend Gladys's house. He had to borrow his brother's car to drive to his job. The next day, his brother brought him there to get his car, but I didn't return until I was ready to pack my bags and leave him. When Gladys and I went to pack my bags, Leon was not home, that made it easier for us. On the way back to her house, Gladys and I discussed what my next step would be.

Sweet home California! I decided that I would return to California, but it would take a while because all my money was gone. I am so glad that my friend Gladys allowed me to come to stay with her. She lived in a small apartment and she had a lot of children. I only stayed with her until I found a small kitchenette apartment near Youville Hospital where I worked. It was a very depressing place to live. There was a shared bathroom near my room and a small kitchen downstairs in the basement. It had a dirty refrigerator that we all shared as well. I was afraid to use the stove or the refrigerator, even to go downstairs at all. Nearly every day I went to the pizza place down the street. They served pizza by the piece. I either ate in the hospital cafeteria or at Piece o' Pizza, which was the name of the business. That was no life. The only reason I was still there is because I needed to earn money for my plane ticket.

Like Morton Salt, when it rains it pours! In July of 1975, I almost had enough money for the purchase of my plane ticket to California. I figured that I should work a couple of extra weeks longer so I could have some pocket change for other things. In the hustle and bustle of life in Boston, I didn't realize that my period had not come. I decided to ask my friend Gladys to purchase a pregnancy test kit from the pharmacy, which was near her house. When I took the test, it was positive, and again I was face with the decision as to what I would do. Of course, staying in Boston and having the baby was out of the question. I already had a son in California that I could not take care of. I also did not want to tell Leon about it, because he had a child from a previous relationship. I must say that I did wonder how he would handle the news.

A friend of Gladys told us that in cases where due to lack of finances a person could not afford to pay, the county hospital might perform a free abortion. I called and inquired about it, and I qualified and was scheduled to have the abortion. After the abortion, I called Leon and told him about my returning to California. He took me out for dinner where he proposed. He didn't want to live with his brother anymore. He also told me how unhappy he had been since I left, and he wanted to share his life with me. Really!! Why would I want to marry him? He slapped me once, he will do it again. Even though he apologized, I didn't believe him.

Why is my life so wrapped up in killing my babies? It was always about me, myself and I. Where does it end? When will I care enough to put my baby's life before mine? My baby, my only son, DD, has been abandoned twice. I needed to once and for all prove to him that I loved him. He's been living in foster care for almost two years. I need to get my act together and be a real mother. By the way, I turned down Leon's proposal and booked my reservation to go back home where I belong, with my son.

Initially, I had to stay with my sister. I also went to the school district and I got my job back. Soon after I got my first paycheck, I found and moved into a nice one-bedroom apartment. The next thing was I petitioned the courts to regain custody of my son.

My petition was conditionally approved. I would first have to do weekend visits in order for DD and I to get reacquainted. The visits worked well, and my son was allowed to come stay with me permanently. I also resumed my therapy sessions. Mrs. Lamette agreed to be my babysitter and made herself available to us whenever she was needed. We both called her mama, and there were times when we were all in the same room and DD called out for mama. We weren't sure which of us he was calling, so we both look up. He got a big kick out of it, and sometimes he did it just to tease us.

My son and I started our life together again. He was now nine years old. We did just about everything together. We went to church, shopping, movies, horseback riding, the park etc. DD loved church, and I believe he loved God as well. Before his ninth birthday, while he was still living with Mrs. Lamette, D.D. invited Jesus into his heart as his lord and Savior. He always told the truth and would even yell at me when he answered the phone and I'd told him to say that I'm not home. He'd say, "Mama, God doesn't want me to lie." He was a perfect child. He was very easy to love, he was obedient, anything I say to him, he'd say, "Okay, mama."

Once, the neighbor's son hit him in the face, and he came home crying. "Mama, Jojo hit me."

I said, "Did you hit him back?"

He said, "No, God said to turn the other cheek."

When another child pushed him off his new bike and ran with it, I said, "I'm sure you fought to get it back, right?"

He said, "I did not, maybe he needed it more."

DD had many positive traits about his character. I was in awe of him sometimes. He was very smart, understanding, caring, generous, and loving. One day, DD's school had a blood drive. Everybody who wanted to give had to be tested before they could give blood. DD's test results revealed that he was positive for sickle cell anemia. I had never even heard about sickle cell anemia prior to this. The school instructed me to have DD tested by his primary care doctor. The positive test was also confirmed by our primary care doctor. Of course, I was devastated after learning how serious the disease was. DD started having sickle crisis episodes; he would have excruciating pain in the joints that required him to be admitted to the hospital.

His life from that point on was a series of painful crisis. Every other month or so, he was in the hospital from three days to seven to ten days at a time. I was back and forth to the hospital. During the time at the hospital, I wanted to make good use of my time. I started to crochet scarves and booties for the nurses that were taking care of DD. I would also stay with my son until he fell asleep then head to my part-time job and home for about three to four hours of sleep and more of the same the next day. I also had another part-time job on weekend. I had three jobs, one fulltime and two part-time jobs.

I wanted a good life for us, and I didn't want him to be deprived of any good thing. Before DD's tenth birthday, in 1977, we bought a two-bedroom house, with one bathroom with a den, on Baring Cross Street, near Manchester, in Los Angeles. It wasn't in the nicest of neighborhood, but it was ours and that's what we could afford at the time. We were very happy there. That was our first stepping stone.

Early that year, I'd asked God as my birthday present to give me a house, a new car, and a sewing machine. A house because I was tired paying rent and moving all the time. A new car because ever since I had to return the new Firebird to the dealer, I've been buying old cars that broke down all the time. A sewing machine because I loved to sew. My mother taught us how to sew and mend by hand. I can make new outfits by hand and without a pattern, but, I wanted a sewing machine.

My prayers were answered. My bank account grew really fast because I worked hard and did not waste the money. The Lord gave me all the energy to work and enabled me to purchase the house, escrow closed in November 1977. It was not a mansion, that's a fact. We had to put sheets in the windows, and my brother helped to paint it. We bought our stove and refrigerator at a secondhand store. That was enough for us until we could do better. To be honest, if I had to do it over again, I would not have worked this hard, but that's the path that life had taken me on.

While working these jobs and taking care of DD, I always found time for dating, and I went to church whenever possible. Every time the pastor gave an altar call I would always go because I felt so guilty. I didn't have the strength to stop sinning. The load of sin was weighing so heavy on me. God was tugging on my heart, and I felt the pull. But every time I went to the altar, I purposed to stop, I repented, but I wasn't fully committed. I was still promiscuous. My sins were stronger, and they always pulled me back down. I have had a few proposals, but I didn't think I would be good at marriage. Later on, then I thought if I got married and had a family, I wouldn't need to sleep with more than one person, and I would stop sinning.

Through it all, God's face shined on us. His grace and mercy saving and restoring us. The Lord was always there for us and with us. I had a road map to follow, but at times I chose my own way. I stumbled and I fell, but he picked me up, cleaned me, and send me on my way. He gave me strength to carry on. I pray and walk close to God. I find and know the strength, love, the fullness of God, who is able to do more than we can ask or even think.

While life was going on, with its ups and downs, a lot of good things had happened for us. With the permission of my little man DD, I had joined the US Armed Forces. With life experience credit, I entered the US Army with the grade of PFC or private first class, and DD was so proud and happy about that. For enlisting in the army, DD and I both became US citizens once I completed basic training. All I had to do was to be interviewed and answer some pertinent questions. We became citizens of the United States of America in 1977.

We lived in our first house for three years, and with the help of God, a realtor friend and our savings, in 1980 we were able to purchase another piece of property, a fourplex in Inglewood, California. Our property was in a much better neighborhood. We moved into one of the two-bedroom apartments and still able to keep our little house as a rental.

On my job at the school district, I received a promotion to the payroll department. I worked a lot of overtime plus I still had two part-time jobs, my reservist duty with the army, and I also worked for greyhound as a reservation sales agent.

Things are not always as they seem. In 1981, through a mutual friend, I met my third husband. We'll call him Chaz. It would be a short courtship. Chaz, who said he was a Christian, didn't believe in premarital sex. That sounded great, hallelujah! Finally, someone following God's law. He seemed nice. He was a machinist by trade and an auto mechanic. He had a very good job. That of course was one of the prerequisites of any prospective suitor. To my surprise, Chaz proposed, and we were married within six short weeks. Why? What's the rush? I should have heard that warning bell ringing, seen the red lights flashing, but I was deaf and blinded by my need. I wanted a husband, a family, a father figure finally for my son. I thought Chaz would be the one to fulfill all three. In the end, Chaz would prove to be none of those.

His sister had warned me against him, but did I listen? No, because he'd warned me that they hated each other, she can't stand to see him happy, and I fell for it. I married him anyway, and it only lasted three months. Sister dearest had told me that he was after my money. He found out about the fourplex, and he wanted his name on that deed. The only thing that kept it from being a total disaster? His sister suggested that I have Mr. Gigolo sign a prenuptial agreement, which I did.

Later, he took me to court saying that he signed under duress. His excuse was that I was pregnant (no premarital sex, remember?) and that I told him if he didn't sign it, I would abort his baby. Here it is again! This word "abortion" coming back to haunt me; and this time, I am not even guilty. It's a proven fact that I have murdered my babies, but there was no baby to abort even if we had slept together which never happened because when I found out that DD had sickle cell anemia I had my tubes tied. He was such a liar.

He was a cheat, a liar, and a swindler. He had moved into my apartment, teamed up with my tenants, and he tried to collect rent from them. When they refused, he told them not to pay me either. It took forever to get rid of him. He wouldn't move out of the apartment, and the law says that he didn't have to move unless he was evicted. I started divorce proceedings, and he had to go. His own attorney had to fire him because he was so obnoxious. Even set the divorce aside, he sued me for community property. Even though he did not prevail in his attempt to take my property, he continued to harass me and did everything that he could to make my life a living hell. Even to the point of breaking all the windows in my car and cutting all four of my tires. If that wasn't enough, he broke into my house and stole jewelry and important documents.

This madness went on for about four years until the divorce was finally granted, and that's the last I saw of Chaz. In the end, my son and I we were alone again, but we were happier because no more fights. No more bickering and no more Chaz. Thank God for deliverance.

CHAPTER 16

The Relentless Stubborn Love of God;
The impossible dream! The mind is a field
of dreams, there is no expectation too far out of
reach, no dream too big. "Nothing is impossible
to those who believe!"

With man this is impossible,
but with God all things are possible.

—Matthew 19:26

Fever in the morning, fever all through the night. I had a male friend. We were so close that he was like my "girlfriend." My BFF. His name was Marshall. He had been in love with me for the past ten years, and he was too shy to make his feelings known to me. In a way, it was for the best because I would have chewed him up and spat him out. Besides that, I was not attracted to him; and at the time life was giving me sour grapes, which caused me to hate men.

Over the course of my life I had endured many painful things at the hands of men. I had come very hardened toward them. Therefore, each one had to pay for what others had done to me, except for Marshall. I could never hate him. We used to commiserate and shared many things about each other. He knew everything about me. I told him everything a female would tell a girlfriend—we were that close. I felt free with him. He would just sit there and listen, no judgement, no condemnation. We ate together, exercised together, we did all sort of things together like besties. He adored me, and I love the way he loved me, at a distance but yet so close that I think he could feel my heart beats.

I think if my heart stopped, his would beat for me. We were just that close. I loved him, but not in a romantic way, and he knew it and didn't want to spoil a good thing. He just adored me from afar, for ten long years. Like they say: "he had the patience of Job!". He knew about the men I dated, and there were many. I would just love them and leave them. (Remember I was in search of the impossible dream, the perfect man.) I kinda slept with them. (I hated men for what Sully, Joseph, and Chaz had done to me).

Most of the relationships that I was involved in didn't mean anything to me. At times I would make two, three dates, and I had no intention of keeping them. When they came to pick me up within five minutes of each other, I would be in the house, watching them through the peep hole but wouldn't answer the door. I would notice a puzzled look on their faces as they were leaving. While trying to get revenge, I think I might have hurt myself in the process. I could have had a better, stress-free life with someone nice if I'd only given them a chance.

I still went to therapy once in a while when I couldn't handle my juggling act. Whenever I felt myself getting close to someone, I had to let him go for fear I might fall in love or get hurt again. I think Raymond was one of them. He called me "my Marie." I was working as a personnel clerk at the school district, and he called to make an appointment to get fingerprinted and be processed before he started working at one of our high schools. We kinda started to fall for each other on the phone, and we began an affair that same day. He was married, and later on as our affair progressed, he told me that if it was legal in America, he would have made me his other wife. I never tried to hurt him.

Marshall started to visit me more after the swindler moved out. He came to offer support and maybe to just watch over me like a big brother, even though I was older by three years. We always hugged each other, and engaged in a friendly kiss. One week, he came over every day, and I always made him feel welcomed. I didn't know it, but I was lonely for companionship. On a particular evening, as he was living, he kissed me in the mouth. I stopped him and said, "No, that can't happen. You want to throw ten years of friendship away! You know how I am with men. You'd be gone out of my life in no time, let's just be friends."

He took my advice, and he left. I thought he was out of his demented mind. I got a pen and paper and wrote him a letter, planning to give it to him the next time we see each other. I said, "We've been friends for a long time, and I don't want to jeopardize that. I don't want to lose you (trying to put him down gently). I am not physically attracted to you. We don't have anything in common aside for our friendship, and you know I hate men. Furthermore, you seem very fragile. I can chew you up and spit you out and don't feel anything. Losing what we have is a chance I don't want to take. Don't ever try that again. Love, Marie."

The next day, he came back. We hugged and had our friendly kiss. I gave him the letter and told him to read it when he leaves. We decided to order a pizza since that's something we both love. While waiting for our food, he came near and rubbed my feet, something

I loved for him to do. He got a tub of water and proceeded to soak, massage, and dry my feet with a towel, which took a lot of my stress away. Just as he was finishing off, the doorbell rang. It was our dinner. After we finished eating, we talked for a while, and he left after giving me the usual friendly hug and kiss good night.

Not much time had passed before the doorbell rang, and it was Marshall. He had forgotten the letter, and he returned to get it. Just before turning to leave, he kissed me again; this time in the mouth, and I responded. I tried to stop him, but I didn't really want him to stop. We kissed with uncontrolled passion, like something had been building up, and we couldn't stop. I felt so desperate, so needy for him, like I'd die if he let go of me. I could feel the strength of his arms around me. I wanted him to make love with me, but I thought that I should be careful, take it slow. I know he won't hurt me on purpose, but I was still scared.

I said, "Can we please stop before we do something we might both regret?" Having said that, we stopped and he went home.

It was almost Valentine's Day when he called me to ask me if I would join him for dinner, and of course I accepted his invitation. Believe it or not, I still have the outfit I wore that night. It was a red jumpsuit with the "genie" kind of legs, and high heels. My hair was in long flowing curls. I also wore a beautiful heart-shaped pendant that fell just above my bosom. He came to pick me up. When he saw me, I could almost feel him undress me with his eyes. He swallowed and wet his lips. I wondered what was on his mind, and I think the feeling was mutual.

At the restaurant, we sat facing each other, and that was a mistake. I couldn't look at him in the face. When our eyes met, I melted every time. He had made reservation at a seafood restaurant on the marina because he knew that I love seafood. This must have been a sacrifice for him because his money was a bit tight. He didn't bring flowers, but what he brought was plentiful. Our 10-years friendship, his listening ears, and great companionship are worth a lot more to me. I didn't eat much those days. I watched every bite because I was vain about my body. Vanity was my middle name. I had carved the perfect body. I walked, ran, and exercised every day.

After dinner, we walked on the pier for a little while. The air was crisp. He put his jacket over my shoulders and kissed me. When we arrived at my apartment, he took the key and opened the front door, and just as we got inside the door, we started to peel off each other's clothes. But he stopped me. You might be wondering where was D.D. when all this was happening? My son spent a lot of time at "Mama", Mrs. Lamette's house. Most of his friends lived near her house, he went there every chance he could. He loved her very much. There were times when I was envious of their relationship.

Mrs. Lamette

Marshall said, "Let's take it slow. I'd like to undress you if you let me."

When he said that, my body trembled with desire. He picked me up and carried me to the bedroom, laid me on the bed, and began by taking off my shoes, then my stockings.

Then he said, "Do you know how long I've waited to do this?" I can imagine, but I'm dying with anticipation and trembling with desire. We went on to make passionate love. Our sinful behavior continued every time we were together. We could never have enough of each other.

Sin will take you farther than you want to go, keep you longer that you want to stay, and cost you more than you want to pay. I had become absorbed, oblivious to the sins in my life, the works of the flesh; because Satan had blinded my mind so that I could not see the light, I couldn't turn away from my darkness. I tried to push down what was troubling me, but it drew me to sexual immorality. Addicted is not something you want to be. Addiction is a place you find yourself in, after you have experienced some of the pleasures of sin (no one is exempt); you linger on too long and you are trapped in the clutches of the enemy, in the dark recesses of your mind.

Darkness is real, even to those who are trying to follow the light. Many of us, with the help of the enemy, have fallen prey to some "thing" that we like more than we should, then, it becomes a habit. Whether it is alcohol or drugs, sexual immorality or even food; anything in excess is a sin. Sin is pleasurable for a reason. Anything that gets first place in our life becomes our 'god', and that is idolatry. That is sin. Sin has to be exposed, brought to light in order to be free from it.

It is very hard for me to reopen the wounds of my past, the vile and despicable things that I have done. I am revealing the truth, exposing sin for what it really is; so that God may use my suffering, through my pain many might find a way out of theirs. Keeping sin hidden gives you an excuse to continue to live in darkness. No matter who we are or what we've done, God's heart remains the same toward us.

By sharing the details of my sins, I am in no way condoning my behavior. I have broken God's laws repeatedly and acted as if it didn't matter; as if I did nothing wrong. After being raped, in addition to sexual and other abuses that I endured in my life, I had become addicted to sexual sins. In so doing, I thought I was getting revenge, I was trying to hurt someone back, when in effect, I was hurting God and myself. I hated myself and detested my actions. Even though I often found myself giving way to my fleshly desires, I also experienced an overwhelming sense of guilt and shame when I thought of how God must have felt about my behavior. Sometimes, even as I am sharing my story, I have trouble understanding why God continued to extend his grace and mercy in my life.

Every time I thought that I had done my worst and that I needed to stop; I wanted to, and I tried to change, but I couldn't. When I thought that God would never forgive me this time, and I repented; He always picked me back up, He took me by the hand and we'd walk together again. Then I pulled away. The cycle repeated itself and I was back where I started from; until I met my husband.

One day, God decided to end my misery, he sent a godly man into my life. By God's grace and mercy, I was able to follow the light, and I have been free to live the life that God had created me for, a life of truth and godliness.

God, the one who is Omniscient, who created me and know me inside and out; from whom I cannot hide anything, chose to love me and give me his grace and mercy. Something I cannot firmly grasp! (Psa. 139:1-18, 23-24)

For example, God gave DD and me favor when he allowed us to purchase our third home, which was a three-bedroom house on Ninety-Fourth Place in Los Angeles. We moved out of the fourplex and got a new tenant. The house on Baring Cross and the fourplex were self-sufficient; they were paying for themselves and for the house we just bought. Marshall and I cleaned up the vacant apartment and got it ready for the new tenant.

Chaz had been following me, to my job, and everywhere. He also followed Marshall, and one day when Marshall was at work, he went to his mother's house and warned her about what would happen to her son if he didn't leave me alone. He went as far as cutting up the tires on my car. One evening at the new house, he threw a big rock through Marshall's windshield. He would leave nasty messages on my answering machine. None of his actions stopped us from continuing the affair. Marshall was all I wanted. I had eyes for no one else but him, so I thought.

Things got kind of boring after a while, and I had admirers everywhere, especially at work. I'd vowed never to date coworkers, specially the boss. There was one individual, Bob, he was the manager of a different department, not my boss. He'd been trying to get at me for a long time, and each time I gave him the same answer. When you don't work here anymore, give me a call.

One day, he said, "I'm at the main office now, I transferred to grand."

I thought he was teasing, but it checked out. Bob asked to take me out, and we went to dinner and a show. Right away I could tell this wouldn't last. He was too stingy, and I told him so, but he said, "I was being frugal." So just to prove me wrong, we had a few more dates, then we went on a long weekend to Pismo Beach, and we had lots of fun. I found out that he was estranged from his third wife. He loves them, marries them, and leave them; wife number 1 was white, number 2 Hispanic, number 3 Chinese born in Hawaii, and now he wants to make me number 4. I also found out that he participated in orgies, and he didn't care that I was cheating on my boyfriend. I don't believe in orgies, and I don't believe in cheating once you're married. I can't believe that I've cheated on Marshall, my best friend, my best lover.

Bob took me on a trip to the Mexican Riviera, and we had the best of times. Before we left on our trip, he gave me a detailed budget on how much I am allowed to spend on each meal and each drink. When I told him that proved his stinginess, he replied, "Without such planning, we wouldn't be on this vacation in the Riviera." I would have helped if necessary.

I followed the plan and managed to stay under budget. Food and drinking were not my cup of tea, shopping and jewelry were. I spent my own money when we went shopping. He bought me a bathing suit and a pinky ring with the face of the Mexican emperor on it. I purchased a couple of gifts for Marshall. I guess by now, he must have realized (I'm sure he knew not to fuss with me.) that if he wanted me, he had to take me just as I am or leave me. I was not trying to hurt him. He is the last person that I would hurt.

When I returned from the weekend spent in Pismo beach with Bob, I didn't think it was important enough to tell Marshal where I was. He asked me where I had been. I asked him if he wanted the truth or a lie. He said truth, and I told him. He was hurt and he left. My sister told me that he had called looking for me. The next day, he came back. We talked about it and made him aware of what was missing in our love affair. It was at that moment in our relationship that I realized that sex is not always the reason for infidelity in any relationship. Partners need to inquire of each other, speak freely and honestly with one another, probe deep in order to find out what is the glue that is holding them together, and do their best to provide it for the other.

Christians have a door stopper. God's word is what's keeping them from going astray, even they, sometimes will lose their way when tempted. What about those who follow Satan who will lead them to paths that end in destruction, who will save them? Only the Lord Jesus can, if they repent and accept him as Lord.

CHAPTER 17

Wedding Bells Are Ringing; O happy days! Two hearts beating as one. Let love lead the way!

*Above all, love each other deeply, because love
covers over a multitude of sins.*

—1 Peter 4:8

The Lord will save them. I had never believed in paying tithe. I always thought that the tithe and offering was going to the pastors, not the Lord's business, and I refused to pay ten percent of my income to make the pastor rich. We didn't pay tithe when I was growing up because at the time, we didn't have much, we only gave whatever we could. I was in the habit of giving an offering.

When my financial situation got better and better, all I could think about was my own bank account. I was trying to amass as much as I could. My goal was to acquire as many houses as I could, invest my money, and never be poor again. I didn't think of helping others or give financial support to church ministries. I was very self-ish. My mindset was I worked hard for my money, why should I give it away to people that refuse to work.

I should have been thinking of the Lord's work, he is the one who gives us the ability to earn our living. I'm always asking the Lord for things, what did I give him back? Nothing, I was too busy to pursue a close relationship with him, but he always answered my prayers, his presence was always felt. I had asked the Lord to allow me to retire at age forty, not really stop working, but not needing to work and live on my savings.

DD kept having those painful sickle cell crises. Almost like clockwork, every two to three months, he was hospitalized, and the cycle continued all the way to adulthood. He was a very strong boy. He kept up with his school work that I picked up from his teachers, and also with the help of a tutor I hired. His physical activities were limited, yet we managed. He wasn't spoiled, and he helped around the house as he was able. He liked doing his chores and got paid for it. He enjoyed spending his money on me, never on himself.

He said, "Mama, you give me everything I want. I don't need anything."

He started working at age fourteen, OJT or on-the-job training, at the sickle cell foundation, where he earned high school credits and still got paid. That's a win-win, situation, so sweet! He had a bank account, and when he turned eighteen, he got a credit card. The first two weeks of summer, he would go to camp with the sickle cell foundation, and when they got back he went to work. He always dressed up for work, shirt, tie, and he always cared about his appearance. He had a tie for every day of the week, his friends envied him for having a mom who crocheted his ties and made his scarves to keep him warm during the winter.

He never cashed his own paychecks. He brought them to me (only by choice). Once, around Christmastime, He told me that he was going to the bank to deposit his own check. I didn't ask why, and I said okay. I found out later that he used the money to buy me a television for my room. We had two TVs one for the living room for both of us to enjoy and the other in his room, for him to enjoy when he would get sick and had to stay in bed. He decided to change that by getting me my own television. That was so thoughtful of him.

He said, "I wanted you to have your own tv in your room too."

Things kept getting better and better for us financially. With God and the help of Mrs. Lamette, who was always available when we needed her, we were looking pretty good. DD obtained his driver's license at age sixteen. I gave him my Opel and got myself another car. When I'd asked God for a new car, what I forgot to tell you is that, there was a clause in my request, which is that I would pay cash for the car and that from then on I would live debt free, except for mortgage payment of course.

The thing about our God is that he loves to give us good gifts. He wants us to bring our needs to him; he hears and answers our prayers, but also—though he knows what we need and want—he wants us to be specific, knowing that he is the only one who can. Philippians 4:6 says, "Be anxious for nothing, but in everything, by prayer and supplication with thanksgiving, let your requests be made known to God." I have always been specific with God, and I thank him in advance for it because I know that he can and he will.

DD was driving himself to school now. He was attending an integrated high school in the valley, and it was a long ride. He used to be bussed to school (I think that was called desegregation bussing.), but it's better now that he is driving, and it gave him a chance to mingle with other kids in a different neighborhood. God did make it happen. The Opel was new and a cash purchase, and this vehicle that I was driving has been paid in full as well. Ever since my 30th birthday when I made my request to the Lord to be debt free, I have been debt free; except for my mortgages.

The familiar realtor nearby. There was a real estate office not far from our house. The broker was as crooked as they come, but very friendly (I guess that's how he traps his pigeons in.), so friendly that he called just about everyone brother or sister. When new people move into their farm (area), they'd send little gifts, trinkets to welcome them in the neighborhood. Sometimes they come to your door (They are called pop by now.) just like this one did in my case. His name seems to escape me, let's call him brother. Brother befriended me and invited me to his office for a business proposition.

He said, "My specialty is investment property where you can turn them around and make a good profit within six months. If you are interested, there is one available in Carson, it's a two-story, four-bedroom, two and a half bath. You'll only need twenty thousand to acquire it, and I can guarantee you at least five thousand or more return within six months."

That peaked my interest, because I love properties, and I love quick returns. I thought about it for a couple of days, and we purchased the property. When I started advertising for renters he told me, "No, on quick turnarounds, we can't rent them they have to be available to prospective buyers and ready to be sold."

He had me to sign the necessary papers in case we find a buyer right away. I would not sign the grant deed. He accused me of not trusting him, and the truth is I didn't, so we left it at that. Since we can't rent it, who is going to pay the mortgage? I inquired. He said, "I will, don't worry about it. I can get it back from the proceed when it's sold."

I thought that was cool. He was still baiting me, and I did not suspect anything. The next month came, and the property wasn't sold, and the mortgage was due again. Then he called and asked me if we probably could split the costs every other month. I told him no, I could not, that I prefer to rent it and let it pay for itself, adding it was not necessary for me to get a quick return if I have to keep putting more money into it; that would cut down the profit or even cancel out the whole thing.

He said, "Don't worry about it, I'll take care of it, and I'll advise you when we have a buyer."

I replied, "As long as the bottom line is five thousand or more. That was what you guarantee, right?" He said, "Right."

I had not heard from brother and the six months had passed, so I called to remind him that I was not worried, but it's been over six months. He said, "I am not worried either. I make those deals all the time, a buyer will come."

My phone rang a couple of days later, and the voice said, "Mrs. Pierre, this is Suzie from XYZ Escrow on Manchester Boulevard. Your realtor told me that you didn't want to be disturbed, and that he should receive your Escrow papers. I called him, but he didn't answer. Do you want to come and get them?"

I said, "Yes, I'll be right over."

I rushed to her office driving as fast as I could while whispering prayers under my breath. When I got there, I found out that my property is about to close Escrow, and even the grant deed had been signed. The signature on the grant deed was so well done that tears came down my cheeks because I know beyond the shadow of a doubt that I did not sign it. The Escrow officer told me that she felt the urge to call me. This was the Lord urging her, I have experience God's favor throughout my whole life. If she had not listen to her instinct, brother was going to sell the property right from under me and keep all the money. I asked her to postpone the closing for a few days so I could talk to this criminal.

I found out later that his broker license was revoked. He was working under someone else's license as a consultant. Criminal actions against him were pending an investigation. Finally, the buyers almost backed out of the deal. He was supposed to have gotten a fee from them as well. He told them that he was part owner and promised them that sellers would carry a second, which I knew nothing about.

In order to consummate the deal, Escrow had to redraw the papers where I would carry a small amount with a balloon payment in six months. I did get my investment money plus the five thousand dollars profit, and he got his commission as a consultant. One year later, I passed the real estate exam. While reading a realtor magazine, I recognized his name on the license revoked column. This article confirmed what I already had known.

Marshall and I are still an item, but I wanted more than he could offer. When Bob and I returned from our vacation in the Mexican Riviera, I decided not to see him anymore, and that we should break up. He insisted that I should give him another chance. I said that I would think about it.

There is a new sheriff in town. While seeing Marshall and Bob, Donald, who happened to be white and with whom I had a short-lived love affair two years prior, came back to the picture. Donald lived forty-five minutes away and worked nights, still smoked like a chimney, and drunk coffee all his waking moment. He was still pining for me. We hadn't seen each other for a long time. While I was visiting my sister in Ontario, California, we ran into each other.

He said, "Hey, lady, is that you?" (He used to call me lady.)

I said, "Hey, Donald, how are you doing? Long time no see."

He said, "Yes, why don't you marry me already and put me out of my misery?"

We went out a few times, and he took me shopping for an engagement ring. I got to pick whatever I wanted. He just loved to watch me try on beautiful dresses. He would buy me the whole rack of dresses if I asked him to. We were engaged, and his father thought that mixed marriages didn't last very long, and ours is not going to be any different. His mother said, "Marie, as long as you make my son happy, you children have my blessings."

DD had graduated from high school. He was working as a proctor at Loyola University in Inglewood where his big brother Dr. Ron, was a professor and also was a volunteer with the Big Brothers of America. Dr. Ron was so kind to my son and took time from his busy schedule to provide my child with what he needed most, a role model, a father figure, and time, precious time. Many thanks and blessings to you always.

We had just purchased our new townhouse in the city of Sunnymead, now known as Moreno Valley in Riverside County. Don lived alone in a three-bedroom house that his parents own. He is going to move with us after he and I get married. The wedding is set for the middle of September. In June, we had a date with the minister to discuss our union. Mom and dad were out of town, and we were house sitting.

That weekend, I discovered that my fiancé was a transvestite. (He called himself a cross dresser.) He is not gay, just has obsession with beautiful women's clothes; that should have given me a clue. I took it very well. When he asked me to teach him how to walk in high heels, I didn't embarrass him. I took him seriously and taught him how to walk in high heels; he already had the shoes. He loved soft clothes, I could live with that, but I panicked. I told him that we should see a therapist together. His answer was, "I am not gay. I don't need a shrink."

He might not, but I did. I had enough of my own drama, to accomplish a task of that magnitude; we needed to be on one accord, we needed professional help. I never judged him. I loved him enough to accept him. He had some knowledge of my issues, and he never judged me. With the help of a good therapist, I think we could have made it. In some very unique way, he was good for me, and I think we were good for each other.

I had a nervous breakdown one evening after we had dinner at his parents' house. They took us to a movie (*Mask*). That movie drove me bunkers. That was the beginning of a psychological breakthrough. Had it not been for Don, I don't know what would have become of me. We didn't want his parents to know what was going on. He drove me around and around for hours while I chewed on ice cubes and poured ice water on my face. I drank ice water and peed in a cup all night. I was hyperventilating, burning hot, and screaming.

What I really wanted to do was go home to my own house. Since Don had to go to work, I decided to call a friend in Los Angeles, whom I asked to come get me. When my friend arrived, I shared my experience with him. He knew my story and understood my situation. When I finally got back home, I felt a little bit better, but the symptoms of my breakdown continued to torment me. Early Monday morning, Don returned to transport me to see my therapist. Even though I received a measure of health from her, I would continue to struggle with bouts of mental illness for many years. I thank God for Don because he was there for me when I really needed someone to be there. Needless to say that Don and I never got married. We decided to remain friends which didn't last very long because he wanted a relationship that I wasn't comfortable with; our friendship slowly died out. I really do hope that in some way I contributed to his life because he definitely contributed to mine.

CHAPTER 18

Never Lend Money to Friends;
Making a gift, that is generosity; making a loan,
that is stupidity, that brings the perfect
friendship to a disastrous end

The wicked borrows and does not pay back,
but the righteous give generously.

—Ps. 37:21

I've been burned, I need a break. One of the reasons for the move was that I didn't like Los Angeles anymore. My old friend Harvey told me about this newer neighborhood in Riverside that he thought I would love. Another good reason was that I thought I was addicted to Marshall and I needed to put distance between us. The bottom line is I needed a fresh start.

About a year before I purchased my first little house on Baring Cross, I had joined a dating club called Dating Game, where I met several nice gentlemen, but one of them stood out, and his name was Harvey. He was much, much older than I was. He called me Miss C. Harvey was a true gentleman, always treated me with respect, like a princess.

When we met, I lived in a beautiful two-bedroom apartment, the nicest one after my son came out of foster care. It was plush with soft white carpet. I remember him coming to my apartment hours before I came home from work to spend time with my son so he wouldn't be jealous when we go out. DD used to appreciate that, and so did I. He said, "I had my time now, you can go have yours." (He was such a special soul.) There were times when he and DD went out for food or a game, and other times when his workers would come with him to shampoo my carpet and clean my apartment.

The day of our first date was so memorable. No one has ever done this for me before. It was a Saturday, I remember it well. DD and I went shopping for groceries. When we got back, we saw a note taped to the front door from the manager, asking me to come to her office for a delivery. There was a big beautiful bouquet of flowers, two dozen yellow roses (my favorite, he must have read it from my profile). I love a man that pays attention to details, especially something as important as this.

The card attached said, "This is a prelude to what's to come. Signed, Harvey. Ps. They are your favorite."

Harvey owned his own janitorial business with many employees working for him. His second business was limousine airport transportation, where his employees picked up passengers and take them to their destination: home, hotel, business, etc. Everywhere he took me was first class. We flew to San Francisco and stayed in five-star hotels, we visited friends, and went to clubs where we danced the night away. We've gone to Las Vegas and stayed at the best hotels, dined at the 700-club in the revolving dining room. The service was top-notch and the food exquisite. We've gone hiking, spent time at his apartment where he was the chef, a great chef.

The attraction was different. Harvey was an intriguing man. He was debonair, patient, and mature. He was knowledgeable when it came to wining and dining and treating a lady with respect. He was very good at what he did (and having the means didn't hurt either). He was like a fine wine that gets better with age. (That's why I liked older men.) He made me feel spoiled and pampered, never bored with him. (He knew what he wanted and how to keep it.)

There is no such thing as a perfect relationship, and every coin has two sides. Shortly after moving into my first house, Harvey said he wanted to talk to me and ask me for a favor. He came to my house. This time we did not go out. He brought take out Chinese food. He appeared ill at ease at the dinner table, somewhat distracted. I asked what the matter was.

He replied, "We are in trouble with the IRS, and my partner is throwing me under the bus."

Harvey had been married with two beautiful children, a girl and a boy; his wife left him for a better pasture. With paying alimony and child support, I gather she was getting the bulk of his money, but I don't know all the details. He was a generous man. He seemed like he would rather pay than fight, that's only my observation. He said, "I am not sure if you are abled or not, but I need a loan of xxxxx dollars." (It was over five thousand dollars.)

I said, "Of course I can, I will go to the bank tomorrow."

That was my reserve funds, my rainy day money, but because he was such a nice guy and he appeared to be honest and trustworthy, I gave him the money. That was the last time I saw Harvey. He even stopped calling. I knew his address, I should rather say that I some-what remembered the location, the street's name, but not the build-ing numbers. I don't recall having "GPS" at that time either, but I wasn't sure I could remember how to get there. That area was foreign to me. He had always picked me up and brought me back to my home. I had driven there only once. I didn't panic but I was worried for him. Did they put him in jail? Is he dead? I tried to call, but there was no answer at first and then his phone was disconnected.

The chickens came home to roost. Three to four years had gone by. I had moved twice. My son and I were spending the Thanksgiving holiday at my sister's house. After a morning walk my sister and I decided to go in the area where I remember Harvey lived, trying to retrace my steps. This was in Riverside, and I lived in Los Angeles. It was not easy, but by the grace of God I found it. He no longer lived there. His manager told me that he had to move over three, four years ago. She recognized me, told me to go to the post office, and send a note to this old address, and if it's not too late they will forward it to the new. She said, "I have it but it's illegal to give it to you. Good luck."

I did just that, and it was a very productive day. I went to the post office and mailed him a letter with my home address and my phone number. I asked him to at least let me know that he was alive. The money was not the main issue because that Lord had already returned to me what the locusts had eaten. One or two weeks later, my telephone rang in the middle of the night. When I picked it up, the caller hung up, and I thought it was my swindler ex-husband. He never stopped harassing me. Sometimes he would call and say, "I know you're there. I dare you to answer, or I'm not done with you yet, or I'm going to make you spend all your money on attorney fees." Each time he brought a lawsuit against my properties, he always lost, then he waits six months and start all over again. If I didn't get a lawyer and respond to his lawsuit, I would lose by default. But that night, it wasn't him.

The next night, the same thing happened, and it was Harvey who called. He said in an apologetic voice, "This is Harvey, was hoping you wouldn't hang up on me, hope I didn't wake you up. It's after midnight, just getting off from work. Can I call you tomorrow during the day?" I said sure, and we both hang up. The next day, he called back and asked if he could come over because what he has to say was very important, and he must say it in person. I said sure. We arranged it for two days later, that was his day off. He came over, explained his past troubles, and the reason for not paying my money. There were a lot of details to his story, and I believed him and forgave him.

When people do you wrong no matter what the reason is, leave it to God. He also wanted to make restitution by doing some work for me. Always knew he was a good person. So I bought the paint, and he painted my house. I set up a payment plan that required him to pay a little each month, until his debt was paid in full.

Sunnymead, June 1985. This brings me to how I found out about Sunnymead. Harvey told me, and I am glad he did. We moved to Sunnymead on June 25, 1985. Marshall and I were still friends, and our lust affair was still going on. But we didn't visit often because of the distance. I also stayed in touch with my ex-fiancé, Don. He seldom came to my house anymore.

I had resigned from my job at the school district because I couldn't deal with the traffic. For more than six months, I lived on my savings only, and was contemplating going back to school.

I applied, interviewed, and secured a job at the Riverside Sheriff Department as a dispatcher. It wasn't an easy job. If you suffer from depression like I did, this is not the job for you. Some of the calls are sad, some dangerous for the officers if you don't handle them properly. The life of the officers and that of the caller is in your hands, depending of the nature of the call. If you give them the wrong address, even the wrong apartment number, there could be blood to pay. I panicked at various times. When there was danger, my heart would beat very fast as if I was going to have a heart attack.

What I didn't tell you about the balance of my money from Harvey is that when I moved to Sunnymead, I was able to go to his job to pick up cash, whatever amount he could give, and only when he was able to give. When I realized that he really couldn't afford to give anymore, God allowed me to give him favor. I told him that he was paid in full. The situation with Harvey reminded me of another friend who borrowed money from me and never even attempted to pay back.

In 1971, I met a couple, Arthur and Joan, who became my best friends. To me, they weren't just best friends, they were like the family I never had. Joan was my very first best friend forever in America. She was smart, beautiful, and a woman of faith, a Seventh Day Adventist. Joan and Arthur were both educated, married, with two small children their younger son was a baby. I think at that time one of them was still finishing their degree. I'm pretty sure it was Arthur.

They were a very happy family as it seemed. They prayed, observed the Sabbath, and they loved others as God asked all of us to do. They lived in a beautiful well maintained, nicely decorated two-story home, with the cars and all the trimmings. When I saw how they lived, this was real to me; the first real, complete family that I had encountered in a long time. I knew in my heart right then and there, that someday that's exactly how I wanted my life to be. I started dreaming the impossible dream, the real, complete and perfect family. I admired them, and even told Joan that when I grew up I wanted to be just like her. I meant that literally even though she was only perhaps three years older than I was. She was a fabulous mom, and a beautiful homemaker, and she also worked outside the home, she was an excellent role model for me. She was the yardstick that I would use to measure what a well-rounded woman/person should be.

I thought they had the perfect marriage, the kind that could stand the tests of time, as far as I could see. I could barely speak or understand English when I met them, but they found a way to communicate with me. When I had a serious medical problem of my own doing, they helped me. They were the kind of people who would do anything for a friend. I felt then and now still do that I owed them a lot, I felt indebted to them. Always felt humbled by their kindness toward me, wished that someday some way I could repay them for all they did for me.

Our friendship lasted a long time. As they say, all good things have a way of coming to an end. Joan always complimented me on my ability to manage and keep money. They made a lot of money and had a very expensive lifestyle. Even though they both made good money with being a college professor and her husband being a therapist, they had trouble holding on to money.

Sadly, over time, there were signs of trouble in paradise. It came in the form of infidelity on the part of Arthur, which opened the door to problems in other areas of their relationship. Then it wasn't long before the toothpick castle came tumbling down. It really hurt me to see my friend's life take such a terrible turn. Things went from bad to worse, and they ended up getting a divorce and going their separate ways after the divorce.

Joan was devastated. Her perfect life became a nightmare. She was financially in need and came to me for help. Oh, how long I waited for a chance to be of help to my friend, my best friend. In the winter of 1985, shortly before we moved to Sunnymead, Joan came to my house one day and asked me to lend her enough money to help her hold on to her health food store in Diamond Bar. So I asked how much. I was in a good place financially and was not very concerned about her answer. She said thirty thousand would be enough because she needed to stack her empty shelves, pay for past due rent, and miscellaneous bills.

I was able to help her out with the proceeds from the sale of my first house. I felt so good, so elated; it was like nothing I had ever experience relating to money. I know now how it actually feels to be a friend in deed. Joan was very happy. Two weeks later, she came back for more and she asked me for another ten thousand. I found out later that she had a nose job that same week. That of course caused me to be very disappointed in her; in fact, I felt used. She had misrepresented herself and taken advantage of my kindness. If the store was in jeopardy, which it was, why would she use the money so frivolously? I concluded that she was a spend junky.

Needless to say, Joan had lost her business. The money was never returned to me. To the best of my ability, I tried to find her, to no avail. I hope she had learned to be a good steward of the talent that God entrusted her with. Life goes on, and my father in heaven is still blessing me. Joan is still nowhere to be found, as far as I know, she never tried to reconnect with me. God is still on the throne, when the right time comes, He will bring us back together, and, Joan has integrity; the person I knew her to be will pay me back. I trust and believe that she will make things right again. In the meantime, I want my friend back. I am still doing my best to manage my talent wisely.

CHAPTER 19

Frog or Prince;
Many a princess has kissed frogs to find their
prince. Searching in the wrong places

*In their hearts humans plan their course, but
the Lord establishes their steps.*

—Proverbs 16:9

What a wonderful God we serve! My job as a dispatcher was short-lived; it lasted about a year and I had to resign. God has and is still enlarging my territory. He enabled me to purchase a fourplex in Riverside, and the returns were very good, and since real estate seemed to be working for me, I decided to become a realtor.

Make a house a home. I decided to attend a weekend seminar that gave a lot of information to help me study for my real estate license. At the end of the seminar, they gave me a lot of material to study on my own time. The materials covered rules and regulations, ethics, math, real estate principles. I also learned about property management, eminent domain, probate, footage, real estate law, and on and on. There is a quiz after each chapter.

Many of the words they used, I had never heard before, and I had to know it know it all. So I went home and started memorizing just like back at school in Haiti, where our lessons had to be memorized. Every night I went to bed with a headache and I woke up with one as well. I would take two bufferin and get back to it and that went on and on.

My beautiful niece, Marie Immacula, whom I admire and I'm so proud of and was going to college at the time, always came to my house after school. My sister owned a townhouse two doors down from mine, and Marie spends her afternoons with me until her mom gets home. She offered to quiz me after each chapter that I studied, and this went really well. I would study and leave the quizzes for later, and we continued this on Saturdays and Sundays after church. One Friday afternoon, Marie Immacula came to my house to quiz me. She took one look at me and saw how tired I was, decided that I needed a time-out.

She said to me, "You are done for the day, Auntie. You need a break." She ordered me to leave the house. She said, "March upstairs, make yourself beautiful, and go out. Have some fun, relax, and we can start again tomorrow." Wise girl!

I said, "Yes, mother," and I did just that. I got myself beautiful and I went out to enjoy some music.

Prince or frog. Our townhouse was located near the March air force base. I had gone on base before with my friend Carol to visit one of her friends. There was a non-commissioned officer (NCO) club on the base, for members only. You must have a military ID or be signed in by a member in order to enter. Before going in to the club, you must be signed in at the gate as well. I wanted to go there, but I didn't have the necessary credentials, nor did I know anyone who could sign me in, but I went anyway in the hope that someone might be willing to let me in.

As luck would have it, I was able to get inside the gate, and when I went to the club, one of their friendly members signed me in. It was not luck. I think for whatever reason, somebody was setting me up. I went straight to the bar and ordered a glass of grapefruit juice. I'm not a drinker. I might occasionally have a glass of champagne or wine, and also, I was driving. I took a seat near the band, which was playing oldies but goodies and popular songs of the time. I got lost in the music while reflecting on my life. I watched the people on the dance floor and enjoyed the music as I sipped on my grapefruit juice. My plan was not to stay out late, since I had to get back to my studying.

A couple of guys had asked me to dance, but I didn't honor their request. I just came to relax for a while, maybe next time. A few minutes had passed, when out of the corner of my eye, I saw someone else headed in my direction and coming near my table. I turned around, and there standing was a gentleman with a pipe in his mouth.

He said, "My name is Charles. Are you here by yourself? Can I buy you a drink?"

I gave him a not-so-friendly look and said, "No, thank you, I have a drink already."

Then he said, "What are you drinking?"

I said, "Grapefruit juice."

He said, "Can I sit with you?"

I said, "No, I'm not going to be here long."

I think he could tell that I wasn't interested, but he was persistent. I have to give him credit for that. Then he said, "You are a beautiful lady, are you married?"

What is this, I was thinking, is this an inquisition? I said, "My name is Marie, and no, I am not married. Why so many questions?" I wanted to say, "Do you see a ring on my finger?"

He said, "I've never seen you here before, and you're so beautiful, I'd like to get to know you. Do you live in the area? Let me refresh your drink for you."

He got up and went to the bar and brought back a glass of grapefruit juice. He put the juice on my table and started talking again. I didn't really want to be bothered, but I also didn't want to be rude. I wasn't attracted to him at all, and the pipe turned me off. I asked him, "Do you only smoke a pipe?" He said, "Oh no, I don't smoke, the pipe is just for appearance." I thought maybe he was lying. He started to tell me why he was at the club. He came to meet a woman who was a no-show, and he's not going to stay long either. Then he said, "I've been stationed here since 1980. I'm from Florida, my hometown is West Palm Beach. I would like to see you again. May I have your phone number?"

I said, "No, I don't give my number to strangers. I am ready to leave now. Thank you for the drink." I got up and started walking toward the door.

He followed me to my car and kept talking. He told me about his ex-wife and two children, that his divorce is about to be finalized, and that morning he had to go to the post office to mail some money to support his children.

I was thinking, "Shut up, man. I don't need to know all that." Then I said, "Okay, thanks for walking me to my car, good night."

For the second time, "Can I have your phone number?" he said.

I replied, "Oh no, again I don't give out my number to strangers, but you can give me yours, maybe I will give you a call. If I think about it, I'll call you."

He wrote down his phone number on the green card from the registered mail from the post office. And I remember thinking that was stupid, the card contained personal information, why would he want me to know all that? He must not be the sharpest knife in the drawer.

Like a mother, my niece was waiting up for me when I got home. And she said tell all. I said, "There's nothing to tell. I had a glass of grapefruit juice, listened to the music, and came home, that's all."

"There must have been some incident or something!"

Then I gave her the green card that Charles had written his information on. She started reading it. "Amanda, who's that? Auntie, you gave me the wrong card." Then I told her what had happened. She got all exited. "Are you going to call him?"

I said, "No, I'm not interested."

She said, "You should, it'll give you somebody to talk to, go to dinner with or something."

I said, "Are you going to let me go to sleep or not?"

She said, "Okay, but first thing in the morning we are going to talk about it."

I said, "Yes, Mother, pushy, pushy."

And we both soon fell sound to sleep. The next day, I studied and she talked. She quizzed me, and we took a break and we talked about it and I told her that maybe I would call him.

In searching for love. The year was 1986, the month was May, May 30 to be exact. It was a Friday; it was the day that Ashley Slaney and Nikolay Bodurov were born, the year when the Oprah Winfrey show started, and the song "Lady in Red" (by Chris de Burgh) was released. What more can I tell you about that year? That was the beginning of the end of my search for true love, commitment, contentment, and friendship. I met Charles Edward Dukes, on May 30, 1986, at March air force base in Moreno Valley, California. Charles later became my friend, my lover, my husband. At first, I was not attracted to him at all. He wasn't what I was looking for. Looking back, I think that he was chosen for me; if it were up to me, I would not have made that call. I accepted his phone number because he was so persistent. I just wanted him to leave me alone. I had no intention of calling him

Lady in red. My niece pestered me and made me call him. When I called the number he gave me, someone else answered. I said, "Hello, is this Charles?"

The voice at the other end said, "No, who is this, you want Charles? What's his room number?"

I said, "Room number? I thought this was his number! You are calling the barracks, lady, the phone is in the hallway for all of us to use." I thought, he doesn't even have a phone! Then he yelled out, "Charles, telephone for you."

Charles came to the phone. He said, "Hello!"

I said, "This is Marie, we'd met on base a week ago."

He said, "The beautiful lady who drinks grapefruit juice, I recognized your voice."

And, "I said oh, you remembered!"

"That's not all I remember," he said, "I remember your beautiful, piercing, amber eyes that hypnotized me."

Wow! He is observant, I thought. "Yeah, this is she."

He said, "I'd like to take you out. Is this Saturday okay?" I said sure. "Can I pick you up at seven? What is your address?"

I said, "You can pick me up at seven but call me before you leave, and I'll give you the address at that time."

He said, "That will do," and I could hear the excitement in his voice.

The song "Lady in Red" was popular at that time. My niece decided that I should wear my red terrycloth dress with a black belt to accentuate my tiny waist. I had a drop-dead gorgeous body. My measurements were 34-23-34, and I weighed 108 pounds, perfect figure, I think. I used to love my body, maybe a little too much; *obsessed* would be a good word. I walked and ran, I did sit ups every day, and ate like a bird.

My date arrived a little early, and he said, "I hope you don't mind, I rather be early than late." (Punctuality, good quality number 1.) His car was a Plymouth Volare; it was an older model but clean. He opened the passenger door and secured me in and walked to the other side. He wore a nicely pressed striped shirt, dark pants, brown shoe on one foot and sandal on the other. When I inquired about the sandal, he told me about a fungus in his right big toe. If it were me, I would have waited until the infection was cleared before going out on a date.

Charles was overweight for my taste. I could see that he had a big belly, and that was not attractive in my book, and I thought, I know how to fix that. I'll get him in shape in no time. We went to the Green Onion restaurant. The food was okay. I didn't eat meat, so I had sopa y ensalada (soup and salad). I don't remember what he ordered, but he ate it all. I am not judging, but it's good manners to leave something on you plate.

The evening went very well. We got acquainted and talked about our respective families, his job, and my interests. He brought me back home to find my anxious niece waiting for me as if I were a school girl on a first date.

"Details, give me details," she said. "Did he try to kiss you?"

I said, "No, he was a perfect gentleman."

Charles called me the next day to thank me for going out with him and he asked if we could go out again. I said, "We'll see."

There was one, and then there was two. Charles was calling almost every day now, and I didn't mind. For our second date, he invited me to attend church with him, and I gladly accepted. He came to pick me up, and we went to a Baptist Church that met on the military base. It was called Chapel Two located at Arnold Heights, across from the Veterans Cemetery. I enjoyed the service very much, and the music was almost angelic, the choir sang in perfect harmony. When the offering plate was passed around, I noticed that Charles opened his wallet and put everything that was in the wallet in the plate. That was impressive to me (good quality number 2), giving to God from your heart.

Charles brought me home after church. He seemed somewhat in a hurry, and he kissed me as soon as we entered the house. I guess he didn't want to lose his nerves. His kisses were delicate, sweet, not rushed but ardently. The earth didn't move underneath my feet, but I enjoyed having his arms around me. I thought going to church together was a perfect way to start a lasting relationship.

Then he asked me if he could use my bathroom to change his clothes. He went to his car and came back, brought back his clothes with him, and changed into a dark blue uniform with the logo "Paloma Security." He told me that his ex-wife got three-fourth of his income, so it required him to work two part-time jobs in addition to his fulltime military job in order to make ends meet. He didn't appear upset about it. He seems to be a man that accepts the hand that life had dealt to him. He seems to be good at making lemonade with the lemons of his life.

He said, "I have to go my shift starts at 1:00 p.m.," and he left.

I think that God was teaching me things through him. Charles is trustworthy, and he is trusting. He doesn't fight even if he is right. He is rooted in the word, and his faith is anchored. He is kind, generous, he is very humble, and most of all he loves God. 1 Peter 2:23 says, "He entrusted himself to him who judges justly." He entrusted all his care upon the Lord. He is quiet, very passive, and for some reason, I can't stand it. Charles is a little too cool, calm, and collected for me. Now, on the other hand, I am the complete opposite. I felt sorry for him at first. I thought he was weak, until I realized that when you give your cares to the Lord, that is inner strength, you don't need outer strength.

I started liking him and began to look for ways to encourage him. We went to church together every Sunday and talk on the phone almost every day. I started a tradition with him by giving each other an anniversary card, weekly, then monthly, until the year has passed. Happy first week, second, and on to one year anniversary. It seemed silly, but it was new and exciting, huh! On one occasion, he came to visit. He was wearing sandals. When I saw his feet, I decided to do something for him. I drew warm water in a foot tub with Epsom salt, and I gave him a foot bath and massage, cut his toenails; they were ugly, long and curly, like they'd never been trimmed before. I dried, lotioned them. He was wearing sandals, and his feet looked gross. I don't know why, but I wanted to put him first and show him that I cared. He was so emotional; I thought he was going to cry.

He said, "No one has ever done anything like that for me before."

What he didn't know was that I was learning how to be unselfish, and I believe that God had sent him to teach me how. I don't think he knew that he was God's instrument in my life. I think I must had feelings for Charles because I would have never touched his feet. I don't like looking at feet; I think feet are ugly, but for some reason I didn't mind touching his.

God had been talking to me through Charles. One night, we attended a revival service at the church, and Pastor John Thomas preached a beautiful sermon. I think it was entitled, "You Must Be Born Again." He kept repeating those words: "You must be, you got to be, can't you see, born again," over and over again. Every time he repeated those words, I felt something pulling me toward the altar. Several times I tried to get up, but I kept resisting. Many people were at the altar, praying the sinners' prayer. Then the pastor made another call for people to learn how to pray in tongues and to receive the Holy Spirit. I responded to that call, and made my way to the altar, although I was still somewhat reluctant. I felt that I needed to go forward. After making my way to the altar, a couple came to help me. The woman asked me if I came for salvation or to receive the Holy Spirit.

I said, "I think I'm saved already. I am not sure why I came. I just felt that I needed to come to the altar." Then they were both laying hands on me and praying in tongues. The music playing was the song "I Surrender All," and I started feeling dizzy, and before I could speak, I was on the floor crying, screaming, and trembling as if the earth underneath me was shaken. I wasn't sure what had happened, but I think I had fainted for a moment. When I came to, the couple told me that I had been slain in the spirit. I was a little bit scared. This was the first time I had experience that sort of thing. Then they took me to another room, where I prayed the sinner's prayer and I rededicated my life to God. I placed my faith in Christ for the forgiveness of my sins.

I continued to attend church services and became a member of Chapel Two. Every Wednesday night, I went to Bible Study and I became an usher. Through the Lord's help, I learned how to be a good steward of my talents. I pay my tithe, but I also learned about the talent that the Lord had given me and how to use them to glorify him. My old life has changed dramatically when I started to walk closely with the Lord. My Christian journey had begun a long time ago when I was very young. My steps were not sturdy; I stumbled and fell many times, had gotten up and fell again and again, but God never gave up on me. I was created for greatness and destined for abundance.

CHAPTER 20

Location! Location! Location!; You can't improve on perfection. The fact is, there is no such thing as perfection

The boundary lines have fallen for me in pleasant places; surely, I have a delightful inheritance.

—Psalm 16:6

I studied and took the real estate exam, which by the way was very hard, but I passed at the first try. I have heard that people have given it many tries and failed. One lady told me she didn't get her license until the eighth time. It is now 1986, and from the looks of things, you can tell that I had taken a break from men, and it feels great, I'm not missing it. It feels like I am being drawn elsewhere. I'm settling down, I am maturing. I go to church more and working in the real estate field now.

Being a realtor is not as easy as it seemed. Before I'd even found out that I passed the exam, I started receiving letters from brokers who wanted to hire me. I guessed my license was in the mail. My first employer was a broker called Clint Buyers. (He's with the Lord now, may he rest in peace.) He was a very nice person. I didn't learn a whole lot from him because we were only selling repos (REO now). Clint would get the HUD list for us weekly, and we'd view as many properties as possible, each one of us would pick one, put an ad in the *Pennysavers* with our personal phone number, and wait for the phone to ring. We didn't have a home base office; our home was our office, and our phone was our equipment.

To my surprise, my very first ad was my first sell. The prospective client called. They were interested to see the property, so I picked them up, and we proceeded to the property. After viewing the property, they were very excited and wanted to write an offer. After getting excited with them, I suddenly realized that I'd never written an offer and really didn't know how to write an offer; in fact, my broker, Clint Buyers, actually helped me to write the offer for submission.

The way it worked in those days was that after submitting your offer, often you would find out that multiple offers had been submitted on the same property. This normally generated a bidding war, and the highest bidder would end up getting the house. The good news is that after going through that nerve-racking process, my client outbidded everyone and I had sold my first house. We later closed Escrow. I received my first paycheck, and since I was on a fifty-fifty split with the broker, I received half of the commission.

Needless to say, I was very, very happy with my share. I hadn't seen a paycheck for a long time, and because we had been living on my savings for over a year, this commission would help replenish some of it. Praise be to God. Even though things were beginning to move forward in my real estate career, I still had to give attention to other areas of my life.

Catching up. One of the realities I had to deal with concerned my son, DD, who was attending junior college and working at a workman's compensation firm in Colton. He'd purchase a new car but still had the Opel. I told him to get rid of it, but he wouldn't listen. He's becoming a little stubborn and independent, at the ripe old age nineteen. The sickle cell crisis had increased, he had new friends, staying out later than I think he should. It wasn't long before we had a big fight that he moved out and got his own place closer to his job.

Once on his own, he crashed his new car. Ducarmel has been a speedy driver ever since he was learning to drive. When he lived with me, I helped to monitor his goings-on due to his being so sick and so often. As they say, a mother has to do what a mother has to do.

I'd never met DD's boss, whose name was Judith, but we were phone pals for DD's benefit. She'd call me when he was too sick to work, and she also let me know that DD was on the verge of losing his job. Things had gotten so bad between us that he didn't want me at his house. He has had other jobs before this one, but he was always too sick to even pass probation. Judith was very patient and understanding about his illness.

A while back, when I lived in Los Angeles, someone had told me that DD should qualify for disability and that we should apply. When we did apply, the people at the social security office told me that I was making too much for him to qualify. But the disease has progressed since then, and my income should not be a factor now that he is no longer a minor, and he needed help.

I had given DD the option to move back home, but he refused, so I sent money every so often to help him out. But he's not like his mama, he goes through money like people change their underwear. He would give the money away because he can't stand to see people in need. DD would give away his last dollar if he thought someone needed it more than him. When he moved out, he was charging too much on my credit card, one and two hundred dollars dinner tabs, jewelry purchases, and more. I finally had to take back the credit card from him.

One day, after missing work for two days, he went to his boss with an attitude and told his boss he wanted to resign. He also said to her, "You do the paperwork and I'll sign it." She also advised him to give two weeks' notice in case he wanted to return some day. The fact was DD was well liked and a good worker. He had received a large raise in two months before his probation period ended, and I remember the only way he was able to pass probation is because they liked his work. He had integrity. He was precise and very thorough. He'd never leave until his work was done. I still have commendation letters from his previous employers and at on-the-job training at the sickle cell foundation for a job well done.

In reply to the two weeks' notice the boss had suggested, DD said, "Take this job and shove it. I don't want to come back." He left and never went back. Judith called me right away and told me what happened. When I tried to apologize, she said, "Don't worry, I'd still take him back."

Right away, I rushed to his apartment, and at first when he saw that it was me, he wouldn't open the door. I didn't give up. I kept knocking, and he opened finally. I went in. The place was filthy. I started cleaning up for him. He yelled at me and said, "You see that's why I didn't want you here, you're always cleaning, not a hair out of place, everything has to be perfect, I can't do this anymore."

I sat next to him, and I said, "I didn't know you felt that way. Why didn't you tell me? I love you. Why don't you come back home? It can be just the two of us again."

"I'll let you know," he said. In a few days he came back home, and things went back to normal.

A few weeks had passed, and he told me that he was moving back to Los Angeles, and that he was going to stay with his girl-friend. I had never met her, didn't even know she existed. I later found out that the girlfriend lived with her mother. I would never allow a boy living with my daughter under my roof without the benefit of marriage.

The next day, the mother and daughter came to pick him up. I made lunch for all of us. We chatted while we ate, and off they went. I thought he would have called me, but no, and I did not have their phone number. I figured that he or they will call when he needed something they couldn't provide.

They had it all planned. I found out later that they were collecting social security money on his behalf as his payee. That relationship and others just like it didn't work. He was moving a lot, and each time he needed my help, and I gave it gladly. I allowed him to live his life as he pleased. I remember later on, DD asked me once more if he could come home and go back to school. I was too happy to accommodate him because that means he would be home where he belong. When he is away, I often worry about him, his health, about his well-being. When he needed transportation, I got him a car, a demo with a few thousand miles on it, practically new.

One day at school, he picked up a street girl who was in need of a new life, and my son felt that I should provide it for her. I'm not sure if DD knew that she was a prostitute with a pimp; he was so naive and trusting. I got up one morning to find a stranger in my house, and my son introduced her saying, "I didn't want to wake you up last night, but she needed a place to stay I brought her home. I am pretty sure we can help her, can't we?" DD was not interested in the girl, he was just being a good Samaritan.

I invited the girl into another room and questioned her. She told me about her life and how afraid she was of her pimp. I suggested that she should return to her family, and I offered to pay for a bus ticket to where they were. She was only eighteen years old. My son was not satisfied about the way I handled the situation. I gave the young woman fifty dollars, and she left.

When he came back in the evening, he announced that he was moving with friends but not so sure about school anymore. I told him that the car was for school, and if he moved out and stopped going to school, he could not take the car with him. If he had the car with him, he would end up being the taxi driver for everyone. I still had to pay the car note and the insurance premium. He said fine, and I said, "I can take you where you want to go." He said, "No, thanks, it's not far. I can walk." He was gone. Two months later, I found out that he was living in somebody's garage, then he moved to Orange County with his cousin. He didn't get in touch with me himself, but I kept tab on what was going on in his life. I was not happy at all about it. I think he had a wandering spirit. He was looking for something he couldn't find; perhaps he should find Jesus because he is the only one that can fill that kind of void. DD used to have a very close relationship with the Lord ever since he was a child, I don't know what happened to change that. He didn't go to church anymore. He was a totally different person. Christ was missing in his life.

A house is not a home. It seemed like my first sell was my last. It wasn't happening for me. Real estate is not what I thought it would be. Other brokers were still sending letters, so I responded to one and was hired at Tarbell Realtors. This one had an office with computers, phones, something called an up desk, which is when the person at the desk gets all the prospects that called into the office with real estate related questions.

I was introduced to a system design to generate business, called a farm, which is a certain geographical area where the agent goes from door to door. Everyone is assigned a farm, passing out flyers, sending out mailers, and generally becoming familiar with the home owners in their farm area.

I was sent to headquarters for my initial orientation and training on the how-tos of selling real estate. For an entire week, I had to fight the seven-o'clock traffic to Orange County and after-five traffic on the way back, and since I am a team player, I made the adjustment. The week had passed quickly, no time to play, a lot of notes, a whole lot to absorb. Even when I return to the office on Monday, it was more training, but this time with my broker. I really like the way Tarbell ran their office. I devoted most of my time and energy to holding open house, every Sunday. I got tired of that really quick.

They said that it's another way to get prospects. I didn't know what was wrong, but it wasn't working for me, no prospects, no escrows, and no money. Where is the money?

The house in LA and the fourplex in Inglewood are doing great, and so is the fourplex in Riverside, bringing plenty of funds in. When I purchased my townhouse, I put a good size of money down, so my mortgage payment was very low. There was no need to worry financially, but I don't believe in depleting all my reserves. I have to start thinking of another way to supplement my income. In the meantime, Charles and I are still dating, and things are going quite well. He even helped me with posting open house signs and most of the times, he was my "GPS" when I went viewing homes for my prospective clients.

CHAPTER 21

It's Beginning to Feel Like Love;
I am falling, falling so fast; I am terrified.
Somebody, help me, please!

I have loved you with an everlasting love;
I have drawn you with loving-kindness.

—Jeremiah 31:3

My feelings toward Charles were warming up. I'd been noticing how heartily he ate, and I was worried about him, so boldly I said, "You're not too young for a heart attack, you know, and you might need to cut back on so much meat and greasy foods." Ever since I became health conscious, overeating seemed to gross me out. Then I said, "I don't like men with big guts. When I put my arms around my man, I want them to go all around."

He didn't seem to be offended or concerned. He said, "Really? I think I'm okay."

One week later, he'd gone for his yearly physical. His doctor gave him a highlighted printout of many of the things he needed to watch for and ways in which he could curtail his diet. When he came home to me, he asked if I had spoken to his doctor.

"Seriously," I said, "You're in the military, how could I possibly have access to your military doctors? He simply diagnosed what I had been witnessing.?

He said, "That's true, hum?"

I said, "Yes."

Then he said, "Are you going to help me?"

"I could," I said, "but I'm a hard and thorough task master, and you have to do everything I say or the deal is off."

He said, "Okay, I'm ready."

He signed his life over to me, and now I'm going to whip him into shape. And I said: Here are the rules: no more red meat, no pork, no TV dinners, less salt and sugar, you have to brown bag your lunch and exercise every day. He needed to lose 30 plus pounds. He weighed 208 pounds at the time. Also, he had to weigh himself at least once a week. He said okay. I remember thinking, that was easy.

We started a regime. I would run, while he walked. I came back for him and made him run; he couldn't run one mile. Then I slowed down and walked with him, and we did this every morning. I made his lunch and sent him to work. We couldn't eat dinner together because of his evening part-time jobs, but I told him what to stay away from. He was very obedient, military, easy to work with. He followed my orders. Atta boy, kudos! I put him on a special diet, where he ate only certain foods and lost ten pounds in three days, and after that he was to lose two pounds every week. After a while, he had lost so much weight that he needed to have his uniforms taken up a few inches.

Some of the friends, those he used to go to lunch with, called him a henpeck man. They said, "This woman has you wrapped around her little finger." He didn't seem to care what they said. The problem was that he didn't pick his friends carefully. His friends were married, and he would go to their house for dinner, and he followed their eating habits. They ate like there was a food shortage and their bellies were a storage cupboard. There wasn't anyone who cared enough to tell him otherwise.

Charles also told me about when they would go out and wager to see who could eat the most lobster tails; of course he would be the winner. They would spend their weekend nights playing cards all night and drinking Tanqueray gin until zero dark thirty in the morning. The wives were there as well, watching TV and commiserating and drinking too. They took turns on going to each other's house. Charles was single and lived in the barracks because of financial hardship, which could have been nipped in the bud if he had enough balls to challenge the ex-wife. It seemed to me that they were working their part-time jobs to support their drinking habit; it was a case of misery loves company.

I inquired about all these parties, and he invited me to accompany him to one of them. I went out of curiosity. I was so bored that I fell asleep, while the ladies talked about nothing that interested me. Out of the bunch, I could tell that one of the women was different, in her own way. Her name is Mary Levy. Mary and her family moved out of state later when her husband retired. We are in touch with each other even to this day. The women thought that I was snobbish, but I was not, just telling it like it is.

I played my part, I visited with them occasionally, but it wasn't a deep friendship. After being there that one time, I told Charles that it wasn't my kind of thing and that if we were going to be together, his drinking had to go bye-bye. From that time on, whenever he went to play cards with them, he had to carry some grapefruit juice and absolutely no more Tanqueray gin. He did just as I suggested. He was able to work harder on his weight loss regime, once he stopped drinking the pounds came off rather quickly. At the end of three months, he had lost 34 pounds. He weighed 174 pounds and looked like a different person.

Our effort had paid off. I was very pleased and proud of him, and he loved his new looks and better health. Our new plan is to work on keeping the weight off. Charles followed the plan well and was able to reach his goal quickly. He wasn't deprived of nutrition, and we adjusted his portions of the right kinds of foods in addition to daily exercise. Determination and discipline played a big part in our game plan as well. We did it together, as a team. Another thing about Charles that I admire is that he is a great team player, and he rises to the occasion no matter what the situation is; just let him know what the plan is and he will follow through.

Too close for comfort. At this point, our relationship was headed in a different direction, we're turning a corner. I had to allow Charles to move in with me at my townhouse. This wasn't right, but Charles wasn't supposed to be living on base. His boss allowed it because of his financial situation and he could not afford to pay for his own apartment. That was not an excuse, it was the truth. We knew that we were living in sin and sending the wrong message to unbelievers. I had a three-bedroom townhouse. He should have used the extra bedroom, but we allowed our flesh to dictate our behavior. I hate my sins. I regret having taken that route because we knew it was wrong, and still we followed our sinful desires.

Charles's mother reminded us many times that we were wrong, but we kept telling her that very soon we would mend our ways. On one occasion, I told Mother Dukes that Charles could not afford to get a place of his own, his finances were too tight, and her answer was, "Why should you care? What did he do before he met you? You need to make him move and find his own way." She was right, and she was the voice of wisdom, but did we listen? We didn't think we were ready for marriage. Proverbs 22:17 says, "Pay attention and listen to the sayings of the wise; apply your heart to what I teach."

To be honest with you, I was the biggest hypocrite; I wasn't ready. I was not ready to share my wealth with Charles, knowing that it would all go to support his ex-wife. I wanted to wait and see how things would be after the children were of age. I did not want to deal with all his baggage. Looking back, I know that I should have trusted God; he has been my source all these years, and he will continue to provide for me. Furthermore, Charles is God's child just as I am. God's provision is for the both of us, and he would want me to share his bounty with others.

I have repented of my unwillingness to share, and I know that it's under the blood of Jesus and that I have been forgiven. We often fall short of the glory of God. With prayer, repentance, and godly sorrow, when we go to God, he hears us. He gives us mercy and pardon and leads us back on the right track, again and again.

One day, Charles started by telling me about how the military operated, how every so often they would send them away on tours that would last as short as one year or as long as two, three, or even up four years, and they don't guarantee their return back to the same place. I thought he was about to propose to me and take me with him. Right away, I said, "I'm sorry, I like my life the way it is, and I'm not going to change it for anyone. I just met you. I don't even know you." I am not really sure that Charles even understood what I was saying, because his response had nothing to do with the point I was making. He went on talking about how the temporary duty station process worked.

So, he went on to say, "If I volunteered to go before my name comes up, they will guarantee my return here, so I can be with you. I want to always be with you."

"Oh," I said, "do as you wish then. That's fine with me."

I was a reservist for six years, I chose to leave because it wasn't for me, too many rules, too many orders, too many changes. One day you're here and you don't know where you'll be the next. I didn't want to be a military wife who had to follow their husband everywhere, who had no identity of her own, being called his dependent. There is a person who is struggling to stay above water, and I would be called his dependent. I know how to bring home the bacon and how to cook it—I will not give up my independence. I think that was probably pride talking.

When I heard that word "dependent," I immediately associated it with having to give up my independence, something I have struggled to maintain ever since I can remember, but in reality becoming a military dependent has nothing to do with me giving up my independence as a person. I want to take a minute to explain why that word struck a nerve. I am very stubborn when it comes to giving up of myself, especially when I don't feel secure about whomever I am dealing with. I don't believe this is arrogance or pride. I had been through too much heartache already. I didn't want to feel vulnerable, again. So many walls built up over the years that not only did I not want to feel, but I couldn't. I just couldn't bring myself to being vulnerable. If I can handle something by myself, that's easier for me.

I'd heard a pastor say, "Our hearts are the theatre the enemy uses to showcase our wrong doings." When I was with this man, I could almost feel that God was setting me up for something, but every time that I started feeling good about him, Satan was tormenting me about my past relationships, comparing the good things that I liked about them, such as feeling more secure in the area of finances and having a sense of being secured and protected. Another area of deep concern was his ongoing financial responsibility with his ex-wife, and all the baggage that came with his past relationship. All the above issues caused me to feel unsure about the future of our relationship.

Korea here he comes. Well, he talked to his supervisors about the voluntary deployment and the ball was rolling. He did the smart thing. He knew what he wanted. He went about securing it by taking the tour to Korea ahead of time. His supervisors approved his request for an early tour with a guaranteed return to California. In January 1987, Charles went on a one-year tour to Korea. It was sad to see him leave. I surely would miss him. Before he left, I gave him instructions about his diet, exercise, a daily routine. I'd recorded videos of exercise programs for him. I gave them to him. I also told him that when he returns, he should not have gained weight if he followed the instructions I gave him.

I showed Charles a little mercy by allowing him to gain within 5 pounds of his current weigh and believe it or not, he kept it within those 5lbs. He left weighing 170 pounds, and he'd only gained four pounds. While in Korea, he enrolled in karate training, and that helped him a lot. He built up his strength, his stamina, and he became more confident.

I never asked him about his weight or how he was keeping up while he was away, I left it up to him. We talked on the phone once each month, because the military allowed him one free phone call per month to anywhere, and he used it to call me. We set a particular date and time for our talks. We also communicated through voice tapes because he didn't like to write. We recorded our thoughts on tapes and sent it to each other.

I used to be a regular on the radio program "Love Songs" on the KOST, and they would notify me as to when they were going to read my poems on the air, accompanied by a love song of my choosing and dedicated to him. We used to stay up at night waiting to hear the dedication, and I used to listen to that station all the time and now KSGN 89.7 FM has become our favorite station. The core purpose of this station is to share the good news of the gospel with people who have never heard it before, and to bring hope, inspiration, and encouragement to those who have.

Our love was—I can say love now because I think it's getting there and is growing because of the way it started—not rushed. Not like paper on fire, which takes off really fast and *poof* it's gone. Our love affair began slowly; it wasn't lust at least not on my part. I surely didn't lust after him, and I don't know if he lusted after me, after it was marinated for a while, it was slow cooked as to allow all the seasonings to get in.

When he called me from Korea, time seemed to go by so fast. We exchanged greetings, and we would discuss our voice tapes. I'd also record the reading of the poem dedication and the song that I'd picked and send it to him, and we'd discuss that as well. By then our hour was almost over. He told me about the different types of food that he'd eaten. He is a gourmand—he'd eat anything. As our time would come to an end, a voice would come on giving us the one-minute warning before our time was up. That time reminded me of the phone conversations I had with Loulou when he first went to New York. Our feelings for each other were so deep and overpowering, my emotions so ardent, my need to be with him so uncontrollable that it was too painful each time we had to end our calls. With Charles it was different, the commitment wasn't as deep. It got deeper as my commitment with the Lord got stronger and closer.

My life has changed tremendously ever since I rededicated my life to the Lord. I am praying more, slowly but surely, and I am learning how to be a better person. I have learned to care more about others, even though I know that salvation is by grace through faith and not of works. I spend time helping different ministries. My time belongs to the Lord; all that I do now is for his glory. I don't work to fatten my bank account; I make myself available in case I'm needed to serve.

One of the areas I served in was at a free pregnancy counseling center in the city I lived in, another area of ministry I served in was counselling people who were pregnant and considering abortion. Having an unplanned pregnancy is very common, and many people decide to have an abortion. I was long time ago caught up in that vicious cycle.

After the first abortion, my ex-husband Sully kept giving me that little pill, which in effect became my birth control. I think that little pill was the morning-after pill used to abort my child, which each month brought on my menstrual cycle, except for that one time when, out of curiosity, I pretended to take it but did not swallow it. That incident is how my son DD came about to be chosen to be born. That was no accident, that was God. Nothing happens without his knowledge, He wanted to bless me through the birth of my son. God chose _him!_ After Sully left and my life became my own, I had chosen a destructive lifestyle that caused me to have a series of abortions, for which I am very sorry. I am ashamed and sorrowful for that destructive time of my life.

A vast majority of women, including me, who have chosen to have these abortions, go on living and suffering under the weight of the guilt of abortion. Many of the fathers of these children have been involved in the abortion decision. We will never know the impact those decisions have on them. We cannot eliminate or deny the guilt feelings, and we need to resolve them once and for all. A permanent solution would be to call it by its real name, which is **sin.** Owning the part we play and then asking God to forgive and cleanse us from our past.

After learning for myself that abortion at any stage is murder, it is sin—and that God hates it—I decided to do my part to help prevent future abortions with the help of my pastor, Raymond Hahn. When the opportunity presented itself, I went to work for an organization called Loving Options, a free clinic in Moreno Valley. While working at Loving Options, I met and was able to help many women, like myself, who found themselves in the compromising situation of unplanned pregnancy.

I was able to share with these women about my past experiences relating to abortion, and what I had to learn about the sin, guilt, sharing also that they needed to realize, just as I did, that at the point of conception that they were carrying a real person. Finally, I shared with them about the new freedom that is possible through Jesus's work on the cross and his forgiveness. I also shared many Bible verses, like Romans 3:23 and 6:23, Psalms 103:10–14, 1 John 1:9, Romans 8:1, and others. I explained to them that we can look forward to being reunited in heaven with our loved ones, covered by Christ's blood, including our children lost through abortion. Finally, I would reassure them that God has seen us at our worst and he still loves us. No matter what we have done, no sin is beyond the reach of **God's** grace. There is no freedom like being forgiven!

I also did fund raisers, walks for life, bake sales, and other related activities. I did not miss the extra money; instead, I made new friends and I enjoyed the work and had a great time serving. My new life has thought me how to forgive those in my past who have hurt me. The enemy can no longer feed my mind with the things of my past. I have learned to know the source where my blessings come from. Psalms 28:7 says, "The Lord is my strength and my shield, my heart trusts in him, and he helps me. My heart leaps for joy, and with my song I praise him." (Colossians 3:13)

CHAPTER 22

To Err Is Human, to Forgive Divine;
I refuse to hold on to the wrong done to me.
I am moving on to my happy place

For there is nothing hidden that will not be disclosed, and nothing concealed that will not be known or brought out into the open.
—Luke 8:17

*If you forgive others the wrongs they have done to you,
your father in heaven will also forgive you.*
—Matthew 6:14

Cheater! Cheater! Cheater! One of the women from the "Tanqueray parties," where Charles used to go, his friend Richard's wife, Mary, told me about the military midtour travel. This is when after being on tour for half of the time and one might feel home sick, you can take a free trip back home or anywhere else of their choosing. I'm new to this military stuff, so I didn't know about that. So I inquired about it, and Charles decided to come to visit me. I would say that I felt hurt because he didn't share that with me, that I had to ask for it. His midtour would have been in July, and it was already September, but he came anyway, just to make me happy. Looking back, I wonder if he came out of guilt.

I went to Norton Air Force Base to pick him up. It was so good to see him, and it brought tears to my eyes. I didn't realize how much I'd missed him. I can understand now why he told me that he didn't like midtour trips. We had made a promise to each other that we would wait for each other. We were very passionate with one another. And, were getting reacquainted with each other, we discussed everything. I asked a lot of questions about his time in Korea. We chatted about some of the things he did, the different kinds of food he ate, etc... He shared that he had been taking karate classes, he was advancing through the many colors of karate belts; and that he was getting very good at it. He even demonstrated some of the karate moves. We spent the rest of the evening reminiscing on how we met and how far we had gotten in our relationship. His demeanor seamed different throughout our conversation, he appeared somewhat nervous. All of a sudden, it came to me that we hadn't talked about the promise we had made to each other, prior to his leaving for Korea, whether he had developed any other relationships while he was overseas.

I told you. God was setting me up, and I was falling for it. Wait! Wait! I said, "were you faithful to me while you were over there?" He said "Hum! Well, no. no, I was not". He was honest. And I said "what! Why"? I got weak. "We're not married yet". That was the stupidest answer I have ever heard. I was deeply hurt, so hurt that I could not continue with this conversation any longer. I thought to myself, God, what's up with this? I have been a good girl, and now this! It reminded me of when I used to be bad, and I wondered if that was consequences for my past iniquities. We're not supposed to be intimate until marriage anyway, and maybe, that was God's way of telling us that we were both guilty.

So, I went downstairs and exercised until my body cried for mercy. My motto used to be, when nothing else works, exercise. Rather I should say, cry out to God before trying anything else. I used to be a fitness junky, that was my solution for everything.

"When nothing else could help, God lifted me." What are you up to, God? I have a bad temper. I am a yeller. I don't care who is around that can hear me. I yelled, and I yelled loud. I was so angry, and honestly, I still need God to deliver me from anger. I know God's word said, "Be angry and sin not," which lets me know that being angry is not necessarily a sin, but I was so angry that I wanted to somehow get revenge for what Charles had done to me, and that would be a sin. If our anger causes us to violate God's law, then we are sinning. But Lord, please help me, I need you.

After admitting that he cheated on me, he would have been gone in a New York minute. He wouldn't have still been in my house. I would have told him to get out, now, like yesterday now. But I didn't, and I don't know why. After hundreds of sit-ups, jumping jacks, push-ups, and anything else you can think of, I cooled down a bit and went back upstairs to take a shower. Guess what? That cheater was asleep. He didn't have a worry in the world. He was probably thinking what could I possibly do to him.

What's done is done, and if there are any consequences, he would deal with it later. That is the type of person Charles is—he leaves everything for God to handle. I am the opposite. I do go to God, he is the only constant in my life, but oftentimes I try to solve my problems in my own strength before I go to the Lord. I know that's the wrong order. I always have to go back to him and say, "Daddy, forgive me," and he always does. I am so thankful that God understands my weaknesses, and because of his mercy and grace, he never held my sins against me. I thank the Lord for seeking me while I was lost and bringing me back to himself through his Son, Jesus Christ.

I could not let Charles sleep. I woke him up, and said, "I know that you came back because I had asked you to. I also know that you don't have anywhere else to go, so you can spend the rest of the time here. And since you don't have a ride, I will take you to the airport when it's time for you to go back to Korea.

He said, "Okay," with no emotions whatsoever.

When the day came, I drove him to Norton Air Force Base and waited for his plane to leave and came home furious. His behavior left me with a lot to think about. I didn't know what to do. "I need help, Lord," I prayed. I'm not sure if I waited long enough for the Lord to give me the answer. I was impatient and anxious. Anxiety is a sin and I knew it, but Lord it is so hard. Philippians 4:6 says, "Do not be anxious about anything, but in every situation, by prayer and petition, with thanksgiving, present your requests to God." My example was right there, living in my house. (Charles went to sleep without worrying, and I was furious with anger.) He left the matter to the Lord. I needed to follow his leading, but I didn't, I followed my old way of doing things.

Dear John. Did you notice that I didn't tell him to go away and never come back, or that I never wanted to see you again? Why not? Why not? I haven't got a clue. I noticed that when dealing with situations concerning Charles, I am not in control; all my operational wisdom was gone, my resilience was lost or maybe willfully ignored. I felt helpless. It was like someone else had taken over, and had taken charge of the situation. I was not love-struck, nor was I under his power, no way. He had no power whatsoever over me. God is the source of my power. He must have taken over, and I think he is winning; God is wearing me down through Charles.

Charles has gone back to Korea, and nothing has changed, it's life as usual. I am sort of pensive, wondering what I should do about him. After hearing my complaint, Mary Levy told me about the saying "boys will be boys," she also said: "a lot of men have an affair overseas and never think about it again, and their wives never find out, he was honest. If he didn't tell you, how were you going to find out?" What she was saying is true, so I calmed down and thought about it some more.

I received voice tapes and I also sent him voice tapes, but something inside of me had died. The feeling was gone, and it was hard getting it back. I couldn't do the poems anymore because there was no one for me to address them to. When I write, I have to live it, feel it, be in the moment, and I just couldn't do it. When he called me for our monthly talk, the excitement, the anticipation wasn't there anymore, and I knew right then and there that it was over, so I wrote a letter. We hardly wrote to each other; it has always been the voice tape, but desperate times call for desperate measures. I wrote him a Dear John.

> Dear Charles, as you should have expected, this is to let you that you need to start looking for other lodging when you return to California, or maybe you can extend your tour and stay in Korea. You did not keep your promise to be faithful, and now I'm keeping my promise to myself not to live with a cheater. I hope that life treats you well.
>
> Signed,
> Marie.

He called me right away after he read my letter. He begged me to let him come back. He said, "I want to be with you, and you only", and he kept on saying it.

"Well, we'll see about that," I said and hung up. I'm not sure if he had to pay for that call because it wasn't time yet for the once monthly call.

He still called back and sent tapes. I did not respond as quickly as I used to. I thought about paying him back, but it wouldn't have been a payback since in my mind we were no longer an item. I already gave him his walking papers. I am free to do as I wished, but why couldn't I bring myself to do it? It would have taken just one phone call, but something held me back.

It's a new year! The Christmas holidays were here, and they came and went. My real estate career was not going so well, but during my farming, I saw a property for sale. It was a FSBO (for sale by owner), and I was interested in it. It was a very nice four bedrooms, three bathrooms, and a loft, a separate family room, and a sizable backyard in a great neighborhood. I called and talked to the owner who had already moved out. (That's a plus because they don't want to leave it vacant for long.) He gave me a time that a cleaning crew was going to be there when I can see the inside. He also gave me permission to go into the back and look thru the windows, which I did. When I saw the house, it was love at first sight. I met the owner with my offer; it was agreeable to him, and we opened escrow. I did not sell the townhouse; it was added to my list of income properties. Charles came back from Korea just in time to help me move into my new house, and since I was not led to let him go, he ended up staying.

This was 1988. Including that time spent in Korea, we've been together almost two years. New house, new mortgage. Since Charles was in no position to support me and I'm not going to be used by a man again, I explained to him that he had to contribute at whatever capacity to the running of the house, and he gladly accepted. After doing inventory of his budget, we decided on an amount that was comfortable for him and satisfactory to me. Charles and I continued to live together without the benefit of marriage, which was very wrong, but we were just not ready at the time. Little did I know at the time we were depriving ourselves of special blessings from God because God's Word says that "he that finds a wife, finds a good thing, and obtains favor from the Lord" (Proverbs 18:22).

I never had to do grocery shopping, he did it every week on base, and we saved money that way. Our funds were not mingled together. I trusted him but he had too much baggage. He was always in court with his ex-wife. Every six months or so, she took him back to court for more money, and the judge granted her request every time, and he still had to pay her attorney fees. One time, we went to see his attorney who informed us that the court could mingle our incomes in order to give his ex-wife more money, when in my opinion she was already getting too much money.

I said, "Over my dead body. I worked too hard for mine. She needs to get a job and earn her own money. She never worked a day of her life. He had to keep her in the lifestyle she was accustomed to, but I say, it is not going to be at my expense." I told him if that was about to happen, he would definitely have to go. Through all this, he never panicked, he never despaired. He had the patience of Job, as they say. I was glad to have him in my life, because of him and his troubles, I learned patience and how to trust God more. He was truly a godly man.

Mommy's baby daddy's maybe! There were facts, which would be proven later, that the children his ex-wife was charging him child support for were not his biological children. I urged him to ask for paternity testing, but he said he didn't want to hurt the children. The children were conceived while they were married; therefore, legally, he was responsible to pay child support, but since he knew they were not his, he could petition the court about paternity, and probably between the alimony and child support he could get a reduction in the amount he paid to her.

The children were teenagers, and they probably suspected that something was the matter because their mother would keep them from seeing Charles even though he made many attempts to connect with the children. The divorce decree said that child support would continue until nineteen or graduation from high school, and the older child, not sure of the younger one, was behind and did not graduate until nineteen, which added an extra year to the child support payments.

For many years now, the older child, has been living with his biological father, of whom he is the spitting image and who is also the father of the daughter born prior to the marriage to Charles. The second boy, I am not sure if he has knowledge of who his father is. I don't have any ill feelings about the children—they're not responsible for the messes that adults create. I wish them well. Hopefully, they will not let history repeat itself. I have never met the children, and Charles have not seen them since 1985. They were never available to him since the divorce, that left him destitute.

The daughter is a very attractive young lady. I had the opportunity to meet her briefly, very late on the night after my husband's father's funeral in July 2012. The boys did not come to pay their respects even though one of them lives approximately three to four blocks away from Charles's parents' house. I do not judge them for not showing up; it was their choice to make. I believe they were making a statement by not being in attendance. They probably know the truth and wanted to end the charade. They had chosen the route that was less stressful and least uncomfortable for them. If it were my choice to make, I think I would have chosen that same route. I am certain that deep in their hearts, the boys wished Charles and the family well. They never came during Dad's life; what difference would their presence make after his death?

CHAPTER 23

His Family! Her Family!;
Family: It is love, it is acceptance, a source of
comfort, a support system. It is always there,
it is a place to which you can return.

Though my father and mother forsake me,
the Lord will receive me.

—Psalms 27:10

Almost everyone lives in dysfunctional families, whether we like it or not. We wouldn't trade them for all the tea in china. Take my family for instance. There are times when I wish I could wiggle my nose and they would be gone, but at other times, I just want to eat them up like chocolate. You are stuck with them forever. Like it or not, God has placed you there for a reason. Just love them as much as you can, whenever you can, for as long as you can.

The very same applies to your spouse's family; his is yours as much as yours is his. They might pretend to like you, but deep inside they know they have to love you if they obey the golden rule (1 John 4:7), but they resent you for having taken away their son or daughter, brother or sister. Some of them think that you are the reason certain things don't happen. The visits (or the lack thereof), the grandchildren, reunions, financial support, phone calls etc.

Having said that, therefore it makes me feel that I am being accused of something that really isn't my fault. The truth is Charles experienced some things while growing up that had a big effect on why it took fifteen years for him to return home. On many occasions, I would encourage him to go and visit his family, especially at the passing of his grandmother and other family members. Charles is the only one who knows the why behind him distancing himself from his family.

Before I met my husband, I had prayed for a man with a big family, with sisters that I can do things with (since I wasn't doing so well with my own). I am not sure how things would work with the in-laws. First, they show that they care. They say that they love you, and I believe in their hearts and minds they think they do, but other times they treat you as an outsider trying to come and invade their territory. How should one react in this situation? I wanted sisters. I wanted to get close to them, but I am afraid to get burned again. I would rather love them from afar.

I got what I prayed for: my husband has a large family, beautiful people with hearts of gold. When I met them, I thought I had died and went to heaven. My mother in-law was already loving on me from afar before we even met. We were phone pals when my husband was away, on a job-related trip. She called me often. She made me feel special. We talked to each other at least once a week for hours at a time. Truth be told, I was the bridge that brought her son back home to her.

I love people, I love family. I wish that they had tried to know me better and allowed me to show them the real me (before that faux pas in 2000, which I will explain later). I have so much love, but I am afraid to get hurt.

Charles and I visited his family in November 1989, my first visit and his second visit since he left home in 1970. In many ways, Mom and Dad were the best parents any child could ever wish for. They would move heaven and earth to make sure their children were well cared for. But there was one itsy bitsy problem: Mom has a tendency to be controlling. She is demanding, overbearing, meddling, strong-willed, you fill in the blank. She thinks she rules the world. Whatever she decided was law—not only with her children, but with everyone else. She doesn't make much noise, but she is a hurricane when it comes to running and taking over other people's lives. (Sorry, Mom, I couldn't help myself.)

Everyone is afraid of her, even I would too be afraid of her at times, but not anymore. I will not disrespect my mother and my husband's mother. God wouldn't want me to do that, but I will speak my mind in the most respectful way that I can. Once, Mom told one of her daughters who went to visit her, "When you come here, you can park your brains outside. You're not going to need them." That could be very insulting. Having said that, Mom is a very loving woman who loves God, loves others, but she wants to run everyone's life.

My husband left home because he couldn't take it anymore. In addition, he married a woman that the family never really approved of, according to what many have shared with me. It is also believed that she is the reason that Charles never returned home for fifteen years. When I came in to the picture in 1986, after hearing the story, my goal was to help reunify him with his family. It took three years to get there, but it's better late than never.

In 1989, prior to Charles and I getting married, we went to visit his family during the Thanksgiving holiday. They welcomed me with open arms. Everyone moved over backward to make me feel at home. That was so sweet, and I felt right at home. It was a fun family reunion, good times never felt so good. That was the best Thanksgiving Day I have ever had with my new family. When we left to return home, I missed them and wished that I were still with them. I thought this is a family I wouldn't mind belonging to.

From the onset of our relationship, I started calling her mom. One of the sisters teased me, saying that I was more like mom than any of them. I kind of thought so too. (I'm somewhat domineering as well.) We visited whenever we could, and one of the sisters and her daughter came to visit us one year. She is very nice. She was facing hardship of her own, but she thought well enough of us and to spend her vacation time with us. I was grateful, and we did a lot of fun things together.

Mom is a devout Christian. She didn't believe in sex before marriage, shacking up, and other sinful things. When we visited them, we weren't allowed to be together. We were not planning to disrespect her home in the first place, but she lets us know right away, "not on her watch." We were not going to sin. After the visit, each time we spoke on the phone, she would hint how sinful our being together before marriage was. She'd ask, "When are you guys going to get married?" When I explained his financial troubles, she said, "What did he do before he met you? Marry him or make him move. God can't bless you as a couple until you are living by his standard." She was absolutely right—that was good advice.

So we decided to get married. He didn't propose, we decided. How romantic! We kind of made that decision mostly to please Mom; it pleases God as well, and it was the right thing to do even though we were not ready. I had to buy my own ring, but I didn't mind because I knew he couldn't afford an engagement ring at the time. We had to get married twice because we wanted to get married on May 30, the same date that we met. In 1990, it fell on a week day, so we went to the justice of the peace. The judge married us, and that way we were able to keep the same anniversary date as when we met.

We had a backyard wedding with a minister on June 16, 1990. "For they say when you marry in June, you're a bride all your life."

The week prior to the wedding, we decided to purify ourselves before the Lord. We fasted for four days. We prayed and confessed our sins, abstained from sex, and asked the Lord to bless us and lead our path. It was not a big wedding. We invited a few friends and family. We did not send single invitations to each family member; mom had always been the go-to person, but I am sure she told everyone.

She wanted us to go all the way to Florida to get married so the family could attend. We would both have to take time off from work, two plane tickets, and other expenses. It seemed impossible, but I took her request into consideration. I called one day to tell her that we could make it happen if she and the family would start the preparation until we got there so we wouldn't have to take too many days off from work. She said, "I'm not giving you a wedding."

I said, "I'm not asking you to give me a wedding. Since it's your idea to have the family there, I thought starting the ball rolling until we get there wouldn't be a problem for the family, and I'm paying for it." It wasn't an easy conversation. We cut it short, and we got off the phone. Needless to say, we did not have the wedding in Florida. The out-of-town family members did not come. I think it would have been a financial hardship on them. They did send a card with a gift.

We had decided on a small wedding, and we would renew our vows after ten years. The inside of our new gazebo was large enough for a pulpit. The seating area is going to be in front, on either side of the gazebo with twenty-five chairs on each side. EZ UP were used to protect the area from the sun, which ended at the edge of the large patio. The patio was used as the dance floor, and the head table; the gift table, and cake table were on the patio as well. The DJ platform was inside by the patio door. Our favorite song was my marching song, "Almost Paradise." Our colors were pink and white. I wore a pink dress with white shoes. Charles wore a white suit and light pink shirt. My maid of honor and best man (husband and wife) wore dark pink and beige.

We had large supplies of foods, sweets, fruit trays, variety of salads and breads, turkeys, honey-baked hams, fried and baked chicken, étouffée over rice, shrimp cocktail, dips, salsa, platters of cheeses and cracker, etc. We had a champagne fountain and bottles of sparkling cider for the nondrinkers. A couple of friends volunteered to go back and forth to each table to offer refills. Everything was plenteous.

There were two decorated arches, one at the entrance of the gazebo, with a walkway that connected to the other arch. We decorated the backyard and gazebo with loads of flowers, balloons, streamers, and other leafy wedding items. We rented tables and fifty chairs. Exquisite décor, delicious food. The maid of honor provided a four-layered cake. One of Charles's DJ friends did the music for us. Everything was well done and to taste.

It was a beautiful wedding. Every invitee that RSVP'd was present and accounted for. Plus, we had extra guests that forgot to RSVP who came anyway, and they were welcomed. Since we weren't going anywhere, and there was enough food, we invited everyone to stay as long as they wanted, and we all danced and party all night. It was a family affair to be remembered.

We had both taken two weeks off from work to tend to the wedding preparations. We didn't plan for a honeymoon at that time. We saved the honeymoon for our first anniversary. We'd planned to stay at a military hotel, the Hale Koa Hotel in Waikiki, Hawaii. We didn't feel a honeymoon was necessary at that time. I, for one, am conservative when it comes to spending. We had been living together about four years (minus the year Charles spent in Korea). We had consummated our union illegally. Now that we are living under the umbrella of marriage, we don't need a honeymoon to validate our physical relationship.

God was patient with us through our days of fornication, now we can wait to honeymoon in Hawaii. And, Mom, thank you for being who you are. If it wasn't for you, we wouldn't have done it then, and maybe we might not have done it at all. Even when I think Mom is meddling in our lives, I always respected her opinion because I love her; and after all was said and done, I find out that she was right.

CHAPTER 24

Overworked and Underpaid; "Remember the 1980 movie: '9 to 5' Work! Work! Work!"

For God does not show favoritism.

—Rom. 2:11

Bad supervisor. There is a saying, "If you do what you love, you'll never work a day of your life." What this is really saying is that you should choose a career you love. Working with figures is my passion. I had worked for the school district in Los Angeles as a payroll administrator. For eight hours, I process time cards and pay the employees for work performed. My job at the cable company is the same, but with this job, several other duties were added. This position offered less benefits for more work, and my work load was getting larger. My task master was never satisfied; her expectation was beyond comprehension. That makes for anxiety and increased stress. We were picking up small cable systems and added them to ours; that's more work for my one-person department, me.

I requested a part-time assistant, but my boss didn't think it was necessary. It was getting harder and harder to complete my daily tasks. In an effort to handle that situation, I had to go to work one hour earlier every morning with no breaks or lunch, and I brown bagged my lunch and ate at my desk while I worked. When I ask my manager for help a second time, she told me that I should feel grateful to have this position. "Who else do you see with an office like yours?" she said. Then she referenced two other employees and said, "Look at Kathy Shepherd and Dorothy Alexander, they don't have what you have, so stop your complaining."

These two employees were both African-Americans and had lower positions than mine, so I took it that she meant that minorities shouldn't have nice jobs! I had to rush every day to get there early; those extra hours of work were without pay, and I was asked to cover the phones (that was on my own time) in case employees were calling in sick for the day. I did a manual payroll and send to ADP. I did adjustments. My job also called for emergency payroll allowances, where I write check when an employee's paycheck was short because timecards were late coming, I kept up with employee benefits, add what they earn for each pay period, and deduct what they'd used; all these done manually and was very tedious work.

My reviews always looked very good, but that did not reflect on my paychecks. Each time she promised me a salary increase for a future date, and when the time came to put it in writing, she said her boss would not allow her to do it. I did believe her at first, but once, out of curiosity, I marched to her boss's office to find out why Mr. Thomas Scheafer had denied me a raise. To my surprise, I found out that he had never even received a request, nor spoken to my supervisor about giving a raise. She had lied about it all this time.

The stress of working at Cablevision was getting to me, I was having anxiety attacks all the time. On the morning of Good Friday 1991, on my way to work after a rainy night, it was a very dark and cloudy morning, the roads were very slippery, I lost control of my vehicle and crashed into a ditch. The vehicle was destroyed but I didn't incur any physical injuries. I had lost consciousness, and I woke up at Loma Linda hospital. After a thorough examination, I was released the same day. The policeman who took the accident report at the scene said that the car must have flipped over several times. The car was totaled but I did not have one scratch on my body. God spared my life. Could it be that the Lord was saving me for a grandeur purpose? Could it also be that He was sending me a message through this accident, telling me to stop being anxious and trust Him.

I started back seeing my therapist Dr. Miller again. Dr. Miller sent a letter to my boss putting me on a two-week leave of absence and scheduled me to see him once a-week. I wasn't getting better, he changed my schedule to twice a-week. Ms. Lanna (my supervisor) would not let me take the recommended time off. When I stayed home, she threatened to cut my pay unless the work gets done and is on time. (We weren't computerized at that time.) She sent all time cards, my accounting books, my calculator, all the necessary tools to my home, to make sure that my work gets done (No one else knew how to do my job.) regardless of the effect it would have on my mental health. Her decision added to my stress tremendously; it made me more anxious. I complained to my doctor about it, so he called her to explain how her actions would delay my recovery. She ignored him, and he had to send her a letter warning her if she didn't stop he was going to report her to the labor board.

My disability lasted about three months, after which time I started to feel better. I was allowed to go back to work part-time, just to see how well I would perform with the aid of new medication.

Before I was released to return to work, Charles and I wanted to take our long-awaited trip to Hawaii, which was booked almost one year in advance. My doctor approved it; he said that it would be good for me to get away. What was supposed to have been our delayed honeymoon turned out to be a time of convalescing in the hospital. Instead of fun in the sun I experienced anxiety attacks, high fever, headaches, chills, and night sweats. Our vacation was ruined. To add insult to injury, when we decided to cut our vacation short, the airlines charged us extra fees to allow us to change our return flight.

When the time was right, at my doctor's discretion, I resumed my duties at the cable company. Ms. Lanna finally thought best to have another employee cross trained for my job, in case that I should get sick again. While I was recuperating from the accident, I took the time to reflect on what was important. When I returned to work, I found that nothing had changed at the cable company. I was at the end of my rope once again with demands and inhumane treatment from my supervisor. My stress level was increasing. When I discussed it with my therapist, he suggested that I should change jobs. I tried to get a lateral transfer within the company, but my supervisor, Ms. Lanna, would not let me. After careful thought and consideration, I had concluded that my values were not in alignment with that dysfunctional company. It was time to move on in order to maintain my health and my sanity; therefore, I resigned.

I went to the unemployment office to file for compensation in order to get paid while looking for other employment. Ms. Lanna denied my claim, which I appealed. On the day of my appeal, Ms. Lanna was invited to come and give reason for her denying my claim, but she was a no-show, so Ms. Long from the human resources department came to represent the company. She knew all the details of my claim. During the course of my employment at Cable Vision, on two different occasions, Ms. Long witnessed the way I was being treated by Ms. Lanna. She spoke in my favor, and my claim was approved. I was able to collect unemployment benefits even though I had resigned from my position.

I loved my job, and I did it well. I was complimented many times by Mr. Scheafer, my boss's boss, for a job well done. He was surprised when Ms. Lanna refused to sign my request for unemployment benefits; that's why Ms. Long came to represent the cable company instead of my immediate supervisor, Ms. Lanna. I have learned from a reliable source that Ms. Lanna no longer worked for the cable system.

I continued with my therapy sessions. Dr. Miller was very good in his approach toward my recovery. My visits were less frequent, and at the proper time I was able to stop the medication. Through my therapy, I realized that I needed to stop working altogether, at least for a while, which would in turn give me a chance to regroup and find myself again.

Charles and I both love children. Since it was impossible for us to conceive children together, we were considering adoption. One of the reason for my desire to adopt was that I was feeling a great void in my life, and I thought that having children would somehow fill that void. We found out about a program that the county of Riverside was sponsoring, in which you start by being foster parents while in the processing stage of the adoption. They train you in the different aspects of foster parenting. You had to also undergo fingerprinting, physicals, CPR, and first aid classes as part of the prequalifying process.

Charles preferred boys, and my preference was girls, so we started with boys. We welcomed the first child, Benjamin, who was eleven years old. He was very sweet and very needy in that he always seemed to want someone close to him. We worked with him for about six months to allow him to get acquainted before we accepted another child from the agency. It was important to us that Benjamin feel at home before he would have to share us with another child. Benjamin went to a private school out of town, so it was necessary that he'd be picked up and brought home every day. We only spent time together briefly in the morning while I made ready his lunch pail. We had more quality time during the evenings and weekends.

Because we were considered very good foster parents, the placement agency was constantly encouraging us to take on more children. We decided to take on an eight-year-old boy named Roary. He was a sweet and loving boy. I remember him coming to us around my birthday, which is in August. After the honeymoon period was over, he turned out to be a real lion, that's why I call him Roary. He was very nice and cuddly, but when he would get upset it was disaster after disaster waiting to happen. It was a little hard for us to get adjusted at first. Going from no children and now we had two, it felt good being able to give back since our own child had spent two years in foster care. I'd shared with both of them about my son being in foster care, how he loved his foster family, and even after our son came home, we stayed in touch with them until they were both deceased.

Both children came from group homes, which was a stricter environment. A lot of children in groups homes are on mood-altering medications. A foster home setting was the next step toward family reunification. The adjustment was harder for them because they felt unsure about whether they would be accepted in the new home they were assigned to. When the children were introduced to a new home, they would always test their parents to see where their limits were. They make sure that the foster parents knew that they were not going to make it easy for them. They want to know that you love them regardless of their behavior. They want to see how long you're going to allow their bad behavior to continue before giving up on them. They want to know if you're going to send them away like the other homes did. In my country, children are seen and not heard. I didn't want to raise my children that way.

My children are not robots. I want to hear what they have to say, help them feel good about themselves, bring their opinions to the table, and discuss their likes and dislikes without feeling intimidated by big people with bad tempers. Our little Roary was kind of scary. He needed a little more than we could provide, which of course added to my stress because I wanted to be the best mom possible. I think he was not ready yet for foster care, or with my kind of childhood maybe I wasn't ready. Many times, our childhood experiences prepare us for situations we will encounter as adults.

Roary had so much anger built up in him that it didn't take much to set him off. On one occasion, Roary came home from school, went straight to his room screaming bad words, and began tearing up the room. He pulled the draperies down, the paintings off the walls and marked them with crayons. He threw his clothes and shoes out of the window and turned his desk and chair upside down. On another occasion, he got upset and hid in the garage. Since we knew where he was, we didn't panic. Charles checked on him from time to time, until finally he came in and went to his room.

Later when Charles checked the garage, he saw that Roary had keyed my Cadillac from bumper to bumper. Oh, no! Not my new car! Later when we approached him about it, he asked us to send him back. He said, "I want to go back. Aren't you going to send me back?" We told him he wasn't going anywhere, and that if he wants to move out when he turned eighteen, that would be okay, but not now.

Even though Roary's acting out was very difficult to deal with at times, it was not something that we would send him back for. We loved him. He was our son, and he belonged with us. The older boy overheard what Roary said about wanting to leave, and he looked at Roary and said, "They're not going to let you go. I have tried the same thing. It didn't work, and besides, I need a little brother." Roary calmed down a bit, and things started to get better for us until the next time and the next.

They were both good boys. We were blessed to have them in our lives. Charles played sports with them; they both were into baseball. I am not into sports and found out that I can do better with girls. We later welcomed two teenage girls into our home. I enjoyed the shopping, the hair and nails, dressing up, and the things girls enjoy doing. I had a lot of fun with the girls, just as Charles enjoyed hanging out with the boys. Whether boys or girls, Charles and I loved them both the same because they brought joy and life to our home. When it came to the children, our good days far outweighed any so-called bad days. Having them taught me how to never give up or abandon your children.

The girls and I did a lot of things together, such as learning how to cook and bake. We also had slumber parties, attended church, and we occasionally went on picnics together. I never went camping, but the kids went, and when the girls came back, we lay on the floor and they gave me blow by blow details of their fun-filled activities. They made me feel like I had been there and experienced it with them.

I remember one evening, each one of the girls had a friend over, and we had a slumber party, which included pizza and ice cream and lots of chocolate. We each had our own half gallon of our favorite ice cream flavors. We were up eating, watching TV, telling jokes all night long. The part that I liked best was when I was with my children, I could be a kid too. Growing up in Haiti, I don't remember much about my childhood. I don't remember running in the park, playing with friends or participating in any children activities. It seems as if I skipped that part of my life and had to grow up much too fast. Whatever the girls did, I did, and we always found a way to show our love, one for the other.

Parenting is an adventure. You and your children learn a lot of things together, and I always tried to leave myself open to learn from the experience. I look back on my time as a foster parent as one of the best experiences of my life. I have learned that the good things you put into your children help prepare them for their own adventure as future parents.

Although we fostered many children over the years, we never adopted any of our own. We realized that we were both getting older and would be more like grandparents to them. Another reason is when my husband retired, we would want to travel and enjoy what's left of our life together. So we gave up that idea. Our time as foster parents was enjoyable and rewarding. We will always remember our foster children and the wonderful times we had spent with them and the contribution they had made in our life.

CHAPTER 25

Hurt, Ignored, and Rejected;
When you thought you were liked, accepted,
even respected; then, proven you were so wrong.

As you come to him, the living stone – rejected by
humans but chosen by God and precious to Him.

—1 Pet 2:4

Our tenth anniversary. Where did all that time go? It is already the year 2000, ten years since our wedding. We had a small wedding in 1990. Our goal was to renew our vows on our tenth anniversary. We planned to have a big celebration, with all the frills, friends and family.

When the time was approaching, we started making the necessary arrangements in order to guarantee that everything would run smoothly and without a glitch. Our plans were coming along fine, until I received a phone call from my sisters-in-law, saying, "Mom and Dad will have been married fifty years on their upcoming anniversary in September 2000, and we want to give them the wedding they never had, and we thought that we should split the cost into fourths. Each child can pay one-fourth of the cost."

My reply was, "What a coincidence! We were planning to renew our vows this coming May, in commemoration of our tenth anniversary. Maybe we can make it a double wedding." Since we were on a conference call sharing our ideas, I decided to paint them a picture of what I thought we should consider.

I am sure between the three of them, they had already made their decision, which was alright with me. All they needed from me was a yeah, great plan, go for it, we'll send our share of the funds. My proposal must have put a monkey wrench in their plan, because everyone stopped talking all at once, you could hear a pin drop.

Finally, one of the sisters broke the silence, and she said, "I don't think that's a good idea. You might steal Mom's thunder, and the ceremony is to make her feel special. It's Mom and Dad's special day."

I can understand all that, but I said to them, "That would thwart my plans as well, and it would mean that I'd have to postpone my special day. I don't think that we can pay our share of the cost of Mom's wedding, buy two plane tickets, and still be able to afford our own wedding celebrations. Far be it from me to consider my plans before yours, just let us know the date of the wedding and we will do our part."

Family or outsider? The time went by fast. September was here, and everything went according to plan. Needless to say, we did cancel our vow renewal plans and put mom's happiness before our own. We could have charged our wedding expenses to a credit card, but, remember, we are living debt free. We purchased four tickets, two for us and two for Mom and Dad, as their wedding present. They had never visited us the whole time we had been married. Mom always preferred that we visited them—that way the whole family gets to see us, so we always went to them because they were never willing to come visit us. Granted, we did not visit very often, and Mother always reminded us of how long since we had been home.

The time is now and we're going to Florida and on our return trip we wanted Mom and Dad to come back with us for a couple of weeks. We thought if the tickets were in their hands, it would be hard for them to turn down our offer to come with us to California. We wanted to pamper them and show them our town and how beautiful California is, go places, do some shopping, spend some overdue quality time together.

Due to our work commitments, we could not take too many days off, so we did not get to Florida until the evening before the wedding. It was fine with the sisters that we arrived on that day because they had everything under control. The wedding and reception were going to be at Mom and Dad's home church. So a family member picked us up from the airport and took us directly to the church, to help with getting the church ready for the ceremony. Everyone helped to add the finishing touches, and we all went home.

When we got home, after we ate dinner, we all gathered in the Florida room (family room in Florida). My husband and I were very tired and ready to go to bed, but we stayed with them to chat for a while. On the other side of the room, there was a conversation going on between my three sisters-in-law about the seating arrangement at the head table. Mom was in the room with them, but for once she wasn't in charge. The table was being set for Mom and Dad, the three sisters, my husband, and Grandma Daisy, who is my mother-in-law's mother. After hearing that, I was wondering where they were going to have me sit.

So I asked them, "What about me, where am I going to be sitting? Am I not going to sit with my husband?"

They all responded in unison, "The head table is for the family." Then they repeated, "It's for the family! The children."

To that, I exclaimed, "What am I, chopped liver?"

One by one, the sisters said, "Hum! Hum!" And they looked at each other, puzzled, and I left the room.

A peculiar situation. How should a "daughter" react when she finds there is no seat for her at the table? Is there a book that deals with a situation such as this? I don't think so. What did I do, dear reader? I just have to wing it. How selfish of me to want to sit with my own husband at the head table. How unkind of me to want to deprive "the family," "the children," their rightful place at the head table? After all, I'm only an outsider. I was very hurt and disappointed. A Christian home, a Christian family not honoring and respecting our marriage, they were separating a husband from his wife.

I am human, I felt hurt, ignored and rejected. I felt unwelcomed, unwanted, and discarded. My husband was in the room, and he said nothing. He was too afraid to rock the boat. I do not blame Mom for what the sisters had done, but I still think she should have intervened. She always ran the show anyway, and what was different about that time? What I wanted to know is whose idea it was, and who thought of it first? I really didn't want to spoil this special occasion for Mom and Dad; therefore, I kept my mouth shut.

The next day, the limousine service came to transport us to the church. I was silent the whole way there. The church was beautifully decorated. Mom and Dad renewed their vows and were ready to continue their everlasting love for each other. It really was a nice ceremony, and Mom and Dad were so happy, still in love after fifty years. Immediately after, the photographer gathered the bride and groom, and all the family members for pictures. No one even missed me until it was all over, because after all, I was not family.

The main family members were included in the family pictures. One of the sisters saw me sitting in the pews and asked me where I was. "We were looking for you to be in the picture." I said right here, I never moved. They didn't have to look very far. I was right there in plain view—the same spot where I was during the ceremony. My husband didn't say anything; that's just the way he is, he likes to keep peace. I wondered, would he fight for me if danger was lurking?

The story gets better. They moved over to the dining hall for the reception, so I waited behind until everyone was in their seats. When I went into the dining hall, I saw the three sisters were scattered at different tables with other family members and guests. They had rearranged the seating to include Mom and Dad, Mom's brother and his wife, Mom's mother, Grandma Daisy, and my husband. They had rather I not sit at the head table, they preferred to remove themselves instead of adding an extra chair at the head table for me, and there was plenty of room. Was it my presence among "the family", "the children", that was disturbing to them? Or was that their excuse? Was that my punishment for having a husband, since none of them were married at that time? What message were they trying to convey? Maybe they were trying to say that "just because you're married to our brother does not make you our family."

I got the message loud and clear. Once again, that was beyond hurtful. It was also very insulting. I went to the bathroom and threw water on my face. I did not want to give them the satisfaction of knowing they hurt me so deeply. My mother used to tell me to never let them see you sweat.

I went back to the dining hall, took a seat way in the back like nothing had happened. I didn't eat any of their delicacies because the knot in my stomach was too big to allow any food to go down. I had lost my appetite. There was a time when "the old me" would have taken a cab, go to the house, pack my bags, go to the airport, change my tickets and go back to California, alone. Remember, God is changing me, He is making diamonds out of me.

Mom and Dad were very happy and thankful for our wedding gift to them. I stayed to myself during the rest of our time there. A couple of days after the wedding, the four of us traveled together to California, where my husband and I reside. I know as Christians, we are not to hold a grudge because the word of God says to forgive our brother their trespasses just as he has forgiven us ours. I have forgiven them, but the thought of their very hurtful treatment towards me and their unChrist-like behavior keeps coming back to haunt me. Even though I know the Bible says that "love is patient, love is kind, and love does not keep a record of the wrongs" that have been done to you, I still struggle with letting it go.

It has been a long time since it happened. I still feel the pain, but God is bringing me one step closer to a breakthrough each day. Approximately ten years or so after that fiasco, during a conversation with one of my sisters-in-law, we were talking and reminiscing about Mom and Dad's wedding, and I asked her what that was about? Why wouldn't they set a place at the table for me?

She responded, "We didn't know if you were going to be another Amanda" (the ex-wife that everyone disliked). *Hate* is a harsh word, but for the lack of a better word, she was not one of their favorite people. I think, considering the way they felt about Amanda, what my sister-in-law said was like adding insult to injury. You all have been forgiven. God has forgiven all of us. After being burned, please do not judge me if I stay away from the fire.

CHAPTER 26

My Three Reasons for Living;
A message of love, a message of truth and happiness; a miracle coming true. Total assurance that life is worth living

But from everlasting to everlasting the Lord's love is with those who fear him, and his righteousness with their children's children.
—Psalms 103:17

The grandchildren. While dating his wife-to-be, DD had an indiscretion in that after being pursued relentlessly by another woman, in his weakness, had a short affair that resulted in them having a child together. I was told that "it" happened only once, but that's all it took. Due to his sickle cell anemia, DD was so sick all the times. We all thought the chances of my having grandchildren were slim. The young lady became pregnant, and nine months later (while I was still on my knees praying for grandchildren), our first little bundle of joy arrived. His name is Omar Leonardo Pierre. The birth of my first grandchild was one of the most joyful days of my life.

I remember being in the delivery room during the birth. I came straight from work. There was a lot of traffic, I nearly missed the whole event. When I finally arrived, Brenda was being prepped for delivery. I remember feeling such a sense of elation watching our first grandchild being brought into the world. I waited for this moment for a long time, and it's finally arrived. Charles and I were blessed with a grandson, and our cup was overflowing with joy, partly because—prior to the birth of Omar and due to how Brenda's family felt about her giving birth to another child, since she already had five older children—Brenda agreed to allow Charles and I to raise him.

After the baby was all cleaned up and wrapped tightly in his tiny blanket, the nurse asked Brenda if she wanted to hold him at least one time or give him to me. Without hesitation, she responded, "Give him to his grandmother." I was grinning from ear to ear! I suggested that she and I should probably share holding Omar the first time. So I sat by her side in the bed, and we both held our baby. It felt so good to me. Brenda looked at him. The light in her eyes was blinding—she was full of joy.

With a sad voice and tears in her eyes, she murmured, "I want to keep my baby."

I said, "What?" And I knew that I didn't have a prayer.

She cleared her throat and said, "He is so beautiful! I want to keep my baby."

Needless to say, not everyone was happy about the birth of Omar. Because as you remember DD's fiancée, Ieasha, thought that she was the only one in his life, until she found out that DD had gotten another woman pregnant. Of course, she was devastated, even though DD told her it was a one-night stand. Though true, DD's explanation did not diminish the hurt and betrayal that Ieasha felt about the whole situation.

It was one year later that Ieasha would give birth to her and DD's first child, and of course, our second grandchild, Darien Drew Pierre, was born exactly one year to the very day that his brother, Omar, was born. I was also blessed to have been in the delivery room to witness Darien's birth. I was leaping for joy on that special day—that was another one of the best days of my life. These are moments that I will never forget.

Later, DD married his fiancée, Ieasha, and six years after the birth of their son, they had a daughter and they named her Demari D'vyne Pierre. While I was yet on my knees praying for a granddaughter, God blessed me with the desire of my heart. Demari was the most beautiful baby I had ever laid my eyes on. I've kissed every finger and every toe on that baby. She has such a beautiful smile. If you know me, you'd know that I was on cloud nine. I love babies, especially girls. When I was pregnant with DD, I was hoping for a girl, but God chose to bless me with a boy instead, and I praise him for every one of his blessings. I might not have said it before; my son was the perfect child. D.D. was the best thing that ever happened to me.

I got so much pleasure watching my little girl with cute little dresses on, with her hair in ponytails with pretty barrettes and bows. It was also such a beautiful sight to see when I took all three of them to the playground in the park, watching Demari running after her big brothers. They both love her very much, and I just love them. And now I have my very own granddaughter to play with, babysit for, and do things with. I thank God for my three special blessings. My heart overflows with joy and gratitude to God who has blessed us with so many blessings.

DD and Ieasha had their share of problems. They fought, they had breakups, and they moved many times, but they always made it through. They had a different kind of love. When you thought it was over between them, they patched it up and were back together again. Ieasha loved DD since she was very young. He was twelve years older. He was sickly, did not have much money, but that didn't change their love for each other. I was delighted when Ieasha gave my son a son, God had blessed me with another grandson. I always wanted to embrace Ieasha as the daughter I never had. My son loved her and she him, and I loved her best. Despite my efforts toward a better relationship with her, she did not reciprocate my feelings. When her first son, Darien, was born, I thought that was going to be the bridge that was going to draw us closer. Instead, she accused me of loving Omar more than Darien. That is a lie straight from the pit of hell, I love all my three grandchildren equally. I love Ieasha very much. One thing she did for me that I considered precious; she probably doesn't have a clue how much it meant to me. Once, on her way back from a trip, she bought a "few sticks of honey" and sent them to me when the children came to spend a weekend. To me that was priceless! To me that meant she was thinking about me! The size of the gift is not what makes it precious, it is the thought behind it. We are not besties, but I'm praying that one day soon we will have a closer relationship.

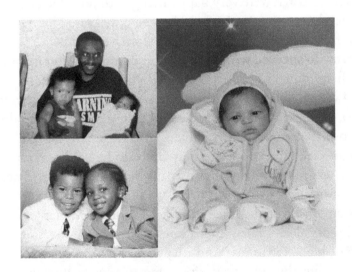

I am grateful for the part she played in my son's life and giving him two beautiful children. I'm not sure what kept them together, but their commitment to each other was evident, and they both loved the children. They finally got a divorce, but even after they were divorced, they got back together as if nothing had happened.

DD's love for his children shine through like in a bright light. I give him the father of the year award because he truly deserves it.

While his ex-wife was working out of town, DD was taking care of the children even though he was really sick. In the year 2009, after undergoing a CT scan, the doctors determined that DD had blood clot on his brain and had to undergo two brain surgeries. The doctors didn't think he was going to survive. We had teams of prayer warriors, on their knees constantly praying for him, and he made it through. His ex-wife was always in his life. She picked him up from the hospital when he was released. He was ready again to resume his responsibilities as a father. When we suggested that it was too much for him to handle, we offered to take over the care of the children, but he refused; he wanted to do it himself. We helped as much as we could by picking up the children from school, doing the grocery shopping, and other chores; but for the most part, he did it himself.

The children were very happy living with him. He helped them with their homework, made sure they were well cared for. He was the best of fathers, loving his children until the very end.

How to succeed with God as your compass. After the purchase of my first home in 1977, I found myself moving almost every three years. I always believed that it was, from the investment standpoint, wise to move up as much as possible. In my opinion, lateral moves can prove to be futile. Each home that I move into more likely was a step up except for properties purchased to be used as rentals. That practice was followed continuously throughout the years. I acquired many homes in the past thirty years and have prospered through my real estate investments. I also dabbled in the stock market at times. My advisors always knew that I am a conservative investor and did not want high-risk funds. And they would make suggestion toward certain acquisition but never force me to plunge into investments that appeared to be a sure thing to find out later that they weren't.

Around 1997–1998, through my local bank, I worked with an advisor that did not know me well. He insisted on a particular high-yield fund that I was cautious about. The fund did very well as he predicted, and my money multiplied tremendously. Being busy with other things, other investments, and in addition I was working with a new advisor, to be honest, I failed to keep track of how he was managing my stock portfolio.

At the end of 1998, we were in the process of moving once again to a new home that we loved very much. It was everything we wished for and thought this is it we'd probably live there forever. We picked up that property for a very good price. God put us at the right place at the right time. I'd allowed my RE license to expire when I was really sick and didn't think I was going back to selling real estate. I hired a very knowledgeable realtor friend who was keeping her eyes open for me. She called me immediately when this property became available. It was a beautiful two-story home with five bedrooms, four baths, 4,770 square feet on three quarter of an acre land. We hired a decorator, purchased extra pieces of furniture, and then we were done with the furnishing and decorating our dream home.

Our home was located on the north side of Moreno Valley. It was about one year new, the backyard was bare, with no fencing around it. Not long after moving, we put new grass, planted an orchard, a vegetable garden, flower beds and trees and put a wrought iron fence around our property. It was beautiful inside and out, and it was in a very nice neighborhood.

In the year 1999 to 2000, the stock market had plunged, or should I say our high-yield funds were doing poorly. I was losing money and didn't know it because when the statements came, I failed to open them. I failed to keep an eye on my investments, and the advisor failed to perform. He did not communicate that fact to me. I don't recall how I found out, but when I did, I went to the bank. I found out that the advisor had left the state of California. The bank manager told me that he no longer worked there, and that someone else had taken over his clients and here is how to contact him.

As they say, easy come easy go. Most of the gain on my investment was gone. The market was plunging and about to get into my original investment. I started to panic. I told them to make it stop, and they told me that on some of the investment, the loss would be greater if they switch funds. I let them know that I wasn't happy with it from the very beginning. I put all the blame on them, and I want my money back. Not only that I wanted my original funds, but I also wanted the gain that was accumulated from the beginning of the relationship with them.

In no uncertain terms the manager advised that it didn't work that way she said. When you go into those types of investments, there are gains but at the same time there are losses. The risks can be low or they can be high, and I understood that. The advisor was pushy, and I was somewhat at their mercy. I asked to speak to his manager whose office was in San Diego, so she gave me a name and a phone number.

I was on a mission trying to recover what was mine. I had been with that institution for over ten years; my home mortgage was with them, safe deposit box, savings and checking accounts with them, line of credit, almost everything was with them. They needed to be held accountable for the mistakes of their employee. They'd also told me that the advisor was in a way an independent contractor, and that he would be responsible for his own mistakes. Why am I just now finding that out?

At the end of the day, however, I had to hire an attorney, the best in the valley area. I also hired a mediator, and they worked together on my behalf. All along I knew that the attorney and the mediator were going to do their very best because they weren't fighting alone, God—who is on my side—was fighting with them on my behalf. There was a lot of work to be done, copies of files, bank statements to be opened and going through, attend depositions with the bank's attorneys and mine. I had to make trips back and forth to Los Angeles, but I was determined to get the victory in this matter.

Another piece of evidence that was in my favor was that I had six to twelve months of statements that were unopened. I'd kept them, but they were not open. How is that evidence you might ask? If I had opened and read them, it would have meant that I knew that the funds were plunging. After almost one year of battle, we won! After paying the attorney and mediator fees, the bank was required to pay their part in the matter and settled with me for seventy-five thousand dollars. Of course, that amount was not enough for all the stress I had to endure because I had lost much, much more, than double that amount; but it is, suffice to say, my strength in pursuing it prevailed, and my trust in the Lord carried me through it all. I didn't allow the bank to treat me like I didn't matter. God is my vindicator, I am a victor not a victim.

I want radical faith. I want to live my life in such a way that I depend on the Holy Spirit for everything. Always desperate for Him; in the big things and the little things. I want revolutionary faith!

My life doesn't make sense to a number of people. For instance, my lack of knowledge, I am not a native American, I'm a foreigner. I have been asked over and over: how have you been able to accomplish so much? It seems impossible! My answer, I live in dependency of the Holy Spirit who guides my every step. I couldn't have accomplished any of it by my own power. I must admit, there are times when I feel so strong that I could pick up and carry a big truck, but, I also know that it is not 'I' doing it. It is only the power of the Holy Spirit working in and through me. I want radical faith!

He is fighting my battles. When I made God my only source, my go-to person, he is my all in all, he has fought every battle I have had to face. When I acknowledge him as supreme authority, knowing that everything that happens in my life had to go through him first, that's when I became me, a victor, the woman that I am today. Romans 8:31 says, "What, then, shall we say in response to these things? If God is for us, who can be against us?"

The Lord has brought me from a mighty long way. He's brought me from a life of nothingness without Christ to one of plenty, overflowing with his love and faithfulness, a life of truth and forgiveness. Now, in shortage: I only see supplies; in lack: I see more than enough, abundance; in times of trial: I see deliverance. With Christ in my life, I have learned to praise God in the good times and in times of testing. The flood gates of heaven have been opened, God's face is shining on me. He has given me beauty for ashes.

The bank sent me a check and made me sign a confidential affidavit concerning the matter. I deposited their check into my account and turned around and sent them a check for the total amount. I asked them to apply it toward the principal balance of my mortgage. I always win when the Lord fights my battles.

Moving on up. We enjoyed our gorgeous home on Chateau Court for seven years, from 1998 to 2005. We had purchased and sold many homes through the years. If memory serves me right, between twelve to fifteen properties, and there was a two-and-a-half acre parcel of vacant land. As they say in real estate, location, location, location. I always kept my eyes open for properties in Riverside; in fact, I lusted after a particular area in Riverside called White Gate. My realtor friend had shown me several exquisite properties in the area in the past. I was not sure if we were ready for a mortgage of that magnitude, but at the moment it felt like it was perfect timing.

We listed our residence, the house in Los Angeles, the parcel of land for sale, plus there was plenty of money from other cash investments to be used as down payment in order to bring the mortgage amount down. We looked at many properties, and none of them was "the one." Then one Saturday morning, I started going from one open house to the other, and I turned on one street and I saw an open house sign with one of my realtor friends' name on it.

I followed the sign and went inside the house, but that property didn't do it for me either. Lisa told me about another one of her listings and gave me a flyer and suggested that I should do a drive by. So I share the information with my friend and realtor, Dwight Pledger, who was the listing agent of my property on Chateau Court. After driving by the property, I let Lisa know that I liked it. Just looking from the outside, I was sure that I wanted to see the inside. She showed me the house, and it was love at first sight. I made an appointment to come back later with my husband.

Charles loved it as much as I did. Then he asked, "Can we afford this!?" I told him that with my investments and the proceeds from the sale of other properties and the land, we'd be able to pull it off. So we made an offer, which was not accepted. We had to go back and forth with the bargaining for a comfortable and acceptable price.

When we finally got our offer accepted, we opened escrow to close concurrently with the escrow on the other properties. We had a couple of setbacks at first, but at the end, everything went according to plan. Our Escrow closed on July 29, 2005. We were now the proud owners of the property on Wyndham Hill Drive, in the White Gate area of Riverside, California, one of the most prestigious areas in Riverside. I say that not to impress anyone but to impress upon everyone that no matter how humble your beginnings are, when you put your trust in God and let him lead you, there is no limit to how much he can bless you.

CHAPTER 27

What Is True Love?;
Butterflies in the stomach, weak in the knees, skipping heartbeats, and even sweaty palms

Love is patient, love is kind. It does not envy, it does not boast, it is not proud. It is not rude, it is not self-seeking, it is not easily angered, it keeps no record of wrongs. Love never fails.
—1 Corinthians 13:4–6, 8

Let's start with what it's not. It is not physical. It is not big muscle. It is not money or the big house on the hill. It is not goose bumps when the two bodies touch. It is certainly not being horny and you tear each other's clothes off. It is not career. it is not even the children. It can be all of that combined, but not just one. True love is very hard to find. Sometimes you might have it and don't even know it, and you keep looking.

True love is long lasting. It is learned. It is compromises. It is when you have a bad hair day and he still thinks you're beautiful. It is when he kisses you in the morning and you haven't even brushed your teeth yet. True love is when you grow old together. It is when one of you passes gas in bed underneath the sheets and you have to fan the sheets to let the bad air out and you both laugh about it.

It is when you're both old and grey, one or both is sick, and you gladly take care of the other. It is when his belly gets so big your arms can't go around him anymore. It is when she loses her perfect ten figure and she is not so easy on the eye anymore. It is when one loses a limb to cancer, or because of prostate he can't perform any longer, or hot flashes, breast cancer, etc.

Have you seen the movie *The Notebook* with Ryan Gosling and Rachel McAdams? They gave up everything for one another—that's true love. Toward the end, he just wanted to stay near her, and how they died together. I love that movie. That is what true love is. Have you found yours? If you haven't yet, try washing your lover's feet. That's when I realized that I must love this man because I hate feet. I think they're ugly. Do you know about S-H-M-I-L-Y? It stands for "See How Much I Love You." Google it. I have found mine.

If my one true love had come into my life any sooner, he wouldn't have had a chance. I wouldn't have recognized it because I was not ready. God has perfect timing. I'd tried to send my true love away many times, but he was persistent, he refused to go. I thought he was too fat, he had too much baggage, he didn't have enough status. I thought of him as a glutton, a cheater. I didn't know it, but he had me when he took me to church with him for the first time, when he put all he had in the offering plate.

I thought maybe I would end up supporting him because of the spousal support and child support he had to pay and then when the attorney said that the judge might have to combine our two incomes to calculate the amount of alimony, he definitely lost me there; I said, "Over my dead body." But, as time went along, God began to open my eyes and allowed me to see his heart. I saw the possibilities, and loving him was easier. I had been hurt so many times in the past, and I wasn't going to take a chance of that happening again, but I did take that chance and I don't regret it.

Charles was not lazy, which was a plus, and he was very open, transparent, and vulnerable before me. This helped me to determine if he was the one for me. He had nothing to hide. Without a word, he was saying, "This is who I am. I don't have much to offer you, but

I am workable." Every day that passed brought us closer. I liked him more but was still cautious. For instance, on our wedding day, one of my attendants, Deloris, told me "You don't look like a bride. You have all the trimmings, but you are not glowing." I know I was not ready to get married to him yet, but I did, so we wouldn't be living in sin.

Again, that was God's timing, and he was telling me, through my mother in-law, "to let go and let God." And when I finally let go, I let down my resistance, God moved in and began to bless us as a couple. My money was God's money, which in turn became our money. I was still a little reluctant and had him to sign a prenup. Self-preservation, I realized later, wasn't necessary, and that Charles was not after my money. God had softened my heart and released me from the bondage within.

God showed me through my husband, how to trust again, how to share, how to live life to the fullest. I used to be cautious about overspending. We do not waste, we are good managers of what God has entrusted to us. We live in comfort, and I leave all worries at his feet. Most of all, we tried to remember that God is our provider, he is our source. It is so liberating when you don't have to be in control all the time.

My husband doesn't force his way in. He does not rush in and try to take over. He is very smart in his approach toward me. He allows me the freedom that I need to function at my capacity. I don't feel crowded or inhibited. This is true love, the Christlike love that is boundless, and you can be confident that it's always going to be there. God has been ordering my steps along the road that led me straight to him.

Bless The Broken Road
by Rascal Flatts

I set out on a narrow way many years ago
Hoping I would find true love along the broken
road
As I look back on my 'fast' life, "My Broken Road"
Full of pot holes, dips and cracks,
With its dark alleys and sharp corners,
With many twists and many turns;
I envision Charles (my husband) waiting patiently,
On the other side of "My Broken Road".
My spiritual journey, though it began early,
Moved in slow motion. With bumps and curves,
Climbing high mountains and falling in low valleys;
With so many delays, so many set-backs;
Lasting what seems an eternity.
I envision Jesus, My Lord, my true love;
Waiting patiently, at the end of "My Broken Road".
I truly believe
That God blessed the Broken Road
That led me straight to you.
My vision ended with Jesus lovingly hovering
Over Charles and me in a kiss and tender embrace.

241

Our paths in life have been chosen for us. Psalms 37:23 says, "The steps of a good man are ordered by the Lord, and he delights in his way." When we stray and lose our way, God comes and redirects it to lead us to our final destination. Mine has led me straight to true love, to you Lord.

Mother Kimble. Jeanne Kimble is one of my true love stories. I started working for Amtrak as a reservation sales agent in July 1995. My duties were to book passage for people who preferred to travel by train instead of flying. I loved my job very much, and I excelled at it. There were fifty new employees in my new hire class. On our second day of training, the class was divided into two groups, of twenty-five each. One group worked the day shift and the other the night shift. I think they drew names out of a hat to determine who went where. I prayed to be in the day class, and my prayer was answered.

I met a friend, whose name is Joanne, and she became my sister. We worked side by side for many years. Jo and I, we developed a great friendship. We took our breaks and lunch together lots of times. On a slow day, we were chatting, and she said to me, "I recognize something familiar about you, but I can't put my finger on it."

I said, "What is it?"

"I think you remind me of Jeanne Kimble," she replied.

I said, "Who is Jeanne Kimble?"

She said, "You are just like my mother, the way you talk and conduct yourself, your demeanor, your mannerism and everything you do, remind me of her. She is bossy, and so are you. She's prim and proper, so are you. She is like a princess, and so are you. Need I say any more? I think you two should meet."

I said, "Okay."

"She has a birthday coming up, do you want to come to her party?"

She gave me information regarding the party, and my husband and I went to meet a new friend. (My motto is "A stranger is a friend I have not met.") When we met, it was magical. She was no stranger—she was like my mama. It was love at first sight. She was chic, she was beautiful, she was coquette, she was like my twin, only twenty years older. Joanne was right, I realized it later, and others in her family have told me so too. We are just alike. I call her mom, she calls me princess, and she treats me like a daughter.

Almost right away, Mom and I started a friendship that is out of this world. Sometimes, it feels like our spirits, our thoughts, sort of merged together; we're thinking the same thoughts, we have the same likes and dislikes, same ailments, doctors prescribed the same medications. We are both vain about our looks, very particular about what we eat, and the list goes on and on. I have told her on numerous occasions that if I were given the opportunity to choose my mother, she would be my choice. I love my biological mother very much but I love Jeanne Kimble as well.

God chooses our parents, and I wouldn't have it any other way. But as I get to know Jeanne Kimble better, each day, I realize that I truly meant it when I said I would choose her for my mother. Her personality and my mother's are similar. They are both bossy, dictatorial, firm, practical. They are both beautiful and elegant. I think that the reason that I would have picked Jeanne is because I have found my mother in her. I have my cake and I can eat it too.

The difference between my two mothers is that of culture. When I was in search for a mother figure, I have found a mother and a friend. We are as tight as thieves. I can discuss anything with her. We talk on the phone and we forget that time was passing by. She gives me good counsel, she shows that she cares in so many ways, and I feel at home with her. What we have is a love affair that will last forever.

You might think that my sister Joanne has lost me when I'd found Mom, but no, we are great friends. Joanne and I are even better friends now that she has unselfishly allowed me to share our mom. We love each other very much. We laugh together, we cry together, we fast, and we pray together. There are times when we pray so hard you'd think that we're knocking on heaven's door. When she hurts, I ache for her. When she is sad, I console her, and she does the same for me. We would both drop everything to run to the other's side if there was a need for it.

CHAPTER 28

Have You Considered My Servant Marie?; The biggest challenge anyone will face is having a disease that can only be cured by a miracle

In my distress I called to the Lord; I cried to my God for help. From his temple he heard my voice; my cry came before him, into his ears.

—Psalm 18:6

All that I am, all that I have belong to you, Lord. After having lost seventy-five pounds in the early 1970s, I realized that if I worked very hard at it, I could keep the weight off. And since I liked my new looks, I decided that I could improve on it and look even better.

From that moment on, I became a health fanatic. Diet and exercise became my new way of life. I made a plan to walk and or run every day, in addition to sit ups, exercising with weights, and eating smaller meals. I was not much into desserts, but I made fruits my dessert of choice. Don't get me wrong, I was never deprived; from time to time, I would reward myself with chocolate, perhaps cookies and ice cream.

Meal planning is the most important part of being and staying healthy. I always make sure that I know what goes into my body. I manage every morsel of food that goes in my mouth. I don't eat between meals, and I keep out the "trashy foods" like fried, sugary and starchy, canned foods, and others. I stopped eating red meats in the early 1980s. My protein intake consists of fish, mostly salmon, tofu, chicken, nuts, beans. I drink nonfat Lactaid. I only eat when I am hungry. I prefer to prepare my meals ahead of time; that way, when I get hungry, it's already there waiting for me. Before too long, I had carved a healthy, perfect body that my friends were envious of. I say this humbly, many of my friends solicited my help in getting their own bodies in better shape.

By the time Charles came into my life, I looked like a Barbie doll. Do you remember back in chapter 21, when I told you about how I helped Charles lose over thirty pounds? Well, except for one minor adjustment: Charles wants to have a small steak once in a while. He has learned and adhere to this new way of life. Charles has kept the weight off. We are both healthier. Charles has since made the decision to give up red meat altogether. Our life together has flourished, our love for each other has grown to new and higher heights.

I still give him foot baths because Charles's love language is acts of kindness, and mine is quality time of which he gives plenty. While giving him a foot bath, fulfilling an act of kindness toward him, my husband and I spend quality time together; thereby killing two birds with one stone. He gets his and I get mine. Once a month I give him a foot bath and trim his toenails. He really loves that. I remember a few times when our friends referred to us as Ken and Barbie. We were so very happy together, and we had so much going for us. Every time I thought that things couldn't get any better, God's blessings were chasing us down and overtaking us. In short, we had our life, health, friends, strength, our cup was filled, full, to the overflow; most of all we had God.

Then one night, at the end of July 2011, I had a disturbing dream, or should I call it a nightmare! I woke up from the dream where I was feeling my left breast and noticed a lump that I had found during the dream. Immediately I got up. My heart was racing. I went to the bathroom to check it out further. I felt a tiny lump under my fingertip. It didn't seem like much, nothing to worry about, you would think. So I went back to bed but was unable to sleep.

As usual, when I can't sleep, I get up and start cleaning the house even though Shannon, our housekeeper, does a fantastic job at keeping our home spotless. I can't help myself, always have to make sure everything looks perfect. It was as if this was the longest night of my life. I kept waiting for daybreak, but it was still dark every time I looked. My heart kept beating fast, my mind racing at the speed of light, thinking about what to do and what's going to happen. I was thinking the worse before I even knew what was really going on. It reminded me of a verse in the book of job, which said, "What I feared has come upon me, what I dreaded has happened to me" (Job 3:25).

Doctor's visit. Finally, after completing many chores, much scrubbing, and polishing, the night gave way to the morning light. My thoughts went directly to God, to my Heavenly Father. That's who I should have been calling on from the very beginning.

I went into my prayer closet, lay on the floor, and I prayed. Lord, what is this? What is going on? You know me, Lord, I get anxious easily. I need you right now. Please help me, give me peace in this situation, and be with me through it. I thank you in advance because I know that you hear me and in your own time and your own way you will answer. I'm not sure of the rest of my prayer, but I must have fallen to sleep.

I awoke to the ring of the telephone, and it was quarter past eight. I was supposed to have been at work by eight o'clock. I rushed and got ready and went to work. I told my coworkers about the dream, and some of them felt the lump and encouraged me to call the doctor. I called my primary care physician's office and told the receptionist that I have an emergency and need to see Dr. Pengson. After all the probing questions, she made me an appointment for that day.

Because Dr. Pengson's office is very busy, a two-thirty appointment can turn out to be a four- to four-thirty appointment. I must be very patient, and patience is not one of my virtues, especially not that day. Just about every ten to fifteen minutes of my two-hour wait, I would go to the desk to inquire when I was going to be seen, when it was going to be my turn. I already knew that they always double and triple book their patients, and I couldn't help myself.

My thoughts were drifting on to a lot of other trials that we encounter in this life. A young woman sat her little girl next to me on the sofa, while she went to check her daughter in. That little girl, probably was no more than five years old, just crawled in on the sofa. She was crying very loud, and incessantly. Her face drooped, and from the way the mother communicated with her, she couldn't talk. I tried to comfort her. I made funny faces to get a smile out of her to no avail. I began to wonder, what if they came for me before her mom was done checking in? All at once, I heard a voice saying, "Marie Dukes," and I said, "Oh, that's me," and at that same moment, the young mother came. She said, "Thank you for watching my baby. I saw you keeping her company for me. She is very sick, and she cannot talk yet."

"It's my pleasure," I said, and followed the voice calling for me.

This little girl is just starting her life and she is suffering already. I have lived my life. My problems are nothing compared to what she has to endure, probably for the rest of her life. I am grateful to have been there to offer a little comfort to her. I pray that she gets healed and despite her illness she can live a meaningful and prosperous life.

Dr. Pengson was a very bubbly and a kindhearted man, always smiling and telling jokes to break the ice. He once told me about his family. There are many doctors in his family. When they take their vacations, they go on mission trips, carrying medicine and treating poor people who cannot afford medical care. I think that is so kind of them. He treats his patients like friends.

To make a long story short, I told Dr. Pengson about my dream and showed him where the lump was located. He touched it and did a breast exam, and to my relief and his, it was not the kind of lump to worry about because it was more on the surface.

"To be on the safe side," he said, "let's send you for a mammogram, and I am going to give you a referral to a colleague of mine, Dr. Asseem Attar who is a surgeon. He specializes in the field of cancer."

I took the earliest appointment to see Dr. Attar, which was after the results of my mammogram were received. The mammogram was negative, no lump, yeah! That made me very happy, but I still had doubts. I wondered why would Dr. Pengson have referred me to Dr. Attar if everything was alright?

It was on August 31, 2011 when I went on my first visit to see Dr. Attar. He was a man of few words, mild-mannered and quiet, but at the same time, pleasant. I was comfortable with him. He made me think of my father. Father was a very gentle soul who I don't think he could hurt a fly. I didn't know my father very well, but the few times that I visited in the country, he appeared to be kind. He never raised his voice, he smiled a lot, and there was such a mystique about him. I observed the same thing with Dr. Attar.

Dr. Attar also did a breast exam, and he looked at the films of the mammogram. He said, "Your mammogram looks good. There's no sign of a lump. What you perceived as a lump was only skin deep, more on the surface, nothing to be concerned about." He indicated that he wanted to monitor me, and that I should make an appointment to see him every six months. We will continue to do yearly mammograms, and do lab work every six months to check my CA 15-3, which is short for a cancer screening.

I had been seeing Dr. Attar for almost two years and all was well. Knowing that I was under his care made me feel better with no worries. I had never learned to do my own breast exams. My doctors had instructed me and shown me how to do it. Doing the exam for me was a simple thing made hard because I really didn't know what to feel for. It may be that in reality, it was my way of dealing with the fear of what I might find. Since my doctor did it every year during my annual physical, that was good enough for me. I also knew that God would keep and protect me, which he has done.

He has been with me and protecting me. My annual mammogram was done on March 2, 2013. I had a bad experience with the technician who performed it. She was stern and cold as ice. She squeezed my breasts under the equipment so hard that tears ran down my face. I pleaded with her, "Please, my breasts hurt, can you do it a little gentler?" She said, "The way you feel has nothing to do with me. I'm only doing a job. You shouldn't have come if you were not up to it." So I kept my mouth shut and bore the pain.

On March 6th, 2013, I went for a walk really early in the morning, as I normally did. I walked every day, except for Sundays, five to seven miles that was the norm. When I came home, my husband, Charles, had already left for work. I went on about my regular routine before going to work at the real estate office, to perform my duties as a transaction coordinator for my very successful boss and friend, Misty. Time was on my side, so I could still go to my favorite organic store and pick up some goodies to share with my coworkers. Since I already knew what I wanted, it didn't take long at all. As I was headed to the office, my cell phone rang. I wasn't going to answer it, but I looked just to find out who it was. It was Dr. Attar. Quickly I pulled over to answer the phone.

He said, "Mrs. Dukes, are you at home?"

I replied, "No, I am on my way to work. Is something wrong?"

He said, "I received your mammogram results, and I wanted to discuss them with you."

I said, "Okay."

He said, "But I prefer to talk to you when you are at home. I would like to call you later when your husband gets home."

I knew right then and there that the news was not good. I replied, "Dr. Attar, whatever it is, you can tell me now. I'm turning the engine off."

He asked, "Are you sure?"

I said, "Yes, Doctor, I am sure."

"Mrs. Dukes, the mammogram revealed a tumor. We need you to come to my office so we can discuss it."

When he said the word *tumor*, the first thing that came to my mind was, cancer? My reply to him was, "When?" I also continued with, "Please, let's do this quickly. If I have cancer, I don't want it to stay in my body one moment longer than it has to." I took the very next available appointment that was on his schedule.

The date was March 13, 2013. The past week went so slow it seemed as if a whole month had gone by. The nights were long and restless. I had no appetite, and everything I ate tasted like cardboard. My prayer time was like agony. I did not want to be awake. I just wanted to crawl onto Jesus's lap and fall asleep.

Finally, my appointment date was here. I was very early to Dr. Attar's office, but he was late coming because he had to do rounds at the hospital before coming to his private practice. I felt so humbled in his presence, as he explained the process of what had to be done. Before he gave me any details, Dr. Attar suggested that I could get a second opinion if I wished to do so. I, of course, turned it down. And I told him to schedule the surgery for the soonest available date. He proceeded to tell me that I needed an ultrasound, MRI, and a biopsy. I was also going to need chemotherapy and radiation treatments.

The ultrasound and MRI both went very well. The nurses, technician, everyone that was involved, treated me with kindness and respect. I am not sure if it had anything to do with me having to report the rudeness of the technician who performed my previous mammogram. The truth be told, I want to thank her for squeezing my breast really hard under the mammography equipment because unknowingly she might have done me a favor. Who knows, if perhaps she hadn't, maybe the tumor would not have been seen.

Soon after the results of the ultrasound and the MRI, I went for the biopsy. It is as if God (and I know it's God) had planned every detail and all the appointments ahead for me, because when I said that I wanted to move fast, there was nothing in my way. Dr. Attar's schedule was wide open. The MRI, the ultrasound, and everything, was like one, two, three.

One morning in the middle of March 2013, I reported to the hospital for the biopsy. As I was waiting for the doctor, not sure what to expect, my mind began to wander. Is it a surgery? How are they going to get a piece of my breast without anesthesia? That's going to be very painful, I thought. But then again, what can be worse than having a baby? I resigned myself to take it like a woman. It is for my own good, and best of all, God promised to be with me when he said, "Be strong and courageous. Do not be afraid or terrified, for the Lord your God goes with you, he will never leave you, nor forsake you" (Deuteronomy 31:6).

I am so thankful that it was a female doctor who was going to perform the biopsy. I thought she could identify with my needs on a totally different level. She smiled as she entered the room and called me by my first name. I liked that.

She said, "Good morning, Marie, I'm Dr. Simone Sutton. I'm going to perform your biopsy."

And I said, "Thank you, Doctor, good morning. Is it going to hurt?"

She answered, "Yes, but it will go fast. Before I do the procedure, I'd like to share my story with you."

I said, "Okay."

She said, "Five years ago, I was diagnosed with stage two cancer in one of my breasts. I was scared to death. One of my physicians told me this. With cancer, sometimes it's a matter of attitude, don't take it laying down, you have to fight, it's in you already, it's not going to politely say, 'I'm sorry I'm in the wrong place let me get out'.

You have to decide you don't want it there and fight for your life, and that's what I did. It's your turn now to fight."

And I said, "Thank you so much for sharing. I am ready, let's get to work."

She said, "I will let you know each time I'm going to insert each needle. There are eight."

I said, "Thank you, but don't tell me, just do what needs to be done, and wake me up when it's over." I closed my eyes and I was transported to a place so peaceful, calm, and totally silent. I knew the place, for I had been there many times before.

Just before I closed my eyes, she said, "Here comes the first one. Oh, I'm sorry, not supposed to tell you."

At that time, I heard a noise like a stapler when you try to fasten stack of paper together then I closed my eyes again, and went back to that peaceful place. When I woke up, I asked her about that noise. She showed me the needles; they looked like tiny pipes. She explained that they have a small knife inside. When she thrust them in, they cut a small piece of flesh and bring it back so they can be biopsied. She repeated the process another eight times.

I did not feel any pain because that place where I often go allows no pain—it's my place of escape. Do you have one? I think you should. You don't know when you're going to need it. Everyone should have one, it's being with Jesus.

Next, we get ready for surgery. The day after the biopsy, I had planned a trip to Los Angeles to visit friends. Before getting on the train, I met this wonderful friend. I call her my angel. Why do I call her my angel? Everything that happened seemed mysterious. We sat next to each other as if we were best friends already. Our conversation was pleasant and somewhat familiar, as if we had it before. We talked about my biopsy the day before, and she told me about having to go through the same procedure five years prior when she had cancer. She was such a comfort to me. Her words encouraged me to stand on my faith and let God fight my battle.

We exchanged information. After my breast surgery, she checked on my progress, and we maintained a friendship for a while. Then she stopped calling. I remember the last time we spoke, she said to me, "Get ready for recovery." I believe that our meeting was not by chance and it was not a coincidence; it was ordained, it was God's providence. I have free passage on all Amtrak train lines, but I chose to pay for passage on a Metrolink line that was going to the same destination. Why would I do that if it wasn't to meet my angel?

CHAPTER 29

Have You Considered My Servant Marie Part 2;
Trusting God makes you say: it is well with my
soul, when the hospital calls to say your child's
heart has stopped. He is on life support!

*To be gracious to him and say, "Spare him from going
down to the pit; I have found a ransom for him."*
—Job 33:24

It is so hard to say good-bye. My surgery was scheduled for April 2, 2013. I reported to an annex building located three blocks away from Riverside Community Hospital for a procedure that would allow the surgeon to know exactly where the tumor was located. First, they put in a marker, which is a small chip in my breast, that will show in any future mammograms to pinpoint the location of the tumor. The chip will remain in my body for the rest of my life. Next, they inserted a long tube-like needle in the same area, which for most people is a very painful experience, but I did not feel any pain. They could not give me any anesthesia at that time. Following the procedure, I had to be driven to the hospital, and I had to hold on to and make sure the needle in my breast stayed in place until I get to the surgery room.

I reported on time for the surgery, which Dr. Attar performed very well. The surgery lasted quite a while, and when I awoke, the first face I saw was that of my son, DD, who was there looking so sad. I had no idea that he was going to be there because he was not feeling well for a few days.

I was in the recovery room practically all day while waiting for a room. I would only be there for one night and hopefully be able to go home the next day. Once I made it to my room, I noticed that there was another woman in my room who just had the same surgery. Her name was Tanya Rodriguez. Tanya seems to be experiencing a lot of pain, while I was not. Tanya became my new friend. I felt bad for her. I wished I could ease her pain since Christ had already bore mine. The doctor had prescribed pain medicine for me, but I never had the need for them because the Lord had taken all my pain away from the very beginning.

One month later, I had to have another surgery to place a portal above my other breast in order for me to receive chemotherapy. I had very small veins. The portal was necessary for them to administer the chemo. Again, I felt no pain. This was the second time this happened. They had to leave the wound open because I had to be driven to that same annex building where I went to for the initial procedure before surgery. Once again, after the procedure, they had to leave that needle in so they could start my first chemo treatment. I was very glad they did it that way because they would not have to poke into that raw spot, even though when I return for future treatments they will have to poke me in that spot.

I want to go to heaven. A tragedy happened at the time when I was recovering from the breast cancer surgery. Two weeks after my surgery, on April 18, 2013, my son called to ask me to pick up the children from school because he wasn't feeling well; he was going to the hospital. This happened often because of the sickle cell anemia. I always picked up the children when he went to the hospital. Most of the time, DD would be hospitalized due to being dehydrated, and after being rehydrated, he would be released within a few hours; but not this time because they decided to keep him. The children's mother picked them up from the house and took them with her. I did not get to talk to him because as usual he stays in the emergency room until he goes home. This time was different.

My plan was to go check on him the next morning. There was nothing unusual about this episode because this happens all the time, so we thought. We later realized that this time was different. I remember getting that phone call from the hospital in the middle of the night and hearing the voice on the other end, saying, "Mrs. Dukes, your son's heart has stopped twice. We revived him, he is on life support; but I think you need to come now." My husband and I got up, readied ourselves really quick, and rushed to the hospital.

When we arrived at the hospital, we found out that he was gone. My child was gone. Even though he was on life support, they were unable to bring him back. We never even got to say goodbye. I felt lost. I felt guilty for not having rushed to his side when he asked me to pick up the children. I was in the hallway outside his room pacing back and forth, crying incessantly and uncontrollably. Charles even tried to comfort me, but I refused to be comforted. In that moment DD's whole life seemed to flash before me—from conception to the very moment in which I was experiencing his death.

Even though I have to deal with the shock of my son's passing, I had to also deal with the reality of battling with cancer. When I initially found out that I had the tumor in my breast, I'd asked the Lord to help me, to give me strength, to be with me through it, and he did. He took my pain away. And now, only two weeks later, my child is gone. He's gone to be with the Lord—he is in heaven. I remember saying, "Lord, I know you're not going to leave me now. I can't deal with all this alone. I need you to be in it with me. I am weak and afraid to stand. Please carry me." When I am afraid and I feel too weak to stand on my own, I know that I can fall on Jesus. He catches me and he carries me.

His eye is on the sparrow. God did carry me. He wiped my tears. After that sobbing in the hospital, all tears were gone. My strength was multiplied. I had a lot on my plate. I could not waste another moment. I had funeral arrangements to make, phone calls, deal with my recovery. I wanted to donate my beautiful long hair to the Lock of Love to be used to make wigs for children with cancer (I needed to get the haircut.), get ready for chemotherapy (to start in one week), and radiation (to start after the last chemo session). I wouldn't accept much help because I want to handle it myself. One of my sisters-in-law came from Georgia to lend a hand. She wanted to take care of me during my recovery. That was so sweet of her, I'm forever indebted to her.

One of the first things I did after DD's passing was to contact my church with the sad news about my son and to make arrangements for his home coming celebration. The church chaplain, Dave Cochrane, came to the hospital first to pray with us and comfort us; then camepastor Montia Seltzler—who is the senior pastor at Magnolia Church in Riverside, California—was very supportive and was a source of comfort and encouragement in our time of bereavement.

After all arrangements were made, the children and their mothers, and everything was ready, we had the memorial service on May 3, 2013, at Magnolia Church, which was followed by a wonderful reception, prepared by the church staff and the friends from my Sunday school class. The memorial services were held at the loft and the reception in the Magnolia room. I thought it would be a small gathering, but to my surprise, in addition to family and friends, the room was filled with friends who had invited their friends. I was grateful for the many that came and felt blessed to know that my son, Ducarmel Didier Pierre (Drew to his friends) was so loved.

After so many hugs, I experienced a tremendous amount of love and encouragement from everyone and many people whom I had not even known. I felt a peace like no other peace, a peace that passed all understanding. It was as if the love I experienced was coming from DD himself. In short, I felt energized. The banqueting tables were set, many beautiful dishes were prepared, diverse types of desserts filled the countertop for everyone to enjoy until they were full, and the hugs and kisses continued until I was ready to go home. I think that this kind of fellowship was a little taste of what heaven is going to be like.

It was a beautiful send-off for my son. He was already with Jesus, my loving, kind-hearted, and courageous son was gone. Good-bye, my love, until we meet at Jesus's feet.

After the reception, our three grandchildren and a few out-of-town guests, Laura, Tyrone and other close friends, came to the house and fellowshipped with us for a short while. Speaking of best friends, I met a friend on the phone, whose name is Betty Sams. She is the sister of a very good friend of mine named Charlene. Betty lived in Louisiana. I never had the pleasure of meeting her in person, but we had a lot in common, and we spoke on the phone all the time. In addition to everything else, we both loved the Lord. God is the only introduction we need when making friends with other members of his family. Distance cannot hinder our love for one another. We couldn't wait for the day when we would meet in person. Our friendship grew quickly. It didn't take very long for us to become besties. Our relationship here on earth was cut short. Betty fought a painful battle with cancer, and in December 2009, she died before we had a chance to meet face-to-face. Her memory will live in my heart. I can't wait to see her in heaven.

Our friends did not stay very long. They didn't want to get me too tired because they knew that I had another battle ahead of me.

When everyone had gone home, I too rested. I didn't need to go to my secret place at this time—it came to me. I rested in the arms of Jesus. I felt God's presence surrounding me. I only rested a little while, because there is more to come. The battle is won, but the war was still going on. With the Lord on my side, I am well ready for a fight; I am a victor not a victim. When I surrendered my life to Christ, I was dead to sin and resurrected to live for righteousness. On the cross at Golgotha, when Jesus said: "it is finished", I believe that he accomplished all that was necessary to secure my pardon. I am set free from the penalty of sin. My debt has been cancelled, stamp 'paid in full'. He paid it all so I owe all to him. The crimson stain that was left by sin has been washed, white as snow.

Jesus died and was buried but he didn't stay in the grave. Friday was a very dark day, no worries, Sunday is coming. Jesus defeated Satan, he was resurrected. God placed all things under his feet. All power and authority in heaven and on earth has been given to him; he has given us the same power through his blood. I am saved by grace through faith in Jesus Christ. Faith is the key that unlocks the storehouse of God's blessings; I have received resurrection power to live whole and victorious. "Do not gloat over me, my enemy! Though

I have fallen I will rise. Though I sit in darkness, the Lord will be my light." Micah 7:8

My rest was cut short when I heard little voices in the hallway. Apparently, it was my grandchildren playing together. The voices I heard said, "Is there more stuff for us to do?" The voice was not addressing me, but I believed that it was meant for me to get up and pray, because there was more stuff for me to do. By faith I believe the war with cancer is won, but the battle in the natural was still raging on, so I had to be alert.

I stayed on my knees and thanked God in advance for the victory. Satan's power was broken at the cross, where by Christ's wounds, I am healed and have been made whole.

My son's memorial service was held on Friday the third of May, and it was now the sixth of May, and I am facing some major decision about the cancer. My oncologist said that this type of cancer was very aggressive, so that she had to mix a cocktail of two or three types of chemos, because depending on the type of cancer and what stage it's in will determine the type of chemo to be administer. Also because there would be side effects to the chemo, she put me on steroids to alleviate the nausea and vomiting.

Another side effect for me was that I was hungry all the time. I had to wear a mask, and also to stay away from people with colds. I gained a lot of weight, and I was weak all the time, and even fainted on many occasions. Once I fell and another time my husband caught me right before I hit the ground. My friend Dot bought me a cane to keep me from falling. Many times I would get depressed, I refused to get comforted, I stayed in the bed and couldn't get up. I could barely walk and I was afraid that I would fall. I was home alone when my husband was working.

Before undergoing chemotherapy, I weighed 122 pounds, and within two and a half months, I was at 150 pounds and climbing. My clothes didn't fit, and I would not shop for new clothes. I thought buying new clothes meant that I was accepting the weight and I wouldn't be able to lose it. The weight gain made me even more depressed. With the help of a friend from Charles's job, we have found a place in Oceanside where we could go after chemotherapy, stay a few days to relax, and regroup. That place is now my second secret place, my home away from home.

I needed five chemo sessions, one every three weeks. First, they did lab work before every session. Then they poked me with a needle into the port, which is very painful initially, in order to administer the chemo but the pain subsided after the needle got into the port. This procedure normally takes four hours to complete, until every drop of the chemo goes into your body. I didn't feel any pain once the needle was in place. The chemo drained all my energy. I was so weak that I couldn't get to the bathroom, and after the session I had to drive home. I had decided to go to the chemo sessions by myself so I wouldn't feel helpless. My husband didn't disagree with me because we knew that he would be there if I needed him to help me.

Next step after chemotherapy was radiation, which lasted two and a half weeks, Monday through Friday. Radiation to me was much harder because my body was being burned, and after a few sessions, pus was coming out of the burned area. I could only apply a special type of ointment and wipe off the pus with gauze before applying more ointment to the burnt area on the left side of my chest. It grossed me out. Some patients had to stop the treatment for a while and start over later because their body could not handle it anymore, they needed to take a break. Thanks be to God I didn't have to stop.

When all treatment was over, they gave me a certificate of completion. I continued to see the surgeon and oncologist every three months and then every six months. Shortly after the chemotherapy and radiation treatments, I started having trouble breathing because my lungs were collecting fluids. I needed to use three pillows in order to sleep at night. Even though I am still having trouble with my breathing, I am now taking medications (Tropol) which is helping me with that situation.

After some testing, my doctor told me that I have congestive heart failure, probably caused by the chemo and/or the radiation. There were certain dos and don'ts I adhered to, such as if I drink too much water, my ankles would get swollen, but if I don't drink enough, I would get constipated. Sometimes I didn't know if I was coming or going. I have to weigh myself every day. I have to take (Furosemide) a diuretic, to get rid of excess fluid from my body. Through it all, God is still on the throne.

In May 2017, I had passed the four-year mark, and I was still going for check ups every six months, followed by yearly mammogram. The appointments with the Radiologist stopped after the third year. I felt blessed that it was almost over. I was still seeing my oncologist and my surgeon. They would continue to monitor my progress until at least the five-year mark. I can truly say that without the Lord keeping me and strengthening me, I wouldn't have been able to survive it. I am also grateful to the many people who prayed for and encouraged me throughout the cancer trial and the loss of my son, DD. I am especially thankful for the unwavering support of my husband, Charles, for his unconditional love and prayers.

Having to deal with cancer and the death of DD has thought me that God is always looking out for my best. He is in control of the happenings in my life. I can trust him because he is my one and only source. God is sovereign. He is above all things and before all things. He loves me and he wants the best for me. "In all things God works for the good of those who love him, who have been called according to his purpose" (Romans 8:28). No matter what I face in life, I can take comfort in the fact that God is always on the throne, always in control.

Sometimes we wonder why God has allowed certain things to happen in our life, and at times we blame him for creating them. He does not create them. Nothing goes past him unnoticed. He is well aware of them. He only allows them, and if God allows it, that's okay with me because he promised that he will be there to see me through it. He will never leave me or forsake me.

God allowed two major happenings in my life all at once. What I realized is that without God's help, I would probably have lost my mind. I do not know how I would have been able to cope with the death of my son. But God, in His sovereignty allowed me to have cancer, so that I could cope. I know that sounds odd, but here me out, it will make sense to you too. Therefore, forcing me not to dwell on my loss which would have broken my heart to pieces. Instead, God comforted me while he healed me and made me whole again, so I could refocus and look to him, my only source.

If I had to deal only with the death of D.D. I would have been mortified, consumed, overwhelmed, broken; unable to function. Death would have been my friend. God wanted me to stay and be functional to participate in life; that's why he had to allow something that would counter or be equal to this tragedy. Then again, what if I had to deal with the cancer only? The worry and anxiety would have taken over. I would have been obsessed, out of my mind thinking about death, my health, my grand-children and my family. I tell you, I would have been worthless to the kingdom I so believe in and of no value to anyone else. God knew I needed one to counter the other or I would have been like salt with no flavor, just granule; useless, good for nothing, only to be thrown out and trodden under foot. Matthew 5:13 says: "You are the salt of the earth. But if the salt loses its saltiness, how can it be made salty again? It is no longer good for anything". God would not have me here like that, unable to serve him and accomplish what he had planned for my life. An example would be like having to change two crying babies' diaper at the same time; you'd need to tend to the one crying the loudest, then go to the other.

I did not take the time to grieve the death of my son. (He didn't need me anymore—he was with Jesus.) God wanted me to pick one over the other, the living over the dead. There was not one thing left for me to do for my son. God gave me that time to concentrate on getting healthy again. After taking care of the loudest baby (the cancer), now I can take all the time I need to mourn.

Lately, my eyes can't stay dry. Everything reminds me of DD. I remember his boyish smile. One of the most treasured moments was watching him spread love on his children. Toward the end of his life, he was not able to drive. The children were still living with him. He has walked almost two miles on a hot day, with his children to the park to play with them. DD loved God so much that at age seven, he would not avenge himself against Jojo, the boy next door, who had hit him in the face. He said, "Mamma, God said to turn the other cheek."

DD never allowed his illness to keep him from doing the things he chose to do. He lived as full a life as he could, given the circumstances. My son had beat sickle cell anemia by ten years or more. Most people with sickle cell anemia don't live to be thirty-five years old, but Ducarmel Didier Pierre lived to be forty-five years old. His doctors told him not to exert himself. Besides not playing sports, he has done most of the things he wanted to do. He endured a lot of hardships. He made a lot of mistakes (so have we all), and he enjoyed some of the good things that life has to offer. Through it all, he learned to depend on God. During the summer of 2009, D.D. was very sick. He had blood clots in his brain and he required surgery. They had to operate on his brain twice in one week, after the surgeries his doctor told me that his chances were very slim. There was a prayer chain set up, just about everyone I knew were praying for his recovery. Prayer works. He did recover. He moved back home with us and he rededicated his life to the Lord; from that time on, he committed his life to God until the day he was called home.

I love him. I miss him like crazy. I miss him like the desert misses the rain, sometimes so much so that I want to hold my breath and die, but then I realize that death is part of life and someday we will meet again in heaven. In heaven, where we will live as if every day will be a holiday and the Sabbath Day will have no end.

CHAPTER 30

Faith Proof Mandibular Tori Miracle; If you believe in miracles stand up, wave your hands, stomp your feet and shout amen

Before   After
Christ   Christ

Truly I tell you, if you have faith and do not doubt, not only can you do what was done to the fig tree, but also you can say to this mountain, go, throw yourself into the sea, and it will be done.
—Matthew 21:21

Lord, your word says that "those who worship you, must worship you in spirit and in truth" (John 4:24). Lord, I believe, Lord I worship you.

A poem
Sometimes Lord, I come to you, reluctantly, but
I do trust you
My heart aches, I have many questions,
But, I come to you in faith.
My problems are deep and grievous,
But, I am grateful for all things.
I fear your name, oh Lord,
But, my love for you is immense.
You are Lord over the days, months, and the years.
You also rule over the seasons.
It can be daytime, and hot, in certain areas,
But it is nighttime and freezing cold in others.
I love how the leaves change color,
And drop to the ground in the fall.
The many varieties of beautiful flowers,
Blooming everywhere, in the summertime.
You are in control, Lord.
Your eye is on the sparrow.
I take comfort in your thoughts and your ways.
Your heart is pure, your heart is kind.
You are diversified in all that you do.
You are extravagant with your blessings.
Father, I love you, I praise you and I worship you.
You are the same yesterday, today and forevermore.
Your love never changes, your mercies are new each day.
You are my God, Lord of my life, and I thank you.
I am your servant and I worship you.

What is mandibular tori? (torus singular) Most people don't know what it is. I didn't either until a few weeks ago. It is a bone growth in the mouth. I have had it for five years and didn't even know; in fact, I have multiple of them.

The first week of July 2017, I started having problems with my heart medication that was going down under my tongue; it is so small that I have to use my finger to pry it out. One night, I was getting frustrated with it and I decided to look in the mirror to see why the tiny pill is going there. I saw two bumpy things that looked like big teeth trying to come out of the gum, one on either side of my lower jaw, and there is another one on the roof of my mouth. I panicked.

The next morning, I called Dr. Blackmon's office, my dentist, to make an appointment for a consultation. Dr. Blackmon told me that it was a bone growth, called mandibular tori, and I have had it since 2012. He also told me that I had five of them. They were smaller in 2012, and they had been showing in my X-rays. There is one on the outer, one in the inner part of both sides of my lower jaw, and one on the roof of my mouth. I don't feel any pain, no discomfort associated with this disease, and I can live with them and never have to remove them. Dr. Blackmon also said that the removal of the tori is only necessary if I was getting fitted for dentures. He gave me a referral slip to go see an oral surgeon, Dr. Joseph Danesh.

When I went for my consultation with Dr. Danesh, his assistant guided me to a room in the back to do X-rays. The X-ray machine was hi-tech. They don't need to put the film in your mouth (which is very uncomfortable). My heart leaps for joy when I realized that God does not watch over me, heal me, and protect me because he is obliged to, but because he wants to.

I found out the reason why the X-ray films were so uncomfortable: it is because they sit on top of the tori, and when you bite down on it, the sharp edges of the film felt like razor blades were cutting my gums. This newer X-ray machine goes around your head and takes pictures of your entire mouth. How cool is that? I saw the

X-rays. The tori make them look so unappealing that I wanted them removed out of my mouth as soon as possible.

Dr. Danesh came in the room to discuss my option. Just by being there, he assumed that my goal was to remove the tori. We discussed the length of the surgery, recovery period, and he told me that I could choose not to remove them since they don't hurt. He advised me that after grinding them down, there is a possibility that they could return, but in my case, it would be unlikely because of my age. The recovery period is six weeks. He had me to sign the approval forms for my primary care physician to fill out. His assistant had already contacted my insurance. They will pay for the consultation but not the procedure. The cost is $824 for each side, plus the cost of anesthesia.

There is no doubt in my mind that I want these things out of my mouth. I am confident that Dr. Danesh can do a great job removing the tori. I also know that my father in heaven is in the miracle business—he can do a better work removing them without the help of men. He made the lame man walk, he restored the sight of the blind man, he created me, and every situation in my life is within his control. So I prayed, "God, I need a miracle from you, hear my prayer dear Lord, hear my cry." I was very specific about my need for a special miracle because this is an impossible task, and I believe that only my God can do it and my God will.

I told my friend, Dot, about my prayer. She said that the miracle could be the surgery itself. I told her that it could be so, but I am trusting my God for much more. A personal miracle. Another friend said that a sign from God could be that he provides the funds since the insurance will not cover the cost of the procedure. I said that God has already provided the funds because from his abundant and extravagant provision, we always set money aside for things like that.

I asked my friends to pray with me that God would remove the tori himself, that they would be gone just as they came. I am confident that he heard my prayers and has already answered them. My mustard seed faith can move the "tori mountain." I thank God in advance for what he has done and still yet to do in my life. I continued to pray while waiting on God's perfect timing.

The mandibular tori had appeared in my mouth in 2012 and was growing unnoticed by me until 2017. I have been calling on the Lord, and will continue to do so until he hears my cry. I will keep asking, keep seeking, and keep knocking according to his word. From time to time, I look in my mouth to see if they were gone, but I have stopped obsessing about the tori, not giving them too much attention. I believe by faith that the day will come when I look in the mirror, I will open my mouth and the tori will be gone. That will be a day of unspeakable joy and celebration that I had never experience before.

Do you have a "**tori**" of your own? An illness, a wayward child, an abusive spouse, anything in your life that requires "**his**" special attention? Tell him about it, escape with him to that wonderful place. Feel the joy in his presence, experience the peace that he brings, and if you don't mind, invite your friends too.

I am overwhelmed with joy and gratitude every time I think of the Lord's favor toward me. I cry often and praise God for his many gifts in my life. For this nearness that I have felt since I was a child, for walking with me even when I strayed from the path he had chosen for me.

I left Haiti so many years ago with one hundred dollars and a hope for a better life in America. As I look back over my journey from then until now, I can truly say that what began as a search for tangible wealth and prosperity turned out to be a chasing of the wind, a looking to clouds with no rain, a trusting and depending on men and women that could never satisfy the true longing of my heart. When I finally discovered that man or woman did not live by bread alone but by every word that proceeded out of the mouth of God, my quest was over. I could finally rest from my labors and put all of my trust and hope in the God of my salvation. When I did that, he led me to a wealthy place where I found *true riches*.

There is a place where he takes me, where there is peace and beauty. It is quiet. There is no shame, no worries, where I can rest in his arms. Nothing can disturb the comfort and the serenity of his presence. Only he and I are in the place where I want to stay, but he bids me to go when our time is over. I go there often. When I was younger, I used to run there for safety and never wanted to leave. Now that I am older, my needs have changed. He's taught me how to balance my time, so I escape to that place less often, but our time together is sweeter because my needs are not so immediate. The place I am describing is a place of unlimited wealth, and pleasures abound forevermore; it is the place where *true riches* are found.

Have you ever experience God's love? God's love is beyond comprehension. It is grandiose, it is extravagant, and it is plentiful. It is so much that you can't handle it all—you'll just have to share it. He gives it even though you don't deserve it. If you refuse it, he still makes it available to you. He allows you enough time to change your mind, and he is ready to lavish it on you, all you have to do is to accept it and to cherish it. Will you?

Being so aware of my blessings and the source where they come from, prompted me to write this "psalm" of thanksgiving

My Psalm -- God's love
>I give thanks to the Lord, for his mighty deeds.
>I put my hope in him, I lift my hands up
>And praise him My Savior, My God.
>Like the children of Israel, He delivered me
>From captivity and conquered my enemy.
>He guided me out of darkness and brought me
>Into his marvelous light.
>>His mercies never end.
>With thanksgiving in my heart, I praise him
>I will glorify his name forever.
>I will tell others of his goodness and faithfulness,
>I will tell the story of his great love.
>I will remember his miracles of long ago.

I will meditate on his unfailing love
And all He has done in my life.
    His mercies never end.
He turned my pain and sorrows into joy.
Weeping may endure for a night, but
He fills me with confident expectations
That the sun will shine again tomorrow.
As long as I put my trust in him,
I need not fear, joy will come in the morning.
How great! How great! How great is my God!
    His mercies never end.

The Lord has done so much for me that I refuse to stop praying. I pray that my Prayer life should become so much a habit that I cannot resist it, and that I would continue until my prayer merges into praising his Name, *"Jesus."*

MARIE DUKES SHARES HER PRINCIPLES FOR WEALTH AND WISDOM

In this section, Marie Dukes has put together a variety of meditations, teachings, and life lessons learned. They will give insight and understanding of the concept of *true riches*. Marie is committed to making sure that what she has learned while living on this planet will not be taken with her to her grave.

The late Dr. Myles Munroe's quote—in which he said, "The wealthiest place in the world is not the gold mines of South America or the oil fields of Iraq or Iran. They are not the diamond mines of South Africa or the banks of the world. The wealthiest place on the planet is just down the road. It is the cemetery. There lie buried companies that were never started, inventions that were never made, bestselling books that were never written, and masterpieces that were never painted. In the cemetery is buried the greatest treasure of untapped potential"—inspired Marie to write her life story and to share many of the things found in this section so that when her time down here has come to an end, she will have deposited everything of value into the heart and mind of those who will be blessed to have read her body of work presented here.

MY LOVER AND ME

My soul finds rest in God alone; my salvation comes from him. He alone is my rock and my salvation, he is my fortress, I will never be shaken.
—Psalms 62:1–2

This is the story of a woman in search of her lover. She looks for him everywhere. She traveled by many roads in her quest to find him. It took her a long time before she realized he was near her all along. She was looking in the wrong places.

My Special Place

There is a place where I can go
Where I've found the peace, I've come to know.
Where I would find my friend there waiting,
As if he knew without a doubt that I would be coming;
To meet him, under the tree, we'd sit and tarry together,
Hand in hand, we'd chat, laugh, and enjoyed each other.
Our time together for me is like digging for and finding gold.
He offers scrumptious delicacies of love, hope, and peace,
He tells me his desires for me, we discuss all of my dreams.
He wishes to give meaning to my life and helps me set goals.
I am sure that my friend loves me, he knows that I love
    him too.

Do you have a friend like mine? Would you like a friend
    like mine?
With whom you can spend time and every day dine.
With the meal, he also gives a multitude of gifts and blessings.
He longs to be with you, listens to your cries and wipes
    your tears.
He gave his life for you, he loves you as much as he loves me.
And, I am certain if you accept him, he will be your friend
    too.

My Beloved

In the Bible, Song of Solomon illustrates the spontaneous and exclusive love between a lover and his beloved. His love for her is joy. It is beauty, and it is timeless. It is charm, it is intimacy, and it is the choicest gift a lover can bestow on his beloved.

> Beloved, let him kiss me with the kisses of
> his mouth- for your love is more delightful than
> wine. No wonder the young women love you!
> Take me away with you—let us hurry! Let the
> king bring me into his chambers. (Songs 1:1–4)

In the book of Song of Solomon, beloved knew who she was. Beloved accepted and appreciated lover's many attributes and even flirted back with lover.

Lover—"How beautiful you are, my darling! Oh, how beautiful! Your eyes are doves" (Songs 1:15).

Beloved—"How handsome you are, my beloved! Oh, how charming! And our bed is verdant" (Songs 1:16)

Until you have become either one, the beloved, you cannot
Understand nor appreciate the lover's position. As the
    beloved,
You tend to enjoy all the benefits, all the getting that comes
With having a kind and true lover. As the lover, you tend
    to give
All that you have, take all the steps to ensure beloved's
Happiness, and put up with her many moods, her rejec-
    tion, and her infidelity.

I was getting all the "getting" from my lover. He loved me when I was happy or sad. When I was fussy or fret, he loved me when I was up or down, and it is as if I couldn't do no wrong. He loved me even when I cheated on him. I cheated many times, and he never left my side. Finally, I left him, I ran away to do the things that I knew would displease him, and he waited on me nonetheless. While away from him, I stumbled in the darkness and I fell. When I awoke, I felt his presence surrounding me.

Many times, I thought I was handling things on my own, I was self-sufficient. Then I realized that he was by my side all along. My lover is the force behind all that I do—it's the force that carried me through. He wiped my tears, healed every one of my hurts.

When I cried, he listened and comforted me. My lover calmed my fears and provided for all my needs. When I messed up, he always picked up the broken pieces and put them back together. I also realized that I was helpless without him. I would be nothing without him by my side.

GOD IS ON THE THRONE

The Lord is in his holy temple; the Lord is on his heavenly throne. He observes the sons of men; his eyes examine them.

—Psalms 11:4

Be still and know that he is God! If I had a choice, I don't think that I would want to be poor. There are many things that I would not choose for my life, one of which is that of being born into the family I belong to, and it is not because we were poor. In this world's point of view, my family was poor, but in God's, I was rich; I have always been rich.

"For all the animals of the forest are mine, and I own the cattle on a thousand hills" (Psalm 50:10). My father in heaven is rich, I am coheir with Jesus; therefore, everything he owns belongs to me as well. I am rich. I did not know how rich I was. I thought they were **small riches** until I met Jesus who led me to the father. Then I realized, Oh, the many unfathomable **riches** of Christ, they are all mine. For example, my salvation, his love, his mercy, his kindness toward me, his grace, patience, tolerance, wisdom and knowledge, they are all mine. Also, the fear of the Lord is another one of his treasures.

Being rich is not always financial. One could have lots of money and be considered poor; being wealthy cannot get you to heaven. One could be rich without any money. Being rich is a privilege that many people hope for but very few actually get to enjoy. If I was raised in a rich home, I probably would not be any good for God to use me; it would have hindered God's purpose for my life.

from riches TO TRUE RICHES is the autobiography of a grateful heart, the true story of a young woman who had gone to hell and back and lived to tell about it. Although I call this book my autobiography, it is, in fact, my biography; God is the author. Every chapter has been written by God. I don't exactly know when it began, and I am not sure when it will end.

My life has taken many turns. I have gotten through every one only by the grace of God, who orchestrated them to give me wisdom while advancing his plan for my life. I don't know what God's purpose is for me, but every person I meet, planned or accidental, is part of God's way of using them to draw me closer to himself and to reshape my character so I can become more like him.

As I write in between the chapters of *from riches TO TRUE RICHES*, God allows me to relive every moment, good or bad, every pain feels stronger, every sorrow harder to bear, every scene more vivid. Every willful act of disobedience made me realize how far away from God I was, how broken, how empty I was, and how much I needed his grace. This was truly a work from my heart. As you can imagine, a lot of these papers I wrote on had tears on them as I relived each experience again. It helped to bring closure. Looking back, I can see that God's presence was always with me. He had never left me, not for one moment. I can see his footprint throughout my life's journey.

1. Though she was poor **(riches)**, she had *true riches*, because her daddy owns the cattle on the thousand hills.
2. Though she was hungry **(riches)**, Jesus was her daily bread that sustained her. He was her portion (*true riches*).
3. Though she was naked **(riches)**, Jesus clothe her with his righteousness (*true riches*).
4. Though she was sick **(riches)**, never forsaken; by his stripes she was healed (*true riches*).

5. Though she was down many times over **(riches),** never out, Jesus pulled her out of the miry clay and made her victorious (*true riches*).

6. Though she was abandoned **(riches),** never in despair, God's love empowered her with strength and kept her steadfast in the midst of adversity (*true riches*).

7. Though she was in prison, in bondage with lifelong depression, abuse, and suicidal tendencies, etc. **(riches),** Jesus has loosed her chains, took the shackles off her feet and set her free (*true riches*).

8. Through the power of the blood, the barrier has been broken, no stronghold keeping her back. She is ready for a new beginning (*true riches*).

God and I are a majority. His plan is to give me a future, and the curse of poverty has been broken. There is no limits to what I can accomplish through him. I may have been born in mediocrity and a challenging environment, but with God's favor on my life, I have been able to overcome every significant obstacle before me. I trust him more and more every day; instead of worrying about my problems, I give them over to the Lord, and somehow, he works everything out. He gives me strength to face every situation that at one time seemed impossible. I can overcome every obstacle and achieve all my dreams. God loves me, and all that he has purposed for my life will be fulfilled.

For everything give thanks! "Give thanks to the Lord, for he is good! His love endures forever!" (Psalm 136:1).

The theme song for the movie *To Sir, with Love* goes partly like this: "Those schoolgirl days of . . . but how do you thank someone who has taken you from crayons to perfume? It isn't easy, but I'll try."

How do I thank God for all he's done for me? It isn't easy, but I'll try. He has taken me from being a frightened little girl to being a "**giant slayer**." I say this because as I watched God slay my giants, I grew deeper in faith. My faith has gotten as strong as the mustard seed that can move mountains. My giants were so big that I had to stay on my knees while Jesus was slaying them, and they were **many.**

My biggest giant was my mother, then there was Sully, abortions, promiscuity, worry, depression, anger, just to name a few. I can also remember lust, envy, greed, rape, anorexia, suicide, and I can't forget unforgiveness, cancer, sorrows, pride, and the list goes on.

I am ashamed of the life I lived before coming to know Christ. I thank him for his forgiveness. He has given me a new beginning, and I pray that God uses my testimony to reach many who has gone through or is still going through the same trials that I had to endure.

I have learned that "I can do all things through Christ who gives me strength" (Phil. 4:13), and John 14:12 says, "He who believes in me will do the works I have been doing, and they will do even greater things than these." With his strength, I can do great things. He is the wind beneath my wings, my strength when I am weak, the fountain I drink from. He is my anchor, and his blood cleanses me. He is the ransom for my life.

How do I thank him? I am aware that he is the source of everything in my life, I want to commit the rest of my life to serve him. I want to make him the center of all I do, and I know that when I live a life that is focused on Christ and allow him to take control, he makes amazing things happen for me. I want to tell the world about him, about his love, and about all he has done for me. He is the ruler and the king of my heart.

How do I thank him? I have experienced God in my heart. I have experienced his miracles in my own life, **my personal miracles**. I have had a pain-free biopsy and surgery. My uncle Jacques got out of Haitian prison through prayers. My son beat the odds against sickle cell anemia by living ten years beyond the life expectancy for someone with that disease. I am cured from cancer and life-long depression. By faith, I am believing that the Lord will even remove the bone growths that are in three places in my mouth.

Faith works, and prayer works. "I tell you the truth, if you have faith and do not doubt, not only can you do what was done to the fig tree, but also you can say to this mountain, 'Go, throw yourself into the sea,' and it will be done. If you believe, you will receive whatever you ask for in prayer" (Mat. 21:21–22). Prayer lifts our eyes from our troubles and brings them to our Lord who with compassion and mercy; he delivers us from them all. If we pray according to the will of God, we are directing his healing power to where our needs are. Thanking God should be a privilege for me because he has delivered me from much (just like the woman with the alabaster jar of perfume in Luke 7:36–50).

How do I thank him? God is miraculous, and his miracles are timeless. He is unstoppable, and he makes me unstoppable. When I am scared, I seek shelter in him alone. He gives me courage, and he makes me indestructible. No weapon formed against me shall prosper. I might be down for a moment, but the darkness can't hide me. The enemy's deceit is transient. My bondage has been broken. God's love will find me, his grace will kiss me, his goodness and mercy will follow me all the days of my life. The enemy cannot curse me because God has blessed me.

How do I thank him? I will shout his praises, bow down before him with trembling and humbleness of heart. I will love more, give more, pray more, and serve more. I will surrender all to him. I am blessed beyond compare. I have nothing that God needs, and everything I do have he has given to me. Lord, I thank you. Lord, I worship you, I give you my heart, and I give you my life, my all. Thank you for making me new again. Thank you for restoring me and refreshing my soul.

LIFE'S LESSONS TO PONDER

Two are better than one, because they have a good return for their work. If one falls down, his friend can help him up.
—Ecclesiastes 4:9–10

God gave me a bubbly personality. I make friends easily. He also gave me a killer smile that is so contagious that when people look at me, they can't help but smile back. I'd like to believe that it is the love of Christ radiating from within me. I have truckloads of friends, too many to number. I love them all. I also have a lot of besties that I don't think I can live without. My friends were part of my support system during my times of trials, some prayed, others sent cards, some of them were at my house almost every day with words of encouragement, food, transportation to doctor's office, even foot massages. They were ready to perform any duty, including cleaning my house. My friend Falinda sent a card that said, "**Available**. I can cook, I can clean, I know how to mend clothes, I can even just sit by and be quiet." That was one of the sweetest cards I have ever received.

Prayer is our first line of defense and the most important of our needs, but God also gives us friendship when someone to listen to is all we need. When life turns a corner we didn't see coming, when our hearts seek a place to be loved and understood, most of all, when we need to be reminded of God's goodness and faithfulness. I don't know what I would do without my friends by my side. Laura is one of my besties who is as close as a daughter. She even calls me Mommy. She and her husband were among the first to be by my side during my illness and when my son died.

One of my besties, Von, had moved away from California to her hometown, and I thought I was going to die. I missed her so much. I cried and mourned her absence. That's just the way I am—I have abandonment issues. She called me a cry baby. She loves me just as much. She had missed me too. To remedy the situation, she sent me a plane ticket to go visit with her. I used to hang a plaque at my front door that said, "A stranger is a friend I haven't met yet." I just love people, and I want to always be surrounded by them.

* * * * *

Ten Steps to Realizing Your Full Potential

The secret for this kind of progress in life, this kind of stepping up from the smallest riches to these huge riches, from one hundred dollars to millionaire status, from being empty without him to being filled with his love, from being hungry to being full to the overflow, involves the following:

1. **Love God and put him first place in your life, trust him, and make him your only source**. "Trust in the Lord with all your heart and lean not on your own understanding, in all your ways submit to him, and he will direct your paths" (Proverbs 3:5–6).
2. **Walk with God and pray without ceasing.** Prayer lets God know how much we need him. We are aware of our inability to accomplish anything in our own power, and relinquishing our will to his. A.S.K. "ask, and it will be given to you, seek, and you will find, knock,

and it will be opened to you" (Matthew 7:7, 21:22, 11:24).

3. **Let your petition be made known to God.** God already knows what our needs are. As our father, God allows us to share with him what is in our hearts, our hopes, our dreams, and our desires. He wants us to tell him our deepest yearnings. "Do not be anxious about anything, but in every situation, by prayer and petition, with thanksgiving, present your request to God" (Philippians 4:6).

4. **Don't steal from God.** Be a good steward of your talents and be a cheerful giver. God gave us his very best, his only Son. "Oh, the depth of the riches of the wisdom and knowledge of God!" (Romans 11:33).

5. **Give God your heart.** When God has your heart, he has your treasure. Store up treasure for yourself in heaven rather than on earth. "For, where you treasure is, there will your heart be also" (Matthew 6:21).

6. **Set goals for your life.** Not goals that you can't achieve, be reasonable and realistic. Plan your work and continue to work your plan. Write them down and stick to them. Do not let anyone deter you from them. "The plans of the diligent lead to profit as surely as haste leads to poverty" (Proverbs 21:5, 24:27; 2 Chronicles 15:7; Luke 14:28).

7. **Be confident of who God is.** Know that God is capable of accomplishing great things, in your life. Do not doubt yourself, because God is working with you side by side. "I can do all things through Christ who gives me strength" (Philippians 4:13).

8. **Hard work.** Be willing to work for it and wait on God for the increase. Hard work never killed anyone, and it takes hard work in order to achieve greatness. "All hard work brings a profit, but mere talk leads only to poverty" (Proverbs 14:23).

9. **Be grateful.** The most important step is to be thankful, also, be generous with your resources. You are blessed, so you can be a blessing to others. Generosity comes from gratitude. "In everything give thanks, for this is the will of God in Christ Jesus concerning you" (1 Thessalonians 5:18; Psalm 136:26; Psalm 106:1, 100).

10. **Be extravagant.** The size of our gift is not what makes it extravagant. God sees the attitude of our hearts (consider the widow's mite in Luke 21:1–4).

What Jesus wanted us to learn from this story is that the rich gave out of their abundance and the widow out of her poverty. The poor widow gave all she had—that's extravagance! This also shows us that she is trusting God for his provision. Extravagant giving breaks the curse and opens the windows of heaven for your own blessings. God always rewards generosity; he is always waiting to bless his children.

If these ten steps are too hard to follow, consider going back to step one and move slowly, one step at a time.

Some people might think that they have to be poor to be a good Christian. God did not create us to be poor, and Christians don't need permission to succeed in life. What is success anyway?

Having a lot of money is not what success is all about. Wealth is not success. The measure of success is the ratio of talents used to talents received (not money). Anything that the Lord gives you is talent, and what you do with it will decide whether you are successful or a failure. What are you doing with what you have? The person doing the most with what he's got is truly successful.

Someone might say, "Ask and God will work a miracle," but that's not the way it works. God is the one who brought cause and effect into being. Usually, right results come from right actions. If you work, you expect to get a paycheck. Luke 10:7 says, "The worker deserves his wages." In the same manner, you have the right to expect good results when you intelligently and diligently use the talents that God has given you.

Give God your heart, worship him with your talents. Oswald Chambers says, "You have nothing except for that which you have received" God is the giver of all good things. Give him back a portion of what he has given you. Worship is when you give God your very best. God deserves our very best because he is God! And, he has given us his best, Jesus Christ, his Son.

Year-by-Year Inventory of Life's Accomplishments

While taking a closer and looking back at my life from when I first entered the United States, I realized that something major had happened every year. First evidence was I left Haiti in 1970.

1. August 19, 1970 new venture, travelled to the United States.
2. January 15, 1971, marriage to Vital, run away from New York, travel to Los Angeles (out of the frying pan into the fire)
3. October 1972 travelled back to Haiti to acquire my green card and bring DD to America, and move into our first apartment
4. 1973 moved again, visits with psychiatrist (Dr. Pender) began
5. 1974 first job with LAUSD, new car Firebird, DD in foster care, moved to Boston, Massachusetts
6. 1975 left Boston, Massachusetts moved back to Los Angeles, California
7. 1976 new position with LAUSD, DD moved back home with me, new apartment

8. 1977 DD diagnosed with sickle cell anemia, bought new car, purchased new home
9. 1978 DD's first sickle cell crisis, transfer from job to Gardena and promotion to payroll
10. 1979 loaned money to Harvey and he disappeared
11. 1980 purchased fourplex Inglewood, move out first home, new tenant
12. 1981 marriage to Chaz, separation, my car got broken into
13. 1982 new job at Hughes Aircraft
14. 1983 new home Ninety-Fourth place, DD is licensed, bought new car
15. 1984 new job LA police department, sold fourplex Inglewood
16. 1985 sold and bought home, loaned forty thousand dollars to J Henry, moved to Moreno Valley
17. May 30, 1986, met Charles, acquired my real estate license, bought new Nissan Stanza, bought fourplex in Riverside
18. 1987 Charles military assignment to Korea, started working part-time at Tarbell Realtors
19. 1988 Charles returned from Korea, purchased new home in Shadowbrook, new employment at Cablevision
20. 1989 sold fourplex in Riverside, bought new Cadillac, visit prospective in-laws
21. 1990 got married, job became very stressful, back in therapy, sold two of LA properties
22. 1991 car accident, bought Charles new Toyota, honeymoon in Hawaii, anxiety attacks, hospitalized in Hawaii
23. 1992 resign from cablevision, sold townhouse, foster children two boys
24. 1993 my health got worse, foster boys went back to group home
25. 1994 purchased house for DD, Charles retired from military, quit part-time jobs, new postal job, two foster girls
26. 1995 new job Amtrak, new rental property in Moreno Valley

27. 1996 DD's new interest Ieasha, our house remodeled, DD moved out of his house, new rental
28. 1997 sold DD house, new Lexus, our house was broken in to.
29. 1998 moved to Chateau Court, new tenant at Shadowbrook, two aggressive and bad investments at Wells Fargo
30. 1999 money lost on invest, gave DD Toyota, Charles new truck, first grandson, Omar (Mat), new fencing at Chateau, new car Lexus
31. 2000 birth of second grandson, Darien, Shadowbrook tenant died, property sold, bought new car for DD and Ieasha, attending new church, in-laws vow renewal
32. 2001 new income property Moontide, start mediation process with the bank
33. 2002 ending of mediation with bank, victory
34. 2003 DD and Ieasha got married, Ieasha joined the army, resurfaced driveway, put Chateau up FSBO
35. 2004 purchased land on Lasalle, remodeled Chateau
36. 2005 sold all (land, LA house, Chateau) bought Wyndham Hill, moved
37. 2006 sick, hospitalized, retired, birth of granddaughter, Demari
38. 2007 new Mercedes, two foster children girls, son's family moved into Moontide
39. 2008 hospitalized nine days, painful court, Charles new Nissan.
40. 2009 son's family finally moved out, my mother died.
41. 2010 brother died from big earthquake in Haiti, new job, RE license, started to work in real estate again, Charles's mom's hip replacement, new rental at Potomac
42. 2011 New tenant Moontide, for closure Moontide
43. 2012 Charles's father died, trip to Florida
44. 2013 Breast cancer, DD died, chemotherapy, radiation treatments, new foster granddaughter, Layla from Evelyn.
45. 2014 Charles retired from postal system, remodeled the backyard waterwise.

46. 2015 refinanced Potomac take money out
47. 2016 new foster grandson from Evelyn
48. 2017 new twin foster granddaughters from Jessie, writing the book.

Prayer Changes Things

Since I was a child, my days have always started with prayer. I was raised to pray and thank God for giving us new mercies every day. It is such a blessing to wake up to see another day, another opportunity to give God the praises that he so rightly deserves. I always pray to the Lord before going to bed, asking him to watch over us while we slumber. As children of God, we must make prayer part of our daily routine.

I always thank God for the many blessings he has so richly bestowed upon my life. From time to time, I include fasting as part of my spiritual cleansing. There are times when I get up in the morning and the busyness of life tries to shift my priorities, and I forget to put first things first, I forget to pray. I would experience a sinking feeling gnawing at me until I realize, oh, I did not pray today. Then I stop whatever I am doing for a few moments and say, "Dear Lord, forgive me of my sins. Be with me today in all that I do and say, and may it all be pleasing to you and bring glory to your name. Amen." Believe me when I say prayer changes things.

God loves us, and he is seeking a relationship with every one of us. We are saying to him that we trust him and rely on his love and guidance. It is very important to communicate with God through prayer. For those of you who drink coffee, can you imagine going a whole day without a cup or two? Please let me invite you to join me in including prayer in your daily plan. Make an appointment with God every day and put it on your calendar. You will not regret it.

To be continued...

NOTES

NOTES

NOTES

ABOUT THE AUTHOR

Marie Cathrie Dukes is a bubbly, cheerful woman who loves God and people. Every stranger is a friend she hasn't met yet. She always has a smile on her face. Her passion is real estate. She loves cooking and entertaining, and she is also a fitness fanatic. What gives her the most pleasure in life is serving in different areas of ministry. She has served and is serving at Set Free Prison Ministry. She has also served as a pregnancy counselor, children's leader, Sunday school teacher, and in other capacities at various organizations. She views her service to the Lord as food for her soul.

Marie and her husband, Charles, have been together for over thirty-one years. They are both retired. During their leisure time, they enjoy cruising, entertaining, traveling, and spending long peaceful weekends at their beach villa. Most of all, they take pleasure in loving their three grandchildren.

To share your comments, thoughts, and feedback, please send those to the author at Marie Cathrie Dukes, PO BOX 56448, Riverside, CA, 92517.

CPSIA information can be obtained
at www.ICGtesting.com
Printed in the USA
FSHW021450280119
55224FS